Other A to Z Guides from Scarecrow Press

The A to Z of Catholicism by William J. Collinge, 2001
The A to Z of Hinduism by Bruce M. Sullivan, 2001

The A to Z of Buddhism

Charles S. Prebish

The Scarecrow Press, Inc.
Lanham, Maryland, and London
2001

SCARECROW PRESS, INC.

Published in the United States of America
by Scarecrow Press, Inc.
4720 Boston Way, Lanham, Maryland 20706
www.scarecrowpress.com

4 Pleydell Gardens, Folkestone
Kent CT20 2DN, England

Revised and updated text based on Charles S. Prebish's *Historical Dictionary of Buddhism* published by Scarecrow Press, 1993. The earlier hardbound edition contains full bibliographical citations.

British Library Cataloguing-in-Publication Information Available

Library of Congress Cataloging-in-Publication Data

Prebish, Charles S.
The A to Z of Buddhism / Charles S. Prebish.
p. cm.
Includes bibliographical references.
ISBN 0-8108-4069-3 (pbk. : alk. paper)
1. Buddhism—Dictionaries. I. Title.
BQ130 .P73 2001
294.3'03—dc21 2001031184

∞ ™ The paper used in this publication meets the minimum requirements of American National Standard for Information Sciences—Permanence of Paper for Printed Library Materials, ANSI/NISO Z39.48-1992. Manufactured in the United States of America.

For my father, whose unflinching sense of morality still fuels my work more than three decades after his passing, and for my mother, whose support, confidence, and encouragement provide constant joy.

Contents

Preface

When I was invited to prepare *The A to Z of Buddhism* volume for Scarecrow Press, I was both pleased and eager to begin what I anticipated to be an interesting, but not especially lengthy project. After all, I was a veteran of one highly successful textbook/reference venture: *Buddhism: A Modern Perspective* (University Park: The Pennsylvania State University Press, 1975), had what I presumed to be an expansive knowledge of and interest in the Buddhist tradition, spanning ancient India to modern America, and had already produced much bibliographic and terminological material. Depending on one's perspective, my anticipation was either naïve, arrogant, or both . . . but certainly not neither!

Much to my dismay, the time frame I had selected for the project was simply insufficient. One of my colleagues at the Pennsylvania State University, Professor William Duiker, told me that preparing the *Historical Dictionary of Vietnam* was *intimidating*, despite his many decades as a Vietnam specialist. It was an appropriate word he chose in describing his travail. The dilemma one confronts squarely at the outset is the overwhelming mass of material to be assembled and the enormously hard choices that must be made in determining just precisely what to include. For a religious tradition like Buddhism that moved out of its Indian homeland early in its history and became diffused throughout Asia within a millennium, there is an absolutely staggering geographic space to confront. To further complicate the task, within the past two centuries, Buddhism has made serious progress in moving beyond Asia, establishing a significant presence in Europe, North and South America, and Australia.

There are few scholars in Buddhist studies whose particular specialty is globally extensive, either in perspective or philological sophistication. As such, some significant aspects of a project like this necessarily fall outside the range of any researcher's preparation, with the recurrent sense of insufficiency providing continual annoyance.

The task at hand is especially complicated and frustrating linguistically. Buddhism offers a variety of so-called canonical languages: Sanskrit, Pāli, Tibetan, Chinese, and Japanese. Of course Sanskrit and Pāli are closely related, as are Chinese and Japanese. Nonetheless, these two sets of languages come from language families that are as different as can be. If one factors in secondary literature in Sinhalese, Thai, Laotian, Burmese, Vietnamese, and so forth, the difficulty escalates exponentially. Obviously, choices for the *Dictionary* had to be made in a fashion that is useful and constructive for the reader. That naturally limits the amount of technical terminology that can be utilized.

Needless to say, the series editor has offered comprehensive guidelines. Yet, even heeding his concern to limit selections to such topics as events, persons, places of historic significance, religious institutions, ritual practices, doctrines, heresies, missionary movements, and the like still leaves the author terribly hard choices.

I have tried to minimize some of the difficulty for the reader by providing a pronunciation guide that is rather explicit for Sanskrit, Pāli, and Chinese terms, and which at least introduces the Japanese and Tibetan alphabets. Additionally, an overview of the Buddhist scriptures in the Indian, Chinese, and Tibetan traditions is presented at the outset. To help the reader keep perspective, both geographically and historically, I have provided a chronology and a map.

A rather substantial number of individuals have offered advice, assistance, and data input during the preparation of this manuscript, and to be sure, they are too numerous to cite individually. I should note, however, that the Pennsylvania State University has been remarkably helpful in obtaining the specialized computer software, and the hardware to support it, that enables me to incorporate Sanskrit diacritics directly into my word-processing program. Without their willingness to support my research effort through a significant funding contribution, this project would have taken very much longer to complete. Finally, I should thank my family for surviving this past year with me. I hope they will readjust to normalcy and find other endeavors with which to fill their time, now that they no longer will be conscripted for alphabetizing, proofreading, and other tasks no sensible person would coax his family into doing.

Pronunciation Guide

SANSKRIT AND PĀLI

The majority of technical terminology utilized in this historical dictionary appears in either Sanskrit or Pāli. This is certainly not surprising since India is the birthplace of Buddhism and these two languages represent the major linguistic heritage of ancient India.

Pāli is utilized exclusively as the canonical language of the Theravāda school of Buddhism. Theravāda is one of the early so-called Hīnayāna schools, and eventually spread from its Indian homeland first to Sri Lanka, and then throughout South and Southeast Asia. Sanskrit appears as the literary medium of the remaining Hīnayāna schools in India and in Mahāyāna literature. Thus, Sanskrit was the chief literary medium of Mahāyāna Buddhism as it eventually came to pervade all of East Asia.

Both Sanskrit and Pāli are generally written in Devanāgarī script. Since the Devanāgarī alphabet contains more than the twenty-six letters of the Roman alphabet, a series of diacritical markings must be added to the Romanized letters in order for us to pronounce them correctly. The following chart summarizes the information necessary for correct pronunciation.

1. *Vowels and Diphthongs*

a	pronounced	like **u** in nut
ā		like **a** in farm
i		like **i** in pit
ī		like **ee** in peek
u		like **u** in rule
ū		like **u** in brute
e		like **e** in grey
o		like **o** in tote

ai	like **i** in pile
au	like **ou** in plough

2. *Consonants*

(a) Consonants with dots under them (**ṭ, ḍ, ṣ, ṛ, ḷ**) are generally referred to as "cerebral" or "retroflex" consonants. These consonants are made by placing the tip of the tongue on the roof of the mouth just behind the upper teeth as the sound is produced. Thus, **ṣ** in dveṣa, sounds like dve**sh**a.

(b) Aspirated consonants (**kh, gh, ch, jh, ṭh, ḍh, th, dh, ph, bh**) are produced by breathing heavily into the sound as it is being produced. Thus, **th** in ar**th**a is pronounced as in ar**t-h**ouse.

(c) Nasal consonants are generally of two types. First, **ñ** is pronounced as in Spanish. As such, **ñ** in prajñapti sounds like praj**ñy**-apti. Second, **ṅ** and **ṃ** are quite close in sound quality, resembling the **ng** sound. Consequently, **ṃ** in saṃvara is pronounced sa**n**-**g**vara.

(d) A few miscellaneous notes are also important. **Ś** is pronounced as **sh**, so **Ś** in **Ś**ata is pronounced **Sh**ata. **C** is pronounced as **ch**, so **C** in **C**akra is pronounced **Ch**akra. At the beginning of words or between vowels, **v** is virtually identical to the English sound, but combined with other consonants, its sound is about half-way between **v** and **w**. Consonants that are doubled are generally **each** pronounced.

(e) Other letters are sounded as in English.

CHINESE

Until 1979, the traditional form of Romanization for Chinese characters was the Wade-Giles system. In 1979 the People's Republic of China officially adopted a new system known as Pinyin. In either case, pronunciation is extremely difficult because the writing and sound systems between English and Chinese are so different.

Two recent publications are helpful in applying the Wade-Giles and Pinyin systems in Romanization to actual terminology. *The Shambhala Dictionary of Buddhism and Zen* (Boston: Shambhala, 1991), compiled by Ingrid Fischer-Schreiber, Franz-Karl Ehrhard, and Michael S. Diener is useful for understanding Wade-Giles, while *Timeless Spring: A Soto Zen Anthology* (New York: Weatherhill, 1980), edited and translated by Thomas Clearly is effective for Pinyin.

The Shambhala Dictionary of Buddhism and Zen offers the following pronunciation chart for Wade-Giles on page ix:

ch	pronounced	j
ch'		ch
e		short *u* as in *fun*
j		like English *r* as in *ready*
k		g
k'		k
p		b
p'		p
t		d
t'		t
ts		dz
ts'		ts
hs		sh

It notes that vowels are pronounced as they might be in Italian or German.

Timeless Spring: A Soto Zen Anthology offers the following explanation for Pinyin on page 170:

> In this system, the letters C, Q, X, Z Zh are of special note: C resembles TS in catsup, Q resembles CH in cheer, X resembles S in sure, Z resembles DZ in adze, ZH resembles DG in judge.
>
> Other consonants, except r, are similar to English. R is perhaps the most difficult for English speakers; it is like a simultaneous combination of r in roll and s in leisure.
>
> An i, as final letter of a syllable beginning with ch, sh, zh, or r, sounds like er in her. Two-syllable names are elided as one word; hence the name Shitou, for example, sounds like the English words shir toe.
>
> Final i following c, s, or z sounds like u in put.
>
> Elsewhere i is as in Italian.

For a useful and complete comparison of the Wade-Giles and Pinyin systems of Romanization, consult *Moon in a Dewdrop: Writ-*

ings of Zen Master Dōgen (San Francisco: North Point Press, 1985), edited by Kauaki Tanahashi, Appendix B, pp. 225–230.

JAPANESE

The system of transliteration for Japanese terminology is known as the Hepburn system. Its orthography compares readily to English usage with exceptions being made in the case of vowels. Macrons over vowels, such as **ō** in k**ō**an, simply prolong the duration of the sound (as in Sanskrit). Diphthongs are also held longer in time, as in long vowels.

TIBETAN

Tibetan terminology is exceedingly difficult, both in transliteration and pronunciation. The most widely used system of Romanization of the Tibetan alphabet is that developed by Turrell Wylie and published as "A Standard System of Tibetan Transcription" in the *Harvard Journal of Asiatic Studies*, 22 (1959), pp. 261–267. Wylie's system, however, has nothing to do with pronunciation; it merely transliterates. Herbert Guenther gives a brief pronunciation guide in his translation of sGam-po-pa's *The Jewel Ornament of Liberation* (Berkeley: Shambhala, 1971; first published in 1959), pp. 277–281. It is too complicated to be reproduced here. Some useful suggestions for unraveling the disparity between transliteration and pronunciation are offered by Jeffrey Hopkins in *Meditation on Emptiness* (London: Wisdom Publications, 1983), pp. 19–22.

The Buddhist Scriptures

THE PĀLI CANON

The Pāli Canon is the complete scripture collection of the Theravāda school. As such, it is the only complete set of scriptures for any Hīnayāna sect, preserved in the language of its composition. It is often called the *Tipiṭaka* or "Three Baskets" because it includes the Vinaya Piṭaka or "Basket of Discipline," the Sutta Piṭaka or "Basket of Discourses," and the Abhidhamma Piṭaka or "Basket of Higher Teachings." There is an especially good summary of the Pāli Canon on pp. 265–276 of *The History of Buddhist Thought* (2nd edition; New York: Barnes and Noble, 1963) by Edward J. Thomas.

I. Vinaya Piṭaka ("Basket of Discipline")
   A. Suttavibhaṅga ("Analysis of Rules"): Rules of the Pātimokkha code with commentarial explanations.
      1. Mahāvibhaṅga ("Great Section"): 227 rules for monks.
      2. Bhikkhunīvibhaṅga: ("Division for Nuns"): 311 rules for nuns.
   B. Khandhaka ("Sections"): Chapters relative to the organization of the saṃgha.
      1. Mahāvagga ("Great Group"): Regulations for ordination, Uposatha (Observance) Day, rainy-season retreat, clothing, food, medicine, and procedures relative to the Saṃgha's operation.
      2. Cullavagga ("Small Group"): Regulations for judicial matters, requisites, schisms, travel, ordination and instruction of nuns, history of the first and second councils.
   C. Parivāra ("Supplement"): Summaries and classifications of the Vinaya rules.

II. Sutta Piṭaka ("Basket of Discourses")
   A. Dīgha Nikāya ("Collection of Long Discourses"): 34 suttas.
   B. Majjhima Nikāya ("Collection of Middle Length Discourses"): 152 suttas.
   C. Saṃyutta Nikāya ("Collection of Connected Discourses"): 56 groups of suttas, grouped according to subject matter.
   D. Aṅguttara Nikāya ("Collection of Item-More Discourses"): Discourses grouped according to the number of items in an ascending list.
   E. Khuddaka Nikāya ("Collection of Little Texts")
      1. Khuddaka-pāṭha ("Collection of Little Readings"): short suttas for recitation.
      2. Dhammapada ("Verses on Dhamma"): Collection of 423 verses, in many cases concerned with ethical maxims.
      3. Udāna ("Verses of Uplift"): 80 solemn utterances spoken by Buddha.
      4. Itivuttaka ("Thus it is Said"): 112 short suttas.
      5. Sutta-nipāta ("Group of Suttas"): 70 verse suttas containing legendary material.
      6. Vimāna-vatthu ("Stories of Heavenly Mansions"): Suttas concerning heavenly rebirths.
      7. Peta-vatthu ("Stories of the Departed"): 51 poems on unfortunate rebirths.
      8. Thera-gāthā ("Verses of the Male Elders"): Verses attributed to 264 male disciples of Buddha.
      9. Therī-gāthā ("Verses of the Female Elders"): Verses attributed to about 100 female disciples of Buddha.
      10. Jātaka ("Birth Stories"): 547 stories of the previous lives of the Buddha.
      11. Niddesa ("Exposition"): Commentary on portions of the Sutta-nipāta.
      12. Paṭisambhidā-magga ("Way of Analysis"): An Abdhidhamma style discussion of doctrinal points.
      13. Apadāna ("Stories"): Verse stories of lives and former lives of various monks and nuns.

14. Buddhavaṃsa ("Lineage of the Buddhas"): History of 24 previous Buddhas.
15. Cariyā-piṭaka ("Basket of Conduct"): Jātaka stories emphasizing a bodhisatta's practice of the perfections.

III. Abhidhamma Piṭaka ("Basket of Higher Teachings")
- A. Dhammasaṅgaṇi ("Enumeration of Dhammas"): Discussion of mental and bodily factors, with reference to ethical issues.
- B. Vibhaṅga ("Analysis"): Continued analysis of various doctrinal categories.
- C. Dhātu-kathā ("Discussion of Elements"): Ordering of various factors under a variety of major categories.
- D. Puggala-paññatti ("Designation of Human Types"): Classification of individuals according to a variety of traits.
- E. Kathā-vatthu ("Subjects of Discussion"): Polemical treatise concerning doctrines disputed by rival schools.
- F. Yamaka ("Book of Pairs"): Pairs of questions addressing basic categories.
- G. Paṭṭhāna ("Book of Relations"): Analysis of causality in 24 groups.

THE CHINESE CANON

The Chinese Buddhist Canon is called the *Ta-ts'ang-ching* or "Great Scripture Store." The first complete printing of the "Three Baskets" or *Tripiṭaka* was completed in 983 C.E., and known as the Shu-pen or Szechuan edition. It included 1,076 texts in 480 cases. A number of other editions of the Chinese Canon were made thereafter. The now standard modern edition of this work is known as the *Taishō Shinshū Daizōkyō*, published in Tokyo between 1924 and 1929. It contains 55 volumes containing 2,184 texts, along with a supplement of 45 additional volumes. A fine chapter titled "The Chinese Tripitaka" can be found on pp. 365–386 of *Buddhism in China* (Princeton: Princeton University Press, 1964) by Kenneth K.S. Ch'en.

I. Āgama Section: Volumes 1–2, 151 texts. Contains the equivalent of the first four Pāli Nikāyas and a portion of the fifth Nikāya.
II. Story Section: Volumes 3–4, 68 texts. Contains the Jātaka stories.
III. Prajñāpāramitā Section: Volumes 5–8, 42 texts. Contains the perfection of wisdom literature.
IV. Saddharmapuṇḍarīka Section: Volume 9, 16 texts. Contains three versions of the Lotus Sūtra and some additional material.
V. Avataṃsaka Section: Volumes 9–10, 31 texts. Contains material on the Flower Garland Sūtra.
VI. Ratnakūṭa Section: Volumes 11–12, 64 texts. Contains material on a group of 49 texts, some of which are extremely early Mahāyāna treatises.
VII. Mahāparinirvāṇa Section: Volume 12, 23 texts. Contains the Mahāyāna version of the conclusion of Buddha's life.
VIII. Great Assembly Section: Volume 13, 28 texts. Collection of Mahāyāna sūtras, beginning with the "Great Assembly Sūtra."
IX. Sūtra-Collection Section: Volumes 14–17, 423 texts. Collection of miscellaneous (primarily Mahāyāna) sūtras.
X. Tantra Section: Volumes 18–21, 572 texts. Contains Vajrayāna Sūtras and Tantric materials.
XI. Vinaya Section: Volumes 22–24, 86 texts. Contain the disciplinary texts of a variety of Hīnayāna schools as well as texts on bodhisattva discipline.
XII. Commentaries on Sūtras: Volumes 24–26, 31 texts. Commentaries by Indian authors on the Āgamas and Mahāyāna Sūtras.
XIII. Abhidharma Section: Volumes 26–29, 28 texts. Translations of Sarvāstivādin, Dharmaguptaka, and Sautrāntika Abhidharma texts.
XIV. Mādhyamika Section: Volume 30, 15 texts. Contains texts of this important school of Mahāyāna Buddhist thought.
XV. Yogācāra Section: Volumes 30–31, 49 texts. Contains texts of this important school of Mahāyāna Buddhist Thought.
XVI. Collection of Treatises: Volume 32, 65 texts. Miscellaneous works on logic and other matters.
XVII. Commentaries on the Sūtras: Volumes 33–39. Commentaries by Chinese authors.

XVIII. Commentaries on the Vinaya: Volume 40. Commentaries by Chinese authors.
XIX. Commentaries on the Śāstras: Volumes 40–44. Commentaries by Chinese authors.
XX. Chinese Sectarian Writings: Volumes 44–48.
XXI. History and Biography: Volumes 49–52, 95 texts.
XXII. Encyclopedias and Dictionaries: Volumes 53–54, 16 texts.
XXIII. Non-Buddhist Doctrines: Volume 54, 8 texts. Contains materials on Hinduism, Manichean, and Nestorian Christian writing.
XXIV. Catalogs: Volume 55, 40 texts. Catalogs of the Chinese Canon, starting with that of Seng-yu (published 515 C.E.).

THE TIBETAN CANON

The Tibetan Canon consists of two parts: (1) the bKa'-gyur ("Translation of the Word of the Buddha"), pronounced Kanjur, and (2) the bStan-'gyur ("Translation of Teachings"), pronounced Tenjur. Because this latter collection contains works attributed to individuals other than the Buddha, it is considered only semi-canonical. The first printing of the Kanjur occurred not in Tibet, but in China (Peking), being completed in 1411. The first Tibetan edition of the canon was at sNar-thang (pronounced Narthang) with the Kanjur appearing in 1731, followed by the Tenjur in 1742. Other famous editions of the canon were printed at Derge and Co-ne. Almost fifty years ago, Kenneth K.S. Ch'en provided a short article on the Tibetan Canon titled "The Tibetan Tripitaka," published in the *Harvard Journal of Asiatic Studies*, 9, 2 (June 1946), pp. 53–62, that is still quite useful today.

I. bKa'-gyur (Kanjur): Translation of the Word of the Buddha; 98 volumes according to the sNar-thang (Narthang) edition.
   A. Vinaya: 13 Volumes.
   B. Prajñāpāramitā: 21 Volumes.
   C. Avataṃsaka: 6 Volumes.
   D. Ratnakūṭa: 6 Volumes.

E. Sūtra: 30 Volumes. 270 texts, 75% of which are Mahāyāna, 25% Hīnayāna.
F. Tantra: 22 Volumes. Contains more than 300 texts.

II. bStan-'gyur (Tenjur): Translation of Teachings; 224 volumes (3626 texts) according to the Peking edition.
  A. Stotras ("Hymns of Praise"): 1 Volume; 64 texts.
  B. Commentaries on the Tantras: 86 Volumes; 3,055 texts.
  C. Commentaries on the Sūtras: 137 Volumes; 567 texts.
    1. Prajñāpāramitā Commentaries, 16 Volumes.
    2. Mādhyamika Treatises, 17 Volumes.
    3. Yogācāra Treatises, 29 Volumes.
    4. Abhidharma, 8 Volumes.
    5. Miscellaneous Texts, 4 Volumes.
    6. Vinaya Commentaries, 16 Volumes.
    7. Tales and Dramas, 4 Volumes.
    8. Technical Treatises: 43 Volumes.
      a. Logic: 21 Volumes.
      b. Grammar: 1 Volume.
      c. Lexicography and Poetics: 1 Volume.
      d. Medicine: 5 Volumes.
      e. Chemistry and Miscellaneous: 1 Volume.
      f. Supplements: 14 Volumes.

Chronology

6th Century B.C.E.	Life of Siddhārtha Guatama, the historical Buddha (563–483).
5th Century B.C.E.	First Buddhist council at Rājagṛha (483)
4th Century B.C.E.	Second Buddhist council at Vaiśālī (383)
	Non-canonical Buddhist council at Pāṭaliputra (ca. 367)
	Beginning of Buddhist sectarianism
3rd Century B.C.E.	Reign of Indian King Aśoka (272–231)
	Third Buddhist council at Pāṭaliputra (250)
	Aśoka's missionary Mahinda converts Sri Lanka (247)
2nd Century B.C.E.	Beginnings of Mahāyāna Buddhism (ca. 200)
	Composition of Prajñāpāramitā literature
1st Century B.C.E.	Pāli Canon written down in Sri Lanka (25–17)
1st Century C.E.	Reign of King Kaniṣka in India
	Fourth Buddhist council at Kaśmīr
	Composition of Lotus Sūtra and other Buddhist texts
	Buddhism enters Central Asia and China
2nd Century C.E.	Age of Indian Buddhist philosopher Nāgārjuna
3rd Century C.E.	Expansion of Buddhism to Burma, Cambodia, Laos, Vietnam, and Indonesia
	4th Century C.E.
	Age of Indian Buddhist philosophers Asaṅga and Vasubandhu
	Development of Vajrayāna Buddhism in India
	Translation of Buddhist texts into Chinese by Kumārajīva (344–413), Hui-yüan (334–416), and others
	Buddhism enters Korea in 372

5th Century C.E.	Nālānda University founded in India
	Age of Buddhist philosopher Buddhaghosa in Sri Lanka
	Chinese pilgrim Fa-hien visits India (399–414)
6th Century C.E.	Bodhidharma arrives in China from India (ca. 520)
	Sui Dynasty in Chinese History (589–617); beginning of golden age of Chinese Buddhism
	Development of T'ien-t'ai, Hua-yen, Pure Land, and Ch'an Schools of Chinese Buddhism
	Buddhism enters Japan (538)
	Buddhism becomes state religion in Japan (594)
	Buddhism flourishing in Indonesia
7th Century C.E.	T'ang Dynasty in Chinese history (618–906)
	Buddhism established in Tibet (ca. 650)
	Chinese pilgrim Hsüan-tsang visits India (629–645)
8th Century C.E.	Nara Period in Japanese history (710–784)
	Academic schools (Jōjitsu, Kusha, Sanron, Hossō, Ritsu, and Kegon) proliferate in Japan
	First Tibetan monastery at bSam-yas
	Great debate between Tibetan and Chinese Buddhist schools
	Ch'an declared heretical in Tibet
	rNying-ma-pa School of Tibet Buddhism begins
9th Century C.E.	Heian Period in Japanese history (794–1185)
	Tendai School (founded by Saichō: 767–822) and Shingon School (founded by Kūkai: 774–835) appear in Japan
	Great Buddhist persecution in China (845)
10th Century C.E.	First complete printing of Chinese Buddhist Canon (983), known as Szechuan edition
11th Century C.E.	Atīśa (982–1054) arrives in Tibet from India (1042)

	Mar-pa (1012–1097) begins bKa-rygud-pa School of Tibetan Buddhism
	Mi-la ras-pa (1040–1123) becomes greatest poet and most popular saint in Tibetan Buddhism
	Sa-kya-pa School of Tibetan Buddhism begins
	Revival of Theravāda Buddhism in Sri Lanka and Burma
	Decline of Buddhism in India
12th Century C.E.	Theravāda Buddhism established in Burma
	Kamakura Period in Japanese history (1192–1338)
	Hōnen (1133–1212) founds Pure Land School of Japanese Buddhism
	Eisai (1141–1215) founds Rinzai Zen School of Japanese Buddhism
13th Century C.E.	Nālānda University destroyed in India (ca. 1200)
	Shinran (1173–1263) founds True Pure Land School of Japanese Buddhism
	Dōgen (1200–1253) founds Sōtō Zen School of Japanese Buddhism
	Nichiren (1222–1282) founds school of Japanese Buddhism named after him
	Mongols converted to Vajrayāna Buddhism
14th Century C.E.	Bu-ston collects and edits Tibetan Buddhist Canon
	Theravāda Buddhism established in Thailand (becomes state religion in 1360)
	Laos and Cambodia become Theravāda
	Tsong-kha-pa (1357–1419) begins dGe-lugs-pa tradition in Tibetan Buddhism
15th Century C.E.	Beginning of Dalai Lama lineage in Tibetan Buddhism
16th Century C.E.	
17th Century C.E.	Control of Japanese Buddhism by Tokugawa Shōgunate (1603–1867)
18th Century C.E.	Colonial occupation of Sri Lanka, Burma, Laos, Cambodia, and Vietnam

19th Century C.E.	Meiji Restoration in Japanese history (1868), marking end of military rule
	New religions begin to emerge in Japanese Buddhism
	5th great Buddhist council in Mandalay
20th Century C.E.	*Taishō Shinshū Daizōkyō* edition of Chinese Buddhist Canon printed in Tokyo (1924–1929)
	Communist persecution and then control of Tibetan Buddhism (1950–)
	Founding of World Fellowship of Buddhists (1952)
	6th great Buddhist council at Rangoon (1954–1956)
	Dalai Lama flees Tibet to India (1959)
	Buddhism comes West
	International Association of Buddhist Studies Founded (1976)
	First electronic Buddhism journal founded: *The Journal of Buddhist Ethics* (1994)
	Pāli Canon available online (1994).

Modern Asia with
Historic Buddhist Sites
CENTRAL ASIA
MONGOLIA
Peking
KOREA
Seoul
JAPAN
Nara
Tokyo
Mt. Hiei
Mt. Koya
Kucha
Yellow River (Huang Ho)
Lungmen
Sian
(Changan)
Loyang
Shanghai
AFGHANISTAN
TIBET
CHINA
Omei Shan
Yangtze River
Lhasa
Indus River
NEPAL
BHUTAN
Ganges River
TAIWAN
Canton
Hong Kong
PAKISTAN
INDIA
Sarnath
Sanchi
Bodhgaya
Ajanta
BURMA
LAOS
THAILAND
Mekong River
Ayudhya
PHILIPPINES
BANGLADESH
Pagan
Irrawaddy River
Bangkok
VIETNAM
CAMBODIA
MALAYSIA
Anuradhapura
SRI
LANKA
Borneo
Celebes
Sumatra
INDONESIA
Bali
Borobudur
Modern cities
Important Buddhist sites
Traditional silk route used by Buddhist pilgrims

INTRODUCTION

BACKGROUND

With a history spanning more than two and one-half millennia, and a geographic scope that now encompasses the entire planet, Buddhism remains one of humankind's most interesting religions, and surely one of its most mysterious. In this regard, I am constantly reminded of Robert S. Ellwood's timely note in the second edition of *Introducing Religion from Inside and Outside* (Englewood Cliffs, N.J.: Prentice-Hall, 1983) that "Religion is made up of gestures that make no sense at all if ordinary practical reality is all there is; if the universe is only matter and space; if humans are only organisms that feed, mate, and die" (p. 8). He goes on to elucidate his rather passionate claim for the value and study of religion more explicitly: "Religion draws maps of the invisible world" (p. 15). It describes the relationship between profane, ordinary reality, and that which is ultimate, what Rudolf Otto called the "mysterium tremendum et fascinans" in *The Idea of the Holy* (Trans. John Harvey; London: Oxford University Press, 1950).

It is clear that human beings become aware of the sacred because *it manifests itself*. In *The Sacred and the Profane* (Trans. Willard Trask; New York: Harcourt Brace, 1959), historian of religion Mircea Eliade refers to this act of the sacred showing itself to us as *hierophany*. He summarizes it concisely: "It could be said that the history of religions—from the primitive to the most highly developed—is constituted by a great number of hierophanies, by manifestations of sacred realities" (p. 11). One of Eliade's foremost students, Frederick Streng, suggests in *Understanding Religious Life* (3rd ed.; Belmont, Ca.: Wadsworth, 1985) that the application of the history of religions approach necessitates two major concerns: "(1) to describe as objectively as possible the conditions and elements of a historical situation and (2) to recognize that the changes in religious life result from interactions with many cultural conditions surrounding a religious event" (p. 223). It is the history of religions approach, and its attendant concerns, that will be utilized in preparing this dictionary of Buddhism.

Religious history occurs in specific space and time. However, if the study of Buddhist religious history is largely an investigation of hierophany, then it is necessary to realize that sacred space is different from profane space, insofar as it often describes existential space rather than geometric space, and sacred time is at variance with chronological time, insofar as it describes the time of religious experience, of religious festival. Thus it is sacred space and sacred time that turn chaos into cosmos. Consequently, while a dictionary of Buddhism must consider the various periods, events, individuals, circumstances, texts, and concepts from which the history of Buddhism takes its shape, it must also consider the sacred sites in Buddhist geography, the festivals, rites, and rituals that configure Buddhist religious practice, the manifestation of Buddhist religiosity as witnessed in biography, art, and mythology, and the soteriological methods employed by Buddhists throughout their history.

BUDDHA'S LIFE

No religious tradition appears in a vacuum, and the one founded by Siddhārtha Gautama, the historical Buddha, is no exception. By the time Siddhārtha was born into the Śākya tribe of the Gautama clan in the mid-sixth century B.C.E., India had a rich religious history. Probably earlier than 2000 B.C.E. a rather sophisticated Indic culture developed in the Indus River Basin, centered in the cities of Harappā and Mohenjo Daro. Within a thousand years, in the midst of internal decay and turmoil, this Indus Valley civilization was overrun by bands of hard-drinking, barbarian, warring nomads known as Indo-Āryans. An amalgam of the two cultures resulted, replete with a new social structure based on a four-class system, the introduction of Sanskrit as the proper literary medium, and a new pantheon of gods (known as devas or "shining ones"). A series of religious texts called Vedas developed over several centuries, outlining sacrificial rituals of varying kinds aimed at winning the favor of the divinities in hopes of establishing cosmic order (ṛta) and obtaining individual boons. By 800 B.C.E., a new and speculative series of proto-philosophic texts known as Upaniṣads appeared as well as an intense series of speculations about the nature of reality, the role of the devas, the proper mode of religious practice, and a variety of social issues. The period of composition of the Upaniṣads lasted several hundred years, and it was into this social and religious environment that Siddhārtha was born.

Possible specific dates for the life of Siddhārtha Gautama abound in the literature, as do speculations about the particular events of his life revealed in both the canonical and noncanonical sources. Nonetheless, the vast majority of the texts agree on the basic episodes of his life. These accounts concur that he was born around 560 B.C.E. to King Śuddhodana and Queen Māyā. Many events surrounding Siddhārtha's conception, gestation, and birth are fraught with mythological overtones, including the death of Queen Māyā on the seventh day following birth. Following the prophecy that the young prince will become a cakravartin or "wheel-turner" (turning either the wheel of the secular law or the religious law), King Śuddhodana marries Mahāprajāpatī, the sister of Queen Māyā. After a privileged youth, Siddhartha marries, fathers a son known as Rāhula, and at age twenty-nine renounces worldly life to go in search of a solution to the human dilemma of old age, sickness, and death. While studying with famous religious teachers of the time and then with a band of five like-minded wandering ascetics, Siddhārtha found no resolution to his predicament. Although he practiced the leading yogic techniques of the period and engaged in rigorous ascetic deprivations for six years, a solution to his quandary regarding old age, sickness, and death was simply not forthcoming. In the throes of a serious but nonproductive fast, Siddhārtha concluded that the solution he sought was not to be found through strict asceticism or the extreme luxury of his earlier life as a prince, but rather by way of a middle, balanced path through the excesses of life. In recognition of equilibrium, he regained his strength, sat down beneath a tree (later to be known as the Bodhi Tree or "Tree of Awakening") in Bodhgayā, and meditated intensely throughout the night. As dawn broke, he destroyed his remaining impurities, eliminated his false views, conquered his desires, and experienced the goal of Buddhahood (literally "the state of being awakened").

Now known as the Buddha (or by several other epithets, including the Tathāgata or "Thus-Come," Jina or "Conqueror," and Śākyamuni or "Sage of the Śākyas"), he began a forty-five-year ministry that was to revolutionize much of the Indian subcontinent. Initially, he preached two sermons to his previous ascetic friends in a Deer Park at Sārnāth, ordained them as the first mendicants in his new community (or saṃgha), and established an eremitical lifestyle of preaching throughout the countryside that was to prevail for the remainder of his life. Recognizing that not everyone was capable of abandoning worldly life in the religious quest, he established both a monastic order of monks and nuns and a community for lay disciples. Allowing himself and his small retinue of intimate disciples to establish fixed residence only in the rainy season, when travel was virtually impossible, the Buddha maintained an aggressive schedule of sharing his teaching, known as the Dharma, with all who chose to listen, converting many thousands of hearers to his path and providing many with the instruction necessary for the attainment of emancipation, referred to as nirvāṇa. His impressive list of converts included not only his father, foster mother (who also became the first nun), and son, but also numerous royal patrons and wealthy laymen of high social standing.

In his eightieth year, following a brief illness and a conversation with his lifelong tempter, the demon Māra, Buddha confessed to his closest disciple Ānanda that he would die in three months. Expressing a desire to end his life in Kuśinagara, the last journey undertaken by the teacher and his disciples was to this village. Prior to his death, Buddha received one final convert into the community, preached a concluding sermon to his followers in which he instructed them one last time about the impermanence of all conditioned things, and suggested that all his disciples remember to work out their own salvation with diligence. He further advised his followers that they could abolish all the lesser and minor disciplinary precepts. Finally, he asked his assembled disciples if they had any final questions, but met with no response. Then, while in meditative repose, he passed into final nirvāṇa, never to be reborn. Seven days following his death Buddha was cremated with the relics distributed to various locations where reliquary mounds called stūpas were constructed over them.

BUDDHIST HISTORY

India

As noted above, prior to his death Buddha suggested that his disciples could eliminate minor disciplinary precepts, and advised them to work out their own salvation with diligence. These two final instructions were to confuse and color the first two centuries of Buddhist history following the Buddha's demise. Since Buddha appointed no disciple to succeed him as head of the saṃgha, trusting the Dharma and Vinaya ("Disciplinary Training") to provide sufficient religious guidance, the community feared that much disagreement would eventually result unless some steps were taken to standardize the teaching of the Buddha.

To facilitate the process of making Buddha's pronouncements canonical, and thus normative for the community, a major meeting was convened in Rājagṛha, in the first rainy season following Buddha's death, on a site donated to the community by Buddha's friend and patron, King Bimbisāra. Although later sectarian records disagree on precisely who attended the conclave, it is at least agreed that the Dharma, as recited by Buddha's disciple Ānanda, and the Vinaya, as recited by the barber Upāli, were established in their integrity. Consequently, the meeting, calling itself the Vinayasaṃgīti or "Chanting of the Vinaya," concluded on a highly positive note. Modern scholars have outlined at least three basic functions in this first council at Rājagṛha. First, it met a clearly pragmatic need in establishing religious authority for the neophyte religious community in the absence of its charismatic founder. Second, it enabled the community to begin its post-Buddha history with disciplinary purity and doctrinal integrity intact. Finally, it conveyed an obvious mythic function in facilitating a religious event that effected a renewal of the social order, marking a new and auspicious mission for the saṃgha. It should also be noted that many scholars suggest that canonical accounts of this event are most likely highly exaggerated, and some even question the actual historicity of the council.

Buddhist historical records are unfortunately silent for the next century. No doubt, the infant community spread extensively beyond its early base in Bimbisāra's domain of Magadha. Most likely, it expanded into Kośala, widely known because Buddha spent his last twenty-five rainy season retreats in its capital of Śrāvastī, and to other kingdoms east of Kośala and north of Magadha. However, one hundred years pass before there is any canonical mention of Buddhist events. One century after the Rājagṛha council, another council was convened in Vaiśālī, at the insistence of a Buddhist monk named Yaśas who believed that the resident monks in the area were engaging in a variety of illicit practices, expressly forbidden by the Vinaya code. With a well-respected monk named Revata as president of the proceedings, the enclave of 700 monks upheld the practices as illicit, condemning their future practice. This council is highly significant for Buddhist religious history for a variety of reasons. Despite the reconciliation effected by the council's decision, it does suggest that within a century of the Buddha's death, serious tensions and disagreements were beginning to appear in the still unified saṃgha. Further, it highlights a conflict between rigorist and laxist disciplinary tendencies in the community, and perhaps even purports to insinuate that there is a movement from sacred to secular emphasis within the saṃgha. Virtually all modern scholars agree that this council at Vaiśālī was a historical event, but there is some disagreement about its import. Until perhaps fifty years ago, the prevailing view, as espoused primarily by Wilhelm Geiger, was that a sectarian split occurred at this event, separating the community into two rival groups: (1) the Sthaviras, closely associated with the traditional Buddhist orthodoxy of the time, and (2) the Mahāsāṃghikas, portrayed as representing the liberal, progressive wing of the community in both discipline and doctrine. This view has now been conclusively discredited by Marcel Hofinger, André Bareau, and Charles Prebish, forcing scholars to look elsewhere for the beginning of Buddhist sectarianism.

Canonical accounts do reveal that by the time of the traditional third Buddhist council, held in the middle years of the Indian King Aśoka's reign (ca. 250 B.C.E.), sectarianism had already beset the Buddhist community. Trying to unravel the beginning of Buddhist sectarianism is perhaps the most difficult problem in early Indian Buddhist history, necessitating a reliance on noncanonical texts composed centuries after the fact, in a variety of languages, and whose reliability or accuracy cannot always be trusted. To avoid complicating an already murky picture, it should be pointed out that there are two leading scholarly opinions regarding the beginning of Buddhist sectarianism. The first, promulgated by André Bareau (but hinted at several years earlier by W. Pachow) concludes that a noncanonical council was held 137 years after Buddha's death in Pāṭaliputra, under the reign of King Mahāpadma the Nandin, and concerning *both* disciplinary laxity and doctrinal issues promulgated by a renegade monk named Mahādeva, ultimately separating the Buddhist community into the rival groups known as Sthaviras (or "Elders") and Mahāsāṃghikas (or "Great Group-ists"). The second opinion, expounded by Janice Nattier and Charles Prebish, argues for a noncanonical conference occurring 116 years after Buddha's death, under the reign of King Kālāśoka, and focusing on unwarranted expansion of the Vinaya rules by the future Sthaviras. Irrespective of which of these rival theories is correct, Buddhism was plagued by a sectarian division early in its second century; by 200 B.C.E. more than a dozen sects were evident in the overall Buddhist community.

In the middle of the third century B.C.E., the Mauryan emperor Aśoka came to rule (possibly from 272–231 B.C.E., although his dates are still disputed). Aśoka is best known for a variety of activities that had direct impact on the Buddhist community in his kingdom. In the aftermath of a bloody battle involving the conquest of Kaliṅga, he seems to have become a Buddhist lay disciple, incorporating into his rule an attempt to maintain the Dharma and emphasize moral practices. Around 250 B.C.E., he sponsored the third canonical Buddhist council in his capital city of Pāṭaliputra, attempting to expel the "heretics" who had presumably been entering the saṃgha, weakening its social and religious structure. Aśoka chose a famous monk named Moggaliputta Tissa (sometimes referred to as Upagupta) to preside over an assembly of 1,000 monks, intending to restore orthodoxy. The so-called "heretics" were expelled from Aśoka's kingdom, and migrated to the northwest of India. They may have been the forerunners of an extremely important sect of Buddhism known as the Sarvāstivādins, particularly known for their erudition in philosophical matters. Finally, Aśoka is important in Buddhist history for his role in expanding Buddhism beyond its early geographical boundaries through a series of missions. Stefan Anacker (in Charles Prebish's *Buddhism: A Modern Perspective*) notes that "It is through these missionary efforts of Aśoka that

Buddhism first becomes an 'international' religion, and they served as a model for later Indian kings to send missionaries across the sea . . ." (p. 28). It is through the effort of Aśoka's son Mahinda that Buddhism was exported to Sri Lanka, and Aśoka is said to have sent other missions to Kaśmīr, the Himalayan regions, and Burma, among others.

Aśoka's legacy appears to have strongly influenced at least one other Indian king: Kaniṣka, the third ruler in the Kuṣāṇa Dynasty. Although we do not know the exact date of his ascension to the throne (78, 103, and 130 C.E. are most commonly suggested), he does seem to retain a certain ferocious and vicious attitude despite his interest in Buddhism. Following Aśoka's lead, he sponsors the fourth Buddhist council, held in either Gandhāra or Kaśmīr. Vasumitra was president of the council, assisted by Aśvaghoṣa. Four hundred and ninety-nine monks were selected to attend, with great debates about Buddhist theory and practice ensuing.

By the time of Kaniṣka's reign and fervent support of Buddhism, the movement begun by Śākyamuni was in the midst of serious reform. In the hundred or so years following King Aśoka, there was a strong feeling in the various Buddhist communities that the religion had become too elitist and ecclesiastic, focusing on the monastic vocation at the expense of the path of the lay disciple. The new movement that was fermenting emphasized a strong commitment to the ideal of compassion and merit shared by all sentient beings, and the suggestion that nirvāṇa represented a selfish goal perpetuated by a rather indulgent monastic order of self-concerned ecclesiastics. It suggested in place of the goal of nirvāṇa and the path to its attainment a new and higher aspiration for full Buddhahood through a path called the bodhisattva path (or path of "future Buddhas"). Its hallmark was the creation of a new literature and the audacity to refer to itself as the "Mahāyāna" or "Great Vehicle," while branding all earlier Buddhism as "Hīnayāna" or "Lesser Vehicle."

Following rather swiftly from the creation of these new texts, known collectively as the "Perfection of Wisdom" (prajñāpāramitā) literature, was a virtual outpouring of new religious documents emphasizing the Mahāyāna ideals of compassion (karuṇā), practice of certain perfections (pāramitās), the notion of the emptiness of all phenomena (śūnyatā), and the bodhisattva path. Of special importance here is the recognition that within a short time, Mahāyāna literature was written rather than oral, thus enabling and encouraging a new and more sophisticated literary and philosophical effort on the part of Buddhist authors. Accordingly, the traditional Buddhist sermons (or sūtras) attributed to Buddha were joined by a new kind of Mahāyāna text known as śāstras or "treatises" and published in the author's own name. It is largely through these latter texts that the complicated Mahāyāna philosophy was fully explicated.

Over time, Mahāyāna divided internally as well. Around 150 C.E., the Buddhist philosopher Nāgārjuna founded the Mādhyamika school, and under his closest disciple, Āryadeva, the school gained the impetus to prosper for several hundred years. Following Madhyamika chronologically, and rivaling it philosophically, was the Yogācāra school founded by the brothers Asaṅga and Vasubandhu. By the sixth century C.E., Hīnayāna and Mahāyāna were joined by yet another school that called itself the Vajrayāna or "Diamond Vehicle" and emphasized practices known as Tantra, and which incorporated much material from folk religion and shamanistic traditions. Vajrayāna flourished alongside the other forms of Buddhism, prospering especially at Nālandā, a Buddhist University located on the outskirts of Rājagṛha. Apart from their philosophic and soteriologic importance for Buddhism, Mahāyāna and Vajrayāna added a new geographic dimension to the tradition. They moved northwest into Central Asia and populated international highways that carried the traditions throughout Asia.

Sri Lanka

Buddhism's first entry into Sri Lanka can be traced to a missionary endeavor of the Indian king Aśoka who sent his son, the monk Mahinda, and daughter, the nun Sanghamittā, along with other missionaries, to convert Devānaṃpiya Tissa, king of Sri Lanka. Upon receiving Dharma instruction, the king was indeed converted. As a result, in the capital of Anurādhapura he donated a park known as Mahāmeghavana as a site for the erection of a great monastery called Mahāvihāra, built numerous Buddhist monuments, and promoted the Dharma throughout the island. Sanghamittā brought a cutting of the original Bodhi Tree from

India to be planted at the Mahāvihāra and relics of the Buddha, which were enshrined in reliquary mounds known as stūpas.

From the above, it is apparent that, from the very beginning of the tradition in Sri Lanka, monasticism is the archetypal model for the proper practice of the religion, and further, that the religion is both sanctioned and protected by the king. The reigning kings were practicing Buddhists who were informed and advised by the saṃgha, and who, in turn, also helped regulate the affairs of the monastic order. Resulting from this symbiotic relationship, Buddhism has had a longer continuous history in Sri Lanka than perhaps anywhere else in the world.

Nonethless, due to its close proximity to southern India, Sri Lanka has regularly relied on India for infusions of cultural innovation, and as Tamils and others migrated into Sri Lanka on a continual basis, the island was also in constant danger of outside control. As early as the second century B.C.E., the island was controlled by Eḷāra the Coḷa who ruled for forty-four years before being conquered by Duṭṭhagāmaṇī (101–77 B.C.E.). A century later the Tamils invaded and ruled until they were defeated by Vaṭṭagāmaṇī (29–17 B.C.E.). In the reign of this influential king, the Pāli Canon, one of Buddhism's earliest scripture collections was committed to writing for the first time. Additionally, he founded another major monastery, Abhayagiri. This new monastery was to rival the earlier established Mahāvihāra politically and religiously.

Within several hundred years, Mahāyāna was to reach the island, as well as the great Theravādin Buddhist commentator Buddhaghosa, whose voluminous work known as the Visuddhimagga is considered to be one of the greatest commentarial masterpieces of Buddhist history. A third major monastery called Jetavana, and donated to Mahāyāna monks, was built by King Mahāsena (334–362). In the ensuing centuries, Sri Lankan history is a mingling of internal rivalries between the three monastic centers and a continual effort to defend itself from external invaders. The situation became sufficiently severe that by the eleventh century a combination of Tamil invasions, monastic disciplinary laxity, and civil war required that the ordination lineage for monks be reimported from Burma in order to restore purity to the saṃgha. Unfortunately, the order of nuns essentially died out at this time.

Eventually, Sri Lanka succumbed to the Portuguese who ruled the lowlands from 1505–1658, converting the people to Catholicism, and subsequently, to the Dutch Calvinists who controlled the same area from 1658–1796. In 1753 the ordination lineage once again had to be reintroduced into the island, this time from Thailand. During this period, the Sri Lankan kings retreated to Kandy, ruling the mountains and supporting Buddhism as best they could. In 1815, the British took over the entire island. From the beginning of British control, Western influences have permeated the island, including the development of a Buddhist Theosophical Society and an international Buddhist organization called the Mahābodhi Society. Sri Lanka gained independence in 1948.

Burma and Thailand

Primarily because it was accessible by both land and sea routes, Burma was especially convenient to a variety of cultures, particularly India. As part of his extensive missionary movement, Aśoka sent Soṇa and Uttara to Burma, where they established a presumably Theravāda community at Thaton. Sri Lankan chronicles also note the attendance of Burmese monks at religious ceremonies in Sri Lanka. In the first century C.E., further Theravāda missions from India reached Burma, and within two hundred years, Sarvāstivāda and Mahāyāna groups were also present. Eventually, Tantric Buddhism entered Burma, and by the ninth century when the Burmans entered north Burma to establish a capital at Pagān, it was the dominant Buddhist form in that area.

King Anawrahtā (1040–1077) of Pagān unified the country, was converted to Theravāda, and put his primary teacher Shin Arahan in charge of the saṃgha. During this period, Burma was one of the world's most thriving Buddhist centers. In 1287, Pagān was conquered by the Mongols and deserted. Although the Theravāda tradition survived, Burma was not united again until 1752, hosting the fifth great Buddhist council in 1868–1871, but in 1886 the British deposed the king and annexed Burma to India. Burma gained independence in 1948, with U Nu appointed its first prime minister. He presided over the sixth great Buddhist Council in 1954–1956.

The original dwellers in what is now called Thailand were the

Mons. During the reign of the Cambodian king Sūryavarman of Angkor (1001–1050), their area came to be dominated by the Cambodians, a circumstance that persisted for over two hundred years. Around this time, the Thais began to migrate into the area from southern China. In the middle of the thirteenth century the area was freed from Khmer rule, King Rāma Khamheng (1275–1317) came to rule, and established Theravāda as the state religion. Over the next four centuries, the Thais had close links with Cambodia, Burma, Laos, and Sri Lanka. In recent centuries, Thailand has carefully avoided European colonization, functioning since 1932 under a constitutional monarchy.

Cambodia, Laos, and Vietnam

The Cambodians or "Khmers" have a history that dates to the first century C.E. with the rise of a state generally known by its Chinese name, Funan. Since it was located on the trade route between India and China, many merchants settled in the area, bringing with them a variety of Indian religions. By the sixth century, Buddhism, particularly Mahāyāna, had spread throughout the area, and there was extensive Mahāyāna exchange with China as well. For the next several centuries, the Buddhist and Brāhmaṇical traditions coexisted in Cambodia. During the twelfth century, a Burmese monk introduced the Theravāda tradition into Cambodia, and after support by the Khmer rulers, it eventually displaced the Mahāyāna tradition. From 1893 until 1975, Cambodia (along with Vietnam and Laos) were all colonies of France. In 1975 the Khmer Rouge seized control, destroying Buddhism and killing most of the monks, a situation that was only tempered somewhat by the Vietnamese invasion in 1975.

The people of Laos seemed to have moved out of their earliest homeland, moving south, eventually settling east of the Mekong River in a kingdom usually referred to as Nan-Chao. By around 800, it had conquered some areas of Burma and established contacts with India. The first Laotian state was founded in the fourteenth century with the help of the Khmers, at which time Theravāda Buddhism was introduced. Within a short time, it became the state religion. By 1975 the Communist Pathet Lao was in power, and many monks joined the Pathet Lao in a variety of roles as the saṃgha lost its status in society.

The Buddhism that found its way into Vietnam came from a variety of sources including China, Funan, the Khmers, and the kingdom of Campā. Along with Confucianism, Chinese Ch'an (Thiên) Buddhism was introduced by the Indian master Vinītaruci who visited Vietnam in 580. His lineage persisted in Vietnam up to the thirteenth century. Another Thiên school was brought to Vietnam by Vô-Ngôn-thông, a Chinese master. The Pure Land tradition also appears, but is largely subsumed into the Thiên tradition. By the eleventh century, there is much Buddhist activity in Vietnam, supported by a series of rulers, and resulting in the construction of a series of stūpas, temples, and shrines.

Following the Ly (1010–1225) and Tran (1225–1400) Dynasties, Buddhism suffered a number of setbacks, with Vietnam eventually coming under the colonial rule of the French. Although there was a Buddhist revival in the 1930s, a number of limiting factors, including a serious lack of funding, truncated the Buddhist agenda. Perhaps the major effort of this unified Buddhist church was the founding of Van-hanh University in Saigon in 1964. Nonetheless, in the aftermath of the Vietnam war, the Buddhist clergy has been seriously harrassed, monasteries and temples have been closed, and the future of Vietnamese Buddhism hangs by a thread.

China

As early as the first century C.E., Buddhism's presence in Central Asia was clearly visible. Moving northwest out of India from Peshāwār, Buddhism traveled along the trade routes, eventually coming in contact with small communities from the Later Han dynasty in China that extended into Central Asia along the Silk Route. Many of the families in these communities were both bilingual and bicultural, thus creating an ideal basis for Buddhism to make inroads into China, particularly via entry at Tun-huang.

It is not at all certain whether Buddhism's first entry into China resulted from the fabled account of the Han Emperor Ming's notorious dream in the middle of the first century C.E., or through some other occasion, but there is a clearly historical account of a Chinese emperor practicing Buddhism by the middle of the second century C.E. Additionally, by 148, a Parthian monk named An Shi-kao settled in Lo-yang to head a team of translators intent on translating Indian Buddhist texts, particularly on meditation, into Chinese. Most of these early translations were of Hīnayāna texts, but the first Mahāyāna missionary, Lokakṣema, worked on a variety of Mahāyāna texts in Lo-yang between 168 and 188.

Despite the fact that the Later Han Dynasty broke apart in the last half of the second century, splitting China into northern and southern parts, the Chinese interest in Buddhism did not diminish. Through the work of innovative figures like Dharmarakṣa, a Chinese-born Buddhist of Scythian lineage, the process of translating Buddhist texts into Chinese continued throughout the Western Chin Dynasty (265–316) and the Eastern Chin Dynasty (317–419). During this period, monasteries were established, monks ordained, and sūtras discussed throughout the south.

Things were not so calm or prosperous in northern China. Under a number of non-Chinese barbarian rulers, nonetheless, Buddhism found favor primarily because it was perceived to be a "foreign" religion, just as the ruling Huns were largely foreign to China. Eager to take advantage of the monks' knowledge of meditation and the so-called powers derived therefrom, these rulers were sympathetic to Buddhist needs. It was fortuitous for the fledgling Buddhist community that sometime around 310, a Kuchean monk named Fo-t'u-teng apppeared in northern China and gained an influential position in the Later Chao Dynasty, serving as court advisor for more than two decades and largely protecting the Buddhist effort.

Fo-t'u-teng is also known for his two chief disciples, Tao-an (312–385) and Hui-yüan (334–416). They encouraged and transacted the translation of a wide variety of Mahāyāna texts, supported a growing Buddhist saṃgha that now included nuns as well as monks, and fostered an intellectual atmosphere that was exciting. Consequently, by the time of the arrival of Kumārajīva (344–413), a great Buddhist translator from Kuchea, the Chinese saṃgha was prepared for a new infusion of Buddhist ideas from India. These early Buddhist translators are generally referred to as Buddho-Taoists because they imparted their uniquely Buddhist message through a largely Taoist vocabulary.

By the time of the Northern Wei Dynasty (386–534), most of the Buddhist elite had fled south, continuing their literary activity. Under the Northern Wei Dynasty, the saṃgha grew prosperous and highly corrupt, eventually becoming victimized by an extensive Buddhist persecution in 446 that lasted eight years. Further, Chinese Buddhism had become highly sectarian with the appearance of a series of "classical" schools: (1) Chü-shê, founded by Paramārtha, (2) San-lun, founded by Kumārajīva, and Fa-hsiang, organized by Hsüan-tsang; "scholastic" sects: (1) T'ien-t'ai, founded by Hui-ssŭ and (2) Hua-yen, founded by Tu-shun; and "popular" sects: (1) Ch'an, founded by Bodhidharma and (2) Ching-t'u, founded by T'an-luan. It was not until the Sui Dynasty (589–617) that China was reunified and Buddhism consolidated.

The high point of Chinese Buddhism occurred during the T'ang Dynasty (618–906). During this period, monasteries grew and prospered, monks and nuns thrived, and Buddhism was profoundly influential in Chinese culture. Yet by 845, in the midst of internal political strife, rivalry between the Buddhists and Taoists resulted in the most severe persecution of Buddhism in Chinese history. During a one-year period, virtually all temples were destroyed, monks and nuns were returned to lay life, texts were burned, and metal objects were confiscated and melted down. Although the proscription had but a brief duration, the results were devastating for Chinese Buddhism: the predominantly intellectual schools of Chinese Buddhism disappeared, the economic base of the monasteries was completely devastated, and the libraries (and the literary histories they preserved) were decimated. Even the practice-oriented schools of Ch'an and Ching-t'u suffered serious losses. And Buddhism never regained its previous status in Chinese history.

Korea

Prior to the introduction of Buddhism, Shamanism was the earliest form of religion in Korea. Buddhism arrived from China in 372 C.E. with the appearance of the monk Shun-tao, sent by the ruler of the Ch'in Dynasty. A monastery named Ibullan was built for Shun-tao, and he was followed by a Serindian monk known as Mālānanda who spread Buddhist teaching to the kingdom of Paekche in 384. By the beginning of the sixth century, Buddhism had established its position, and the practice of sending monks to China for texts and teachings was widespread. In short order, the T'ien-t'ai, Vinaya, San-lun, Satyasiddhi, Nirvāṇa, and Hua-yen schools were prevalent.

During the period of Unified Silla (688–935), Buddhism became a dominant religion in Korea. Ch'an Buddhism was introduced from China, and became the most predominant form of monastic Buddhism. Buddhism reached its apex in Korea in the Koryo Period (935–1392) through considerable construction projects sponsored by the government. In the tenth century the Buddhist Canon was printed, and a new edition printed in the thirteenth century.

During the Yi Dynasty (1392–1910) Buddhism suffered as Neo-Confucianism, adopted from China, became normative. Within several hundred years, Buddhism was severely suppressed, losing its state support and witnessing a reduction in the number of monasteries and sects. Eventually the number of sects was reduced to two: a meditation sect and a textual sect. By 1623, monks were barred even from living in the capital, with this proviso remaining in effect until 1895.

In the aftermath of the Yi Dynasty, the Japanese gradually assumed more and more control over Korean life. While the Japanese control over Korea ended following the Second World War, it was not before the two major sects of Korean Buddhism coalesced into one group known as the Chogye sect in 1935. Religious recovery has come slowly to Korea, but recent estimates indicate as many as six million Buddhists practicing their faith in South Korea.

Japan

Japan's indigenous religious tradition is Shintō, generally referred to as the "way of the gods (kami)." Into this environment, Buddhism was introduced in 538 C.E. from Korea, when emissaries were sent bearing Buddha-images and scriptures. Within half a century, the regent, Prince Shōtoku, declared Buddhism to be the state religion. Some sources even compare Shōtoku to the Indian king Aśoka. As such, close ties between the Buddhist saṃgha and secular power were established.

In the Nara Period of Japanese history (710–784), an extensive program of temple construction was promoted by Emperor Shōmu. Shōmu's daughter Shōtoku continued efforts favorable to

Buddhism. During this period, six academic traditions of Buddhism were imported from China, essentially without modification: (1) Jōjitsu, (2) Kusha, (3) Sanron, (4) Hossō, (5) Ritsu, and (6) Kegon. Study and exegesis of Buddhist texts took place, as well as much emphasis on Buddhist philosophical matters.

By 794, when the capital was moved to Heian (modern day Kyōto), Buddhism was ready to blossom in Japan. Consequently, the Heian Period (794–1185) may well be considered the high point in Japanese Buddhist history. Two more important Buddhist schools were imported from China: (1) Tendai, introduced by Saichō (also called Dengyō Daishi) in 805 and (2) Shingon, introduced by Kūkai (also called Kōbō Daishi) in 816. Saichō set up a training temple on Mount Hiei, utilizing a twelve-year training period for those monks who came to study and meditate with him. His temple prospered, housing as many as thirty thousand monks. Kūkai, on the other hand, established the headquarters of Shingon on Mount Kōya, about fifty miles from the capital. Emphasizing the arts and drawing on his personal brilliance, disciples flocked to study with Kūkai. Combining his writing and systematizing of Buddhist doctrine with a keen aesthetic sense, Kūkai became a court favorite. At one point, Mount Kōya was home to almost a thousand temples, and Shingon became even more popular than Tendai. Nonetheless, by the end of the Heian Period, both schools became decadent. By the middle of the eleventh century, it was felt that a period of decline of the Dharma (known as mappō) had befallen Japan.

In the next period of Japanese history, known as the Kamakura Period (1192–1338), rule was conducted by military Shōguns and a warrior class known as samurai. A number of new schools of Buddhism arose in this period, perhaps in response to a shift in power from the capital to the provinces. Local temples were supported, and both power and culture began to suffuse to the peasant class for the first time. The first new school to appear was the Pure Land School (Jōdo Shū), begun by Hōnen (1133–1212). Moved by the notion of mappō, Honen argued that recitation of the name of Amida would ensure followers of rebirth in the Western Paradise following their death. Hōnen's disciple Shinran (1173–1263) carried this notion one step further by suggesting that one could not *earn* their way into the Western Paradise, but rather it was Amida's vow to save all beings that produced the desired result. Shinran's innovation was thus referred to as Jōdo Shinshū or the "True Pure Land" school. Around the same time, a fisherman's son known as Nichiren (1222–1282) founded a new school named after him. Its basic premise was that the truth of Buddhism was to be found in the Lotus-sūtra, with all other forms of Buddhism being wrong. For Nichiren, salvation was to be obtained by reciting the name of the Lotus-sūtra in the following invocation: Nam Myōhō Renge Kyō ("Homage to the Scripture on the Lotus of the Good Teaching") while staring intently at a diagram known as the diamoku. His program was fiercely nationalistic, intending to deliver the Japanese people from social and political chaos and ruin. Two major schools of Zen were also introduced during the Kamakura Period. Upon returning (in 1191) from a trip to China, Eisai (1141–1215) began Rinzai Zen in which the primary mode of attaining enlightenment (satori) was the use of seemingly nonsensical sayings known as kōans, aimed at moving the mind beyond conceptualization to a direct perception of reality. Rinzai was especially successful among the samurai. More popular with the masses was Sōtō Zen, begun by Dōgen (1200–1253) upon his return from China in 1227. In the Sōtō form of Zen, one practices zazen, or sitting meditation, with the intention of "just sitting" (known as shikantaza), of manifesting the notion that one *already is* a Buddha. Because of its simplicity, it was sometimes called "farmer's Zen." In any case, the Kamakura Period also witnessed a general development of the arts, and particularly the tea ceremony, Noh theater productions, and Haiku poetry.

The Ashikaga Period (1333–1573) divided the country among feudal lords, leading to continual turmoil and eventually civil war. Only the Zen monasteries remained peaceful places in this period. The rest of Japanese Buddhism was singularly militant. Buddhist militancy was extinguished by the Shōgun Nobunaga who destroyed the temples on Mount Hiei in 1571, later decimating the Shingon center at Negoro and the Jōdo Shinshū complex in Osaka.

In 1603 Iyeyasu Tokugawa established a military dictatorship that lasted until 1867. This era, known as the Tokugawa Period, marked a period when Japan completely isolated itself from the outside world. Although there was little religious liberty, various Buddhist schools kept their traditions alive with scholarship and similar efforts. Encouraged by Shintō nationalism, the Meiji Restoration began in 1868, lasting up to the Second World War. In the time since 1945, nearly two hundred new sects have arisen in Buddhism, generally referred to as "new religions" (shinkō shūkyō).

Tibet and Nepal

Nepal has a long history of contact with Indian Buddhism. Apart from being the birthplace of the historical Buddha, Aśoka is said to have visited the region in the third century B.C.E., with his daughter given in marriage to a Nepalese nobleman. More than half a millenium later, the Buddhist philosopher Vasubandhu visited Nepal. Following the Muslim invasion of India, many Buddhist monks resettled in Nepal, bringing with them the Tantric tradition and their heritage of scholarship. Nonetheless, Nepal was primarily Hindu, and by 1000 C.E., Nepalese Buddhism suffered a fate similar to that of its Indian counterpart. Today, one finds remnants of both the Sanskrit and Tibetan traditions of Buddhism in Nepal.

Tibet's first contact with Buddhism comes in the reign of Srong-btsan-sgam-po (616–650). Legend suggests that the daughter of King Aṃśuvarman of Nepal married this Tibetan king and established the cult of Tārā. Equally, when the king conquered Chinese border areas, Tibetans went to China to study. And there is a rich history of contact with Central Asian kingdoms such as Khotan and Kuchā. Sometime around 632, the king sent an emissary to Kaśmīr to establish a script for the Tibetan language.

By the eighth century, King Khri-srong-lde-brstan (755–797) established the first Buddhist monastery in Tibet, had Buddhist texts translated from Chinese and Sanskrit, and brought the renowned scholar Śāntirakṣita from Nālandā University to Tibet. He also brought Padmasambhava, an accomplished Tantric master, to Tibet. One Tibetan Buddhist sect, the rNying-ma-pas ("ancient ones"), claims Padmasambhava as their founder. Precisely because Tibet had contacts with both India and China, there was much controversy, and perhaps even confusion, about Buddhist doctrines and practices. In one famous debate, taking place between 792 and 794, Chinese Ch'an monks debated the Indian master Kamalaśīla about the issue of "sudden" versus "gradual" enlightenment. As a result of the Indian scholar's victory, Tibetan Buddhism continued to owe its development largely to the Indian tradition.

Despite a short interlude in which Tibetan Buddhism was persecuted under the reign of gLang-dar-ma (838–842), the Buddhist tradition prospered in Tibet. Within two hundred years, a great monk-scholar from India named Atīśa arrived in Tibet to infuse new Buddhist understanding into the tradition and to help establish the Tibetan saṃgha on firmer footing. Atīśa's chief disciple 'Brom-ston established the bKa-gdams-pa school, representing the first Tibetan Buddhist school with a *clear* historical origin. Later, the bKa-rgyud-pa school was founded by Mar-pa (1012–1097), a great Tantric master who had traveled to India for his training. Mar-pa's lineage was carried on by Mi-la-ras-pa (1040–1123), a great poet-saint, and Mi-la-ras-pa's disciple sGam-po-pa (1079–1173) established the first monasteries of this new tradition. Also around this time, the Sa-skya-pa school began (1073), emphasizing scholarship.

The last major school of Tibetan Buddhism, known as dGe-lugs-pa, was founded by Tsong-kha-pa (1357–1419). Modeled on the famous Indian monastic universities, the dGe-lugs-pa school established its own major centers near the capital of Lhasa. Members observed a strict discipline, emphasized *both* esoteric and exoteric traditions, and distinguished themselves by wearing yellow ceremonial hats (in contrast to the red hats worn by the other sects). Tsong-kha-pa's third successor was identified as an incarnation of Avalokiteśvara, and was proclaimed the first Dalai Lama, seen as both the religious and political head of Tibetan Buddhism. This lineage continues today, with the fourteenth Dalai Lama having been enthroned in 1950, just prior to the Communist Chinese invasion of Tibet. Over time, Tibetan Buddhism spread to Sikkim, Bhutan, Mongolia, and even into the Soviet Union.

Buddhism in the West

The scholarly tradition of Buddhist studies in the West, dating since before 1800, has been well documented. The development of Buddhism as a global religion, however, is quite another matter, nonetheless spanning more than a century and a half.

By the middle of the nineteenth century, hundreds of thousands of Chinese immigrants appeared on the west coast of North America to work on the railroads and in the gold mines. Within another quarter century, they were followed by large numbers of Japanese immigrants, also seeking employment. This steady flow of Asian immigrants was augmented by the 1893 World Parliament of Religions, held in conjunction with the Chicago World's Fair, which featured a number of influential (and well received) Buddhist officials from the Theravāda, Pure Land, and Zen traditions. After 1900, a continual influx of eminent Buddhist teachers from Asia kept the American interest in Buddhism alive despite various legislative acts limiting the number of immigrants allowed. Within a century of the first Buddhist presence on American soil, virtually every major school of Asian Buddhism was represented, replete with occasional visits from major Buddhist world leaders like the Dalai Lama. It has increasingly become the case that most American Buddhists are Caucasians who have abandoned their traditional Christianity or Judaism in favor of Buddhism. It is difficult to estimate the number of Buddhists in the United States. In my book *American Buddhism* (North Scituate, Mass.: Duxbury, 1979, pp. 13, 59), I estimated a population of perhaps several hundred thousand. By 1987, the American Buddhist Congress suggested three to five million, a figure that is almost certainly inflated. The development of Buddhsim in Canada mirrors that of the United States, although having a much smaller Buddhist population. Peter Harvey, in his 1990 volume *An Introduction to Buddhism* (Cambridge: Cambridge University Press, 1990, p. 310), suggests approximately 50,000 Buddhists in Canada by 1985.

Buddhism has had an active missionary interest in Great Britain since 1893 when Dharmapāla visited. He returned twice more, in 1896 and 1904. He appealed to British scholars, and in 1907 the Buddhist Society of Great Britain and Ireland began with Thomas W. Rhys Davids as its first president. The society was primarily interested in Theravāda Buddhism, and to this end, published *The Buddhist Review* until 1922. Eventually the society was absorbed by the Buddhist Lodge of the Theosophical Society, founded by Christmas Humphreys in 1924. The latter organization continues to publish its own journal called *The Middle Way*. Just as in North America, Great Britain now boasts a more diversified Buddhist population, including groups from virtually all Buddhist countries and sectarian denominations. Of particular interest recently is the Friends of the Western Buddhist Order, founded by the Venerable Sangharakshita in 1967. This group, with more than several hundred members, is especially interested in developing a Western style of Buddhism. As in America, the number of Buddhists in Great Britain is hard to estimate, but the number is certainly less than 100,000.

There is a clearly growing Buddhist presence in Europe, especially in Austria, Belgium, France, Germany, Holland, Italy, and Switzerland. The Theravāda tradition is strongest in Germany, while the Tibetan and Zen traditions have made significant inroads in the other countries. Most recently, Buddhism is also spreading into Scandinavia. Finally, small Buddhist communities are beginning to appear in Australia, South America, and Africa.

BUDDHIST DOCTRINE

Although it would be extremely helpful in any attempt at a general understanding of Buddhism as a practicing religion to be able to pinpoint its basic doctrines *prior* to the development of the sectarian tradition, all efforts to explicate a so-called *precanonical Buddhism* necessarily fail. Consequently, we are directed to the canonical records of the various early Buddhist sects for whatever information they offer regarding doctrines that might have been common to the earliest tradition.

Needless to say, Buddhism arose in an Indian climate that was alive with religious and philosophical speculation. As such, it affirmed a basic worldview that saw time as progressing in a circular fashion, referred to as the wheel of saṃsāra, with rebirth anticipated at the end of each successive life. It accepted the Indian cosmology of the time, including belief in a variety of nonhuman realms. Buddha sanctioned the conviction that individuals were reborn from life to life in accord with the consequence of their accumulated merit and demerit, generally identified as the law of karma. Like other traditions in the various wanderers' communities, Buddhism searched for a way out of the cycle of perpetual rebirth.

Within the context of certain limits, it is possible to postulate that the earliest tradition affirmed the (1) three marks (lakṣaṇa) of existence, (2) four noble truths (ārya satyas), (3) five aggregates (skandha) of existence, and (4) dependent origination (pratītya-samutpāda) as doctrines that directly impact the potential attainment of salvation, known as nirvāṇa. Notions about other Buddhist doctrines of the time are highly speculative and uncertain.

The first of the above doctrines reflects Buddha's general presuppositions about the nature of the world around him, revealed in his second sermon to the five monks at Benares. In this text, known as the Anātmalakṣaṇa-sūtra, Buddha reflected on the nature of the self (ātman), impermanence (anitya), and suffering (duḥkha). Regarding the first issue, Buddha attacked the prevailing Brāhmaṇical notion of the self, arguing that not only does the postulation of a self promote grasping and clinging, items which he felt were inconsistent with the religious attainment of nirvāṇa, but also that the concept was illogical. He suggested that something pure, subtle, and eternal (i.e., the ātman) simply could not be associated with something impure, gross, and impermanent like the physical body. In place of the notion of ātman, Buddha suggested the idea of anātman, generally rendered as "not-self." No doubt, given Buddha's insistence on affirming the concept of rebirth, neither the Buddhist literature of the time nor the literature that followed over the next several centuries ever successfully resolved the issue of precisely how rebirth took place. Regarding the second mark of existence, Buddha simply affirmed that all things in experiential reality (with the exception of nirvāṇa) were impermanent and continually changing. A theory of momentariness was developed in which each moment could be analyzed into an origin, duration, and decay. Nothing was permanent or abiding, and thus, there was actually nothing to act as an object of craving or grasping. The third mark of existence is a more explicit statement of the first noble truth, revealed in Buddha's first sermon, and explained below.

The four noble truths, proposed in Buddha's first preaching, known as the Dharmacakrapravartana-sūtra, are generally cited to be the cornerstone doctrine of the early tradition. The first truth, that of suffering, is dramatically expressed in Buddha's contention that "Birth is suffering, old age is suffering, disease is suffering, death is suffering, association is suffering, separation from what is pleasant is suffering, not obtaining that which one desires is suffering. . . ." In fact, this statement is not so negative as it initally sounds. Buddha is simply telling his audience that all life's experiences are transient, and transcience is necessarily accompanied by the occasion for craving, grasping, and thus, displeasure. Craving, and its attendant grasping, are identified with the second noble truth. No matter whether one craves for sensual pleasures, continued existence, or even nonexistence, the end result of the enterprise is further entrapment in the bonds of saṃsāra. Were Buddha to have stopped here, he would probably have been identified only as a nay-sayer, a nihilist of unlimited scope. It is in the third noble truth that Buddha revealed himself to be optimistic. Here, he simply and directly stated that there can be a cessation of suffering, a permanent stopping of the pain associated with craving. The method, revealed as the fourth noble truth, that of the eightfold path, identified Buddha as a clear pragmatist. He outlined eight steps designed to lead the disciple to the cultivation of morality (śīla), concentration (samādhi), and wisdom (prajñā). The eight steps included (1) right understanding, or understanding the four noble truths; (2) right thought, or thought that is free from the three "poisons" of greed, hatred, and delusion; (3) right speech, or speech free of falsehood and malicious talk; (4) right action, or action that avoided killing, stealing, and general misconduct; (5) right livelihood, or abstinence from earning one's living in a fashion that harms others; (6) right effort, or making an effort to remove evil thoughts from one's mind while replacing them with good thoughts; (7) right mindfulness, or beginning to cultivate the meditative path; and (8) right concentration, or practicing the meditational training that culminates in the four trance states. The great Theravādin Buddhist commentator Buddhaghosa suggested that wisdom is the body of Buddhism, while morality and concentration are the legs that support it.

Since Buddha summarily rejected the notion of a permanent, abiding ātman, his disciples did question him with regard to the basic components that make up the individual, the person. Buddha's response was that an individual was composed of five skandhas, literally "heaps" or "bundles." These aggregates of energy are of two types: physical and mental. The physical aggregate is referred to as form, and represents the traditional four great elements (earth, water, fire, air). The remaining four aggregates are all mental. The first of the mental aggregates is feeling, generally defined as that which results from the contact of our physical organs with the external world. The second mental aggregate is perception, or that which determines the characteristics of an object. The third mental aggregate is called the "mental constituents." It represents the volitional quality of the mind, and accordingly, puts the mind into action. The final mental aggregate is consciousness, that which integrates the other aggregates. Since this early schemata was rather simplistic, it underwent an extensive exegesis and expansion at the hands of the later scholastic Buddhists. Nonetheless, even initially, it gave some picture of what an individual "is" in early Buddhism as well as how function transpired.

In an environment that affirmed the efficacy of ethical conduct based on volitional activity, resulting in a coming to fruition of the karmic "seeds" produced by that activity, it is not unreasonable to assume that Buddha was deeply interested in the notion of causality and precisely how it functioned. His theory of causality, arrived at during the night of his enlightenment experience, is called "dependent origination." It not only highlights the relational aspect of all existent things, but suggests that nothing happens by accident, so to speak. It states, quite simply, "because of this, that becomes; because of that, something else becomes;" and so forth. It applies to all compounded things, and accordingly, nirvāṇa is thereby excepted. In his formal explication of this doctrine, Buddha demonstrated the case by utilizing twelve specific links. Considered in forward order, they explain the truth of suffering. Taken in reverse, they suggest the cessation of suffering. Because of the causal relationship of all links, it is argued that elimination of any one link undermines the integrity of the entire chain. Consequently, Buddha emphasized working diligently on three particular links: ignorance, craving, and grasping. Not only are these links more likely to be undermined than the others, but their eradication results in the main point of the enterprise, destroying our reliance on causality altogether and achieving that which is uncaused: nirvāṇa.

Of course there are many other doctrines mentioned in the early tradition. None seem to be quite so generally supported, or of such significant import as the ones noted above. Needless to say, it is beyond the scope of this introduction to elucidate *all* the doctrines that developed in the various Buddhist sects that arose in the first several hundred years following Buddha's death, but it is important to reiterate that by 200 B.C.E., Buddhism experienced a major reformation in doctrine resulting in the generation of a new kind of Buddhism known as Mahāyāna.

One of the primary concerns of the infant Mahāyāna movement was trying to find a way to return Buddhism to the common people following a rather protracted period of ecclesiastic exclusivism and an emphasis on scholasticism, in part encouraged by the Abhidharma activity which accompanied sectarian expansion.

Among the first concerns incumbent on the Mahāyānists was a reassessment of the position of Buddha Śākyamuni, now several hundred years dead. During his lifetime, his accessibility was one of the chief assets of the system. Not only was he authoritatively available, but he continually addressed the perceived needs of his followers and communities. In the immediate aftermath of his demise, he was still readily available through the legends that grew up quite quickly around his actual history, but more importantly, he was also available through the qualities of Buddhahood that permeated the various sermons that were presumably collected at the first great council, held at Rājagṛha. As time passed, both the legends and the embodiment of teachings lost some of their immediacy in the confusion of a rapidly expanding saṃgha. The Mahāyāna remedy for this problem was to meet it directly, to coax the metaphysical process forward to its logical conclusion, resulting in the development of the notion of *Buddhahood*, sometimes identified by the term *Dharma-kāya*, and equated with ultimate reality itself. Once Buddhahood becomes a synonym for ultimate reality, Buddha Śākyamuni remains popular only as an apparitional, physical manifestation of that ultimacy (called Nirmāṇa-kāya). Indeed, a quasi-physical manifestation, available to instruct bodhisattvas (or future Buddhas) is also developed (known as Sambhoga-kāya). Around 300 C.E., this notion was formalized by the Yogācāra school as the doctrine of the Three Bodies of Buddha (Trikāya).

The path too was problematic for Mahāyāna. Previously, aspiring practitioners followed the eightfold path, cultivating the ethical life, and meditating arduously in the hope of gaining wisdom sufficient for the attainment of nirvāṇa, and with it, the status of enlightened saint or arhant. In the context of ecclesiastic exclusivism, the path of the arhant began to appear rather elitist and selfish to the general Buddhist populace. The Mahāyāna solution was to offer a new path, modeled on Siddhārtha Gautama's course to Buddhahood. In its fully developed form, it was known as the bodhisattva path and consisted of ten stages. Each stage was accompanied by an incumbent practice, referred to as a perfection. The prevailing emphasis of this new path was to cultivate wisdom, compassion, and the skillful means necessary to utilize them. In so doing, the path to complete, perfect enlightenment was opened to *all* Buddhist practitioners, not only those with a monastic vocation. Texts emerged extolling the merits of this new ideal type, such as Śāntideva's Śikṣāsamuccaya and Bodhicaryavatara, which even suggested that bodhisattvas could selflessly *transfer* their merit to other sentient beings. Mahāyāna texts were prudent in pointing out that bodhisattvas, on the attainment of the sixth stage of the path (i.e., the perfection of wisdom), could actually enter nirvāṇa and end their continued rebirth, but rejected this option through the intensity and expansiveness of their great compassion for all beings.

Perhaps the greatest Mahāyāna contribution to Buddhist philosophy was their innovation with regard to the doctrine of emptiness (śūnyatā), designed to radically alter the Buddhist understanding of reality. For earlier Buddhists, it was apparently sufficient to simply argue that everything was without self (anātman). Mahāyāna went further, claiming that all elements (known as dharmas), whether compounded or uncompounded, were empty of any reality in and of themselves; that is, they possessed no inherent own-being (svabhāva). From Mahāyāna perspective, this is simply the logical and proper application of Buddha's law of dependent origination. If dharmas, or the elemental building blocks of reality, were revealed to have no ontological status of their own, then all of conventional reality was stripped void as a potential object of craving and grasping. With nothing to crave and grasp, error-filled conceptualization was undermined and destroyed, yielding an experience of complete, perfect enlightenment, identified with Buddhahood itself, and termed *tathatā* or "suchness."

Armed with a new understanding of the concept of Buddhahood, a new path emphasizing Buddhahood itself as the goal rather than the attainment of nirvāṇa, and a radical new comprehension of reality, Mahāyāna spent centuries expanding and refining these doctrines. Despite philosophical incompatibilities with early Buddhism, Mahāyānists shared monasteries and dwelling places with their rivals, attested to by pilgrims from China and other countries, coexisted peacefully with them, and gradually became sectarian, just as their predecessors had.

Still a third major development appeared in Buddhism, beginning around the sixth century C.E. It was based on a new series of texts referred to as Tantras. In *The Buddhist Religion* (3rd ed.; Belmont, Ca.: Wadsworth, 1982), Robinson and Johnson note that "Buddhist Tantra is a mysticism mixed with magic; amalgamating some elements distinctly Buddhist, others traditionally quite non-Buddhist" (p. 91). Buddhist Tantra was quite popular in India under the Pāla Dynasty of Bengal. It was important at the great Buddhist University of Nālandā, and eventually moved throughout Asia.

It was also referred to as Vajrayāna or the "Diamond Vehicle," utilizing the diamond scepter as one of its primarily ritual implements. Vajrayāna also utilized mantras (i.e., sacred verses) and maṇḍalas (i.e., sacred geometric shapes) as means for promoting realization on the part of adepts. Complex rituals and visualizations were employed, eventually developing into a highly esoteric tradition, revealed only by properly trained teachers to their most intimate disciples. Tantric Buddhism attempted to utilize one's passions to destroy those very same passions. As such, the masters of this eccentric methodology were known as Mahāsiddhas or "Great Accomplished Ones," often manifesting unpredictable behavior, cited by their disciples as "crazy wisdom." Additionally, in Tantric Buddhism women occupy roles that reflect a growing equality with men. Exported from India, Vajrayāna became the prevailing Buddhist tradition in Tibet and Nepal, gained a strong following in China and Japan. Since the Tibetan Holocaust, it has demonstrated a significant visibility in Europe and North America.

BUDDHIST COMMUNITY LIFE

Tradition generally acknowledges that Buddha spent forty-nine days in the vicinity of the Bodhi Tree following his experience of enlightenment. Eventually, he was persuaded to propagate the Dharma by a deity known as Brahmā Sahampati, and upon so doing, his first followers were two merchants who became lay disciples. Buddha moved on to Benares, where he preached his first sermon to five old ascetic friends who had previously wandered around with him for six years practicing austerities. As noted above, this initial sermon was followed by a second, and in short order the five ascetics attained nirvāṇa.

The five ascetics requested both preliminary ordination into monkhood (called pravrajyā) and full ordination as well (called upasaṃpadā). Buddha accomplished this with a simple exhortation of "Come, O Monk!" (ehi bhikṣu). Thus the monastic order was born, and within a short period this monastic community expanded rapidly and enormously. The dramatic growth of the saṃgha, as it was called, required certain adjustments to be made in the ordination procedure, and over time, the entire process became rather formalized. Monks were allowed to confer both ordinations, and the entire process was preceded by a threefold recitation of the following formula:

> I go to the Buddha for refuge,
> I go to the Dharma for refuge,
> I go to the Saṃgha for Refuge.

An order of nuns was begun, perhaps reluctantly, by Buddha with both the monks' and nuns' communities being charged to wander continually teaching Dharma, settling down only during the rainy season when traveling about was simply not practical in India.

Although the monastic vocation was by no means ascetic, in keeping with Buddha's insistence on a "middle path" between asceticism and luxury, it was certainly a serious step that *most* individuals were not capable of making. As such, a lay community grew up early in the tradition, composed of male lay disciples (upāsakas) and female lay disciples (upāsikās).

In order to effect the highest level of ethical conduct from the monastic and lay communities, disciplinary codes for each unit were enacted. For the monastic community, this took the form of a portion of the canon known as the Vinaya Piṭaka. The Vinaya Piṭaka was divided into a general section of rules governing the behavior of individual monks and nuns, referred to as the Sūtravibhaṅga, a general section of rules governing the collective organizational conduct of the monastic community, referred to as the Skandhaka, and a supplement appended to the general text, covering miscellaneous matters. For the lay community, ethical conduct was governed by adherence to five vows, generally known as the pañca-śīla: (1) to abstain from taking life, (2) to abstain from taking that which is not given, (3) to abstain from sexual misconduct, (4) to abstain from false speech, and (5) to abstain from intoxicating substances. In some variants, this formula was expanded to eight and to ten precepts. Additionally, a number of famous discourses, like the Pāli Sigālovāda-sutta, regulate ethical conduct within the various relationships that occur in normal social intercourse.

The rigor of disciplinary rules for the monastic community is easily explained in the context of understanding the symbiotic nature of the monastic-lay relationship. Since the monastic vocation required a retreat from worldly life and an eremitic ideal, the individual monk or nun had to remain worthy of the highest respect in order to retain the support of the laity. In return, the laity received the wise counsel and Dharma instruction from the monastic community.

Initially, the Buddha's plan for community life worked admirably. Monks and nuns settled down during the rainy season (or varṣā) in one of two types of dwelling: (1) a self-constructed hut known as an āvāsa, or (2) a donated hut known as an ārāma. In each case, furniture and requisites were kept to a bare minimum, and the monastic dweller engaged in serious study and meditation for the roughly three-month period of rain retreat confinement. As might be anticipated, within a short time after Buddha's death, the rain retreat became institutionalized, expanding communal needs considerably, and the wandering ideal became largely a fiction in early Buddhism. Large monastic units developed, usually identified as vihāras, and often catalogued by their location as "the Saṃgha of Vaiśālī" or "the Saṃgha of Śrāvastī," and so forth. Although the movement toward settled, lasting monasteries contradicted Buddha's injunction regarding settled permanent dwelling, it did provide the opportunity for the development of Buddhism as a religious tradition. And it was this social institution that was exported by various rulers in the Buddhist missionary enterprise. In time, the monasteries that developed in diverse Buddhist cultures became formidible units, serving as festival and pilgrimage sites and commanding economic and political, as well as religious, respect.

As Buddhism spread throughout Asia and the world, it was the saṃgha that served as its lifeblood. It was the vehicle by which its methodology for salvation was transmitted to hundreds of millions of people worldwide. It remains the contextual basis for modern Buddhism today.

The Dictionary

— A —

⌘ ABHAYAGIRI ⌘

A major ancient monastery in Sri Lanka, founded by King Vaṭṭagāmaṇī. By the 1st century B.C.E., Sri Lanka was in the midst of enormous political turmoil. Almost simultaneously, King Vaṭṭagāmaṇī was dethroned (in 43 B.C.E.), a period of famine ensued, and Tamils invaded from southern India. Vaṭṭagāmaṇī was eventually restored to the throne and ruled from 29–17 B.C.E. Unlike the Mahāvihāra, or "Great Monastery," erected earlier during the reign of King Devānaṃpiya Tissa (247–207 B.C.E.) in his capital of Anurādhapura and given to the saṃgha, Abhayagiri was given to an individual monk. As a result, a conflict developed between the monks of the Mahāvihāra and the monks of Abhayagiri ostensibly focusing on the issue of whether monks could receive gold or silver, but more accurately reflecting a struggle for control of the Buddhist tradition on the island. Reconciliation was not effected, with each unit developing into a separate school, not to be united again for more than a millennium. Mahāvihāra residents were known as the Theriya school, while Abhayagiri residents were referred to as the Dhammaruci school. Under the reign of Parākramabāhu I (1153 1184), a council was held at Anurādhapura in 1165, and a reconciliation between rival schools effected. When Anurādhapura was abandoned around the thirteenth century, the history of Abhayagiri essentially ceased. (See also ANURĀDHAPURA; JETAVANA; MAHĀVIHĀRA.)

⌘ ABHIDHARMA ⌘

See ABHIDHARMA PIṬAKA

⌘ ABHIDHARMAKOŚA ⌘

An Abhidharma text written by Vasubandhu prior to his conversion to Mahāyāna. The text name literally means the "sheath" or "storehouse" (kośa) of Abhidharma. Prior to the composition of the text, Vasubandhu, as a member of the Sarvāstivādin Buddhist school in the north of India, regarded the Mahāvibhāṣā (and its followers, called the Vaibhāṣikas) as the classic text of orthodox Buddhism. Over time, he embraced the views of the rival Sautrāntika school, and constructed the Abhidharmakośa-śāstra as a statement critical of the Vaibhāṣika position. The full text of the Abhidharmakośa is composed of two parts: (1) a bare text of 600 verses, known as the Abhidharmakośa-kārikās and (2) 8,000 verses of prose commentary, known as the Abhidharmakośa-bhāṣya. The text is essentially a compendium, arranged in eight main chapters, discussing (1) elements, (2) faculties, (3) cosmology, (4) karma, (5) propensities, (6) the path to removing defilements, (7) knowledge, and (8) concentration. A ninth chapter is appended that discusses theories concerning the individual (i.e., pudgala). It remains one of the most important texts in Buddhist literature insofar as it provides a thoroughly systematized view of Sarvāstivādin philosophical positions as well as their critique. (See also SARVĀSTIVĀDA; VASUBANDHU.)

⌘ ABHIDHARMA PIṬAKA ⌘

The third and last portion of the Buddhist canon or scriptures, generally rendered as the "Basket of Higher Philosophy." It is a collection of the philosophical and psychological teachings of early Buddhism. While it can be assumed that each early Buddhist school (or nikāya) had its own version of this portion of the canon, only two complete versions have remained intact: (1) that of the Sarvāstivādins, preserved primarily in Chinese and Tibetan, and (2) that of the Theravādins, preserved in Pāli as the Abhidhamma Piṭaka. The period of composition of the Abhidharma Piṭaka spans perhaps half a millennium, beginning around 300 B.C.E. In a sense, the Abhidharma represents a commentary on Buddha's teaching as expressed in the sūtras, and utilizing a methodology that emphasizes impersonal technical terminology as well as an inductive, analytical approach. The texts included in the Abhidharma Piṭaka explained the information included in the sūtras, arranged and classified the material considered, and systematized the various doctrines espoused. Because of its emphasis on mind, the Abhidharma Piṭaka becomes a critical source for an explanation of the process and subject matter of perception. However, insofar as the main purpose of Buddhist practice is religious, the main thrust of the material considered is highly ethical. The seven books of the Sarvāstivādin Abhidharma Piṭaka include the (1) Saṅgītiparyāya, (2) Dharmaskandha, (3) Prajñaptiśāstra, (4) Vijñānakāya, (5) Dhātukāya, (6) Prakaraṇapāda, and (7) Jñānaprasthāna. The seven books of the Theravādin Abhidhamma Piṭaka include the (1) Dhammasaṅgaṇi, (2) Vibhaṅga, (3) Dhātukathā, (4) Puggalapaññatti, (5) Kathāvatthu, (6) Yamaka, and (7) Paṭṭhāna. Eventually, an extensive commentarial tradition grew up to expand and enhance the texts of the Abhidharma Piṭaka. (See also TRIPIṬAKA.)

⌘ ABHIDHARMASAMUCCAYA ⌘

A Mahāyāna text, written by Asaṅga, and devoted to an exegesis of dharma characteristics in the three vehicles. It is divided into five major parts. Unlike the Abhidharma of the so-called Hīnayāna schools, which emphasize the existence and classification of dharmas, the Abhidharmasamuccaya leads its arguments toward the understanding of all dharmas as empty (śūnyatā). Its usefulness arises not only from the importance and sophistication of Asaṅga's argument, but from its existence as one of only very few Mahāyāna Abhidharma texts. (See also ASAṄGA.)

⌘ ABHIJÑĀ ⌘

Supernormal powers, usually six in number, and generally possessed by a Buddha, bodhisattva, or arhant. They include: (1) magical powers, (2) the divine ear (i.e., clairaudience), (3) penetration of the minds of others, (4) the divine eye (i.e., the ability to see in time and space), (5) memory of former existences, and (6) knowledge of the extinction of the "outflows," or (moral) impurities. The first five are generally regarded as mundane, attainable through perfection of mental training, while the sixth is supramundane, attainable only through the development of insight (vipaśyanā). These supernormal powers are identified in both Mahāyāna and Hīnayāna.

⌘ ABHIṢEKA ⌘

Technical term derived from the Sanskrit abhi + $\sqrt{}$ ṣic, and meaning literally to anoint or sprinkle water over one's head. It is part of a consecration ceremony, usually employed at the accession ceremony of a monarch, and eventually utilized to symbolize the attainment of Buddhahood. It is referred to frequently in the Mahāyāna, and in esoteric Buddhism it often marked the initiation of a practitioner into the esoteric portion of the training, this latter item explained rather extensively in the Mahāvairocana-sūtra.

⌘ ĀDI-BUDDHA ⌘

The primordial Buddha. Although the concept itself can be traced to early Buddhism, it is widely acknowledged that the notion of the Ādi-Buddha was fully developed in esoteric Buddhism. In early Tibetan Vajrayāna Buddhism, the Ādi-Buddha is often associated with Samantabhadra who represents the Dharma-kāya. In later Tibetan Vajrayāna, it is Vajradhara who represents the Dharma-kāya. In Japanese Buddhism, the Ādi-Buddha is represented by Mahāvairocana.

⌘ ĀGAMA ⌘

The general title given to those scriptures collected in the Sūtra Piṭaka of the Sanskrit Buddhist tradition. Etymologically, the word derives from the Sanskrit ā + $\sqrt{}$ gam which is usually rendered "is handed down by tradition." Thus, Āgama refers to scripture or canon. Four Āgamas are traditionally cited: (1) the Dīrgha Āgama, or "long discourses," corresponding to the Pāli Dīgha Nikāya, (2) the Madhyama Āgama, or "middle length discourses," corresponding to the Pāli Majjhima Nikāya, (3) the Saṃyukta Āgama, or "linked discourses," corresponding to the Pāli Saṃyutta Nikāya, and (4) the Ekottarika Āgama, or "increased-by-one discourses," corresponding to the Pāli Aṅguttara Nikāya. A Kṣudraka Āgama is mentioned in the literature, but this is generally regarded as a miscellaneous collection of texts *not analagous* to the Pāli Khuddaka Nikāya. (See also NIKĀYA.)

⌘ AGGREGATES ⌘

See SKANDHAS

⌘ AHIṂSĀ ⌘

The principle of not-killing or not-injuring. The notion of non-injury runs throughout Indian religion, possibly dating from the early Upaniṣads, but also advocated by Buddhism and Jainism. In early Buddhism, it is manifested in a variety of ways. It is inherent in the Pāli pañcasīla (5 vows of the laity), for example, in the phrase pāṇātipātā veramaṇī sikkhāpadaṃ which means abstaining from harming living beings is a precept which should be observed. Yet it goes further than this, insofar as Buddhists are enjoined to love all beings and delight in compassion. Emphasized not only in early Buddhism, it is also stressed in a wide variety of Mahāyāna discourses, and since it was primarily Mahāyāna Buddhism that was introduced to China and Japan, the concept is highly visible in those traditions. In circumstances where Buddhist individuals and communities espouse vegetarianism, it is generally based on the principle of ahiṃsā.

⌘ AJAṆṬĀ ⌘

Site of a prominent series of caves in northwest Hyderabad. The location was once a significant one for Buddhism, with the caves being excavated up to around the sixth century C.E. The site was overlooked for over a thousand years until a number of British officers rediscovered the monuments early in the nineteenth century. The earliest excavations seem to belong to the tradition of Hīnayāna, while the later ones reflect Mahāyānist themes. Overall, there are around thirty structures, the vast majority of these being vihāras or monastic dwellings. The wall paintings, for which the caves are famous, depict scenes from a wide variety of Buddhist Jātaka stories, reflecting the former lives of the historical Buddha. There are also a series of sculptures in the caves, also reflecting a high level of knowledge of traditional Buddhist literature on the part of the craftsman.

⌘ AJĀTAŚATRU ⌘

King of Magadha who ruled during the last eight years of Buddha's life, and twenty-four years thereafter. Ajātaśatru was the son of King Bimbisāra, a patron of Buddha who ruled over Magadha for fifty-two years. While still crown prince, Ajātaśatru participated in a double-edged plot, with Buddha's rival and cousin Devadatta, to kill Buddha and overthrow Bimbisāra. Devadatta had wanted to displace Buddha as head of the community, and when he was rejected in his quest, he attempted to murder Buddha, first through the use of hired assassins, and eventually through his own effort. Following the failure of his final attempt, Devadatta provoked a schism in the community, founding a separate congregation, but this latter maneuver also failed, resulting in Devadatta's punishment. Ajātaśatru, in the light of Devadatta's failure, relented, and with the pardon of both his father and the Buddha ascended the throne. Although he mourned the Buddha's death severely, and shared in the distribution of Buddha's relics following the cremation, Ajātaśatru did not feel safe and confident while his father was still alive. As such, he imprisoned his father, and shortly thereafter, Bimbisāra died of starvation (followed swiftly by his Queen Kosaladevī). Eventually, Ajātaśatru was killed by his own son (either Udāyin or Udayabhadra, who ruled for fourteen years). (See also DEVADATTA.)

⌘ ĀJÑĀTA KAUṆḌINYA ⌘

One of the five ascetics who wandered with Siddhārtha Gautama for six years prior to his attainment of nirvāṇa. Along with the others (Vāṣpa, Bhadrika, Mahānāman, and Aśvajit), he was present for the preaching of Buddha's first sermon (known as the Dharmacakrapravartana-sūtra or the "Sermon on the Turning of the Wheel of the Law"). Upon hearing the substance of this discourse, Kauṇḍinya is said to have attained enlightenment, and taken ordination as a monk (bhikṣu) by the simple formula, "Come, O Monk!" Thus he became both the first enlightened disciple and the first monk in the Buddha's new community. Some accounts suggest that he was the leader of the first Buddhist council, convened at Rājagṛha, following Buddha's death.

⌘ AKṢOBHYA ⌘

Earliest of the nonhistorical celestial Buddhas. His name literally means "immovable," and he is said (in the Vimalakīrtinirdeśa-sūtra) to reign over the Eastern Paradise known as Abhirati. His name seems to be first mentioned in the Perfection of Wisdom (Prajñāpāramitā) literature, but eventually finds citations in a wide variety of Mahāyāna and Vajrayāna texts. His most usual color is dark blue, but occasionally golden colored. He usually holds a vajra or diamond scepter in his right hand, while making the earth-touching gesture (bhūmisparśa-mudrā) with his left. He is often seated on a blue elephant. Legend reports that Akṣobhya, while still a bodhisattva, vowed never to manifest anger toward any being, and as a result of his vow, came to rule over the paradise of Abhirati. It is suggested that other practitioners who follow his example will obtain rebirth in Abhirati. While he is prominent in Nepal and Tibet, Akṣobhya is less popular in China and Japan. (See also AMITĀBHA; AMOGHASIDDHI; RATNASAMBHAVA; VAIROCANA.)

⌘ ĀLAYA-VIJÑĀNA ⌘

Literally "storehouse consciousness," the central concept of the Yogācāra school of Buddhism. In early Buddhism, a theory of six consciousnesses was postulated, each applicable to a particular sense organ. Yogācāra (especially in the writings of the brothers Asaṅga and Vasubandhu) added two further items to the list, extending it to eight: (1) manas, a subtle mental element which functions by receiving and disposing of data from the other six consciousnesses, and (2) the ālaya-vijnāna. This so-called storehouse consciousness receives the seeds (known as bījas) of karmic activity and stores them until they ripen and manifest themselves in a process referred to as "perfuming" (vāsanā). In so doing, this consciousness theory of Yogācāra accounts for such mental activity as memory, hard to explain through more traditional theories of consciousness. While the vast majority of seeds that ripen and manifest themselves are "tainted" (āsrava-bījas), resulting in a perception of reality that is delusional, the ālaya-vijñāna also contains a number of pure seeds (called anāsrava-bījas) that emerge from the deepest layer of the ālaya (referred to as the paramālaya). It is the ripening of these pure seeds that establishes the potential for a complete restructuring of experience, known as āśraya-parāvṛtti or literally "a turning over of one's basis," through meditation. Precisely because the ālaya-vijñāna functions as a storehouse, it is sometimes referred to as the Tathāgata-garbha or the "Womb of the Tathāgata." (See also TATHĀGATA-GARBHA; YOGĀCĀRA.)

⌘ AMARAPURA NIKĀYA ⌘

One of the three major divisions of the modern Buddhist saṃgha in Sri Lanka, differing from one another by region, caste, and purity of the monks. This group broke off from the Syāma Nikāya in Sri Lanka in 1803, taking its name from the city of Amarapura in Burma with which it is associated. It lists its founder as A. Ñāṇavimalatissa Thera. Originally intending to travel to Siam in search of ordination for monks other than those of the goigama caste, the founder instead went to Burma where ordination was conferred on him and five companions in Amarapura. Within a few years of return to Sri Lanka, the Amarapura Nikāya subdivided into a number of groups.

⌘ AMBEDKAR, BHIMRAO RAMJI ⌘
(1891–1956)

Former Indian Minister of Law who led a movement of low caste Indians to convert to Buddhism. Although he was from an untouchable caste, he nontheless obtained an education, became a lawyer, and worked diligently to upgrade the status of the untouchable castes in India. By 1935, Ambedkar announced that he would personally convert from his native Hinduism to another religion, encouraging his followers to do likewise. He eventually chose Buddhism due to its ethic of equanimity, and, in 1956, he converted to Buddhism in a public ceremony at Nagpur, along with more than a half-million untouchables. His well-known book *The Buddha and His Dhamma* remains an important guide for the millions of untouchables, known as "Ambedkar Buddhists," who have followed his model.

⌘ AMIDA ⌘

See AMITĀBHA

⌘ AMITA ⌘

See AMITĀBHA

⌘ AMITĀBHA ⌘

The Buddha of "Unlimited Light," said to rule over the Western Paradise of Sukhāvatī. Known in China as A-mi-t'o and in Japan as Amida (from the short Sanskrit form Amita), this Celestial Buddha is the focus of three major texts of Pure Land Buddhism: the (1) Larger Sukhāvatīvyūha-sūtra, (2) Smaller Sukhāvatīvyūha-sūtra, and (3) Amitāyurdhyāna-sūtra. The legend surrounding Amitabha develops from the story of a monk named Dharmākara who, eons previously, aspired to Buddhahood and made forty-eight vows, each concerning the nature of existence whence he becomes a Buddha. Dharmākara, after countless lifetimes of practice, becomes the Buddha Amitābha. Amitābha is generally conceived of in two ways: (1) as an object of meditation and (2) as the embodiment of compassion. As ruler of the Pure Land of Sukhāvatī, he welcomes all who earnestly wish to be reborn there, requiring only a strong commitment of faith in Amitābha's vows. This faith is expressed by the formula (in Sanskrit): Namo Amitābhāya Buddhāya, "Homage to Amitābha Buddha." Known in China as the Nien-fo (Namo A-mi-t'o Fo) and in Japan as the Nembutsu (Namu Amida Butsu), its repetition was a necessary ingredient for rebirth in the Pure Land. In fact, Dharmākara's eighteenth vow, often referred to as the most important of all vows, states quite directly that anyone who desires rebirth in the Pure Land need only recite his name or think of this desire *ten times*, in order to actualize their ambition. Because this tradition relies on faith rather than meditation, it is sometimes referred to as the "easy way" (*tariki* in Japanese). Amitābha sometimes appears with the Bodhisattvas Avalokiteśvara and Mahāsthāmaprāpta on his left and right, respectively. He also appears with Bhaiṣjyaguru Buddha, another of the Celestial Buddhas. An alternate name for Amitābha is sometimes employed: Amitāyus, literally "Unlimited Life." (See also AKṢOBHYA; AMITĀYURDHYĀNA-SŪTRA; AMOGHASIDDHI; DHARMĀKARA; LARGER AND SMALLER SUKHĀVATĪVYŪHA-SŪTRAS; PURE LAND; RATNASAMBHAVA; VAIROCANA.)

⌘ AMITĀYURDHYĀNA-SŪTRA ⌘

Literally "Discourse on Meditation on the Buddha Amitāyus." Along with the Larger and Smaller Sukhāvatīvyūha-sūtras, one of three texts basic to the Pure Land School of Buddhism. The message of the discourse is contextually embedded in the story of King Bimbisāra's imprisonment by his son Prince Ajātaśatru. Bimbisāra's wife questions the Buddha as to a place where she could lead a happy, trouble-free life. In response, Buddha causes all the Buddha-fields to appear to Vaidehī, whereupon she selects the Pure Land of Sukhāvatī. Rebirth in this paradise, however, is dependent on the cultivation of sixteen meditations, of which the ninth, meditation on Amitāyus (the Buddha of Unlimited Life), is most important. In fact, proper meditation on Amitāyus reveals all the other Celestial Buddhas. (See also LARGER SUKHĀVATĪ-VYŪHA-SŪTRA; SMALLER SUKHĀVATĪVYŪHA-SŪTRA; PURE LAND.)

⌘ AMOGHASIDDHI ⌘

Literally "Unfailing Success," one of the five Celestial Buddhas of Mahāyāna Buddhism. Amoghasiddhi is geographically associated with the north. Most often, he is linked with the Bodhisattva Viśvapāṇi. When depicted in paintings, or in iconography, he is green in color, with his left hand in his lap (palm up) and his right hand making the gesture of fearlessness (abhaya mudrā). In Tantric Buddhism he is the personified deity of the fourth aggregate (saṃskāra). (See also AKṢOBHYA; AMITĀBHA; RATNASAMBHAVA; VAIROCANA.)

⌘ ĀNANDA ⌘

One of Buddha's chief disciples and his personal attendant during his last twenty-five years of life. Although there is much uncertainty about his family history and ordination lineage in the various Buddhist textual traditions, it does appear that Ānanda was Buddha's first cousin. According to the Pāli accounts, Buddha made his wish for a *permanent* personal attendant known during the twentieth year of his ministry. Although not initially seeking the position, Ānanda was eventually selected and offered to serve (provided a series of conditions were fulfilled in which it was guaranteed that Ānanda would receive no extra benefits as a result of his position). Ānanda is especially recognized for his role in the establishment of an order of nuns (bhikṣuṇīs). Following Buddha's preliminary decision *not* to establish an order of nuns, Ānanda interceded on behalf of Buddha's foster mother, who desired to enter the homeless life, and convinced Buddha to change his decision, allowing Mahāprajāpatī to go forth as the new order's first member. Ānanda was also revered for his powerful memory, a talent which precipitated his critical role in the proceedings of the First Council, held at Rājagṛha in the year of

Buddha's death. Ānanda was chosen by the council's president, Kāśyapa, to recite all of the sermons preached by Buddha, thus establishing the canonical record known as the Sūtra Piṭaka or "Basket of Discourses." Unfortunately, all members participating in the event were required to be arhants or enlightened monks, and Ananda, by dint of his extensive, time consuming, and unselfish service to Buddha, had not yet achieved that goal. Late into the night prior to the beginning of the convocation, Ānanda attains nirvāṇa, recites all of the sūtras for the council, and establishes one of the major bases of scriptural orthodoxy for the early community. Legend suggests that Ānanda lived to the age of 120. (See also COUNCILS-RĀJAGṚHA.)

⌘ ĀNANDA METTEYYA ⌘

(1872–1923)

British Buddhist, founder of the International Buddhist Society. Born in London as Charles Henry Allan Bennett, he became fascinated with Buddhism after reading Sir Edwin Arnold's *The Light of Asia*. He traveled first to Sri Lanka in 1898, became a novice monk in Burma in 1901, and took full ordination the following year, adopting the name Ānanda Metteyya. On March 15, 1903, he founded the International Buddhist Society (Buddhasāsana Samāgama), based in Rangoon. The Society published a quarterly review called *Buddhism*, and within a few years of its founding the Society established a branch in England. Afflicted with severe asthma throughout his life, Ānanda Metteyya had planned to travel from England to California in 1914, but was not allowed to make the journey, owing to his poor health. He spent the last decade of his life in England, occasionally writing for *The Buddhist Review*.

⌘ ANĀTHAPIṆḌIKA ⌘

A wealthy banker from Śrāvastī who was one of Buddha's chief patrons and lay followers. He built a monastery for the community, known as Jetavana, in Śrāvastī, a site at which Buddha spent the last twenty-five rainy seasons of his ministry. He saw the Buddha regularly, and bestowed so many gifts on the community that he was eventually reduced to poverty. He predeceased the historical Buddha.

⌘ ANĀTMAN ⌘

One of the three marks of existence preached in Buddha's second sermon and literally meaning "not-self." The Brāhmaṇical tradition at the time of Buddha maintained that each sentient being possessed a self (ātman) which was pure, subtle, and eternal, and which transmitted karmic residue from one life to the next. Buddha attacked this notion in two ways. First, he emphasized nonattachment as a key factor in his teaching, thus eliminating the urgency of clinging to the supposed ātman. Second, he suggested that the concept was illogical and argued that something pure, subtle, and eternal like the ātman could not associate with something impure, gross, and impermanent like the body. The above does not mean to suggest that Buddha preached annihilation of the individual at death. Rather, like other Indian traditions of the time, he maintained that rebirth took place and karma was transmitted from life to life. The resolution of precisely *what* is transmitted and *how* the transmission occurs remains unclear. The issue became one of the critical areas explored by the developing Abhidharma or "Higher Philosophy" traditions in Buddhism. One theory, for example, suggests that factors known as "mental constituents" (saṃskāras) are transmitted, at death, to an individual's "rebirth consciousness" (pratisandhi-vijñāna) and that rebirth occurs in a "stream" (santāna). This is dangerously close to positing rebirth consciousness as a pseudo-self, simply titled differently. Additionally, "stream" is only an ordinary language metaphor utilized to accomodate discussion about the self. Equally, the problem is not solved in the famous text known as the Milindapañha in which the clever monk Nāgasena advises King Menander that rebirth occurs just as a flame passes from one lamp to another. Later Buddhist sects, like the Pudgalavādins postulated other ideas about the process of rebirth, which were generally considered and refuted, but the problem has never been satisfactorily resolved either by the Hīnayāna or Mahāyāna sects. Thus, the "self" in Buddhism can be considered to be nothing more than an impermanent, changing personality comprised of the five aggregates (skandhas). (See also ANITYA; DUḤKHA.)

⌘ ANAWRAHTĀ ⌘

Burmese king who ruled 1040–1077, converted to Theravāda Buddhism, and put Shin Arahan in charge of the saṃgha in unified Burma. Anawrahtā was impressed with the simplicity of Theravāda, as taught to him by the young, pious monk Shin Arahan from Thatōn. When Anawrahtā sought to obtain a complete set of the Tripiṭaka from King Manuha of Thatōn, the king refused, prompting a military encounter in which Manuha's capital was destroyed. Anawrahtā attempted to make his own capital of Pagān a center of the pure faith, a feat he accomplished through a series of battles that consolidated Burma. In addition to building many pagodas, he established relations with other Theravāda countries, including Sri Lanka.

⌘ ANESAKI, MASAHARU ⌘
(1873–1949)

One of the renowned early Japanese scholars of Buddhism. He was the chief professor at the Seminar of Religions of the Faculty of Letters at Tokyo Imperial University when it was founded in 1905. He had a remarkable education, having had the opportunity to study in Europe with Paul Deussen, Hermann Oldenberg, Thomas W. Rhys Davids, and others. He held the chair of Japanese Literature and Life at Harvard University from 1913–1915. During his stay in America, he wrote his classic book *Nichiren, the Buddhist Prophet*. Following the great earthquake in Tokyo (1923), he was appointed chief librarian of the Tokyo University Library. He was a prolific author, having written hundreds of articles in Japanese and more than fifty in English. *History of Japanese Religion* remains one of the standard works on the subject today. In addition to his outstanding work on Japanese Buddhism, he was a serious student of both comparative religion and comparative Buddhist studies. He retired from Tokyo Imperial University in 1934, spending much of his time until his death in 1949 working on the life and thought of Prince Shōtoku.

⌘ AṄGA ⌘

An early Theravāda classification schemata of Buddha's teachings into nine categories. In early Buddhism, especially Theravāda, one of the terms utilized to designate Buddhist canonical teaching is *Buddhavacana*, literally "that which is spoken by Buddha." Another of these terms used to speak of Buddha's teachings collectively is *Navaṅga-satthu-sāsana*, the "nine-limbed teaching of the Master." The nine divisions include (in Pāli): (1) Sutta (prose discourses), (2) Geyya (mixed prose and verse), (3) Veyyākaraṇa (expositions), (4) Gāthā (verses), (5) Udāna (utterances), (6) Itivuttaka (quotations), (7) Jātaka (birth-stories), (8) Abbhutadhamma (mysterious phenomena), and (9) Vedalla (dialectical analyses). Precisely because this classification is very early, Buddhist commentators like Buddhaghosa were hard pressed to classify texts of obviously later composition. This latter point becomes quite acute with regard to the somewhat later Buddhist schools that preserved their canonical texts in *Sanskrit*. To account for their texts, three further aṅgas were added (in Sanskrit): (10) Nidāna (introductions), (11) Avadāna (legends), and (12) Upadeśa (instructions). Whether one affirms the 9-fold or 12-fold pattern, this classification invariably stands at odds with the traditional notation of Buddhist scripture as *Tripiṭaka* or "Three Baskets." (See also TRIPIṬAKA.)

⌘ ANGKOR WAT ⌘

A temple complex in Cambodia, built under the reign of Sūryavarman II (1113–1150), a Hindu Vaiṣṇavaite (i.e., follower of Viṣṇu). Once the subsequent Khmer rulers embraced Buddhism, the temple became a Buddhist site. Eventually, Angkor was abandoned as the capital of Cambodia (in 1431), and the temple site was reclaimed by the jungle. Angkor Wat is considered by some to reflect the finest art and architecture of the Khmers.

⌘ AṄGUTTARA NIKĀYA ⌘

The fourth collection in the Sutta Piṭaka of the Pāli Canon, literally meaning the "item-more" discourses. It corresponds to the Ekottarika Āgama of the Sanskrit Buddhist canon. This division of the scriptures contains a series of texts grouped according to the number of items in the text, and in an ascending or arithmetical progression from one to eleven. Most of the discourses are short, and in so doing, exercise greater emphasis on the message being established. The Aṅguttara Nikāya may also have deep links with the other two Pāli Piṭakas. B.C. Law, for example, thinks that some of the suttas of this Nikāya form the real historical basis of the Vinaya texts. Additionally, the foundations of the Abhidhamma can be seen here too, as texts of that Piṭaka, like the Puggalapaññatti, have whole sections that can be found in the Aṅguttara Nikāya. (See also ĀGAMA; TRIPIṬAKA)

⌘ ANITYA ⌘

One of the traditional three marks of existence preached in Buddha's second sermon and generally translated as "impermanence." In its simplest sense, it suggests that everything is in a continual process of change. More explicitly, early Buddhism argued that all elements of existence are composed of fundamental building blocks called *dharmas*. These dharmas are of two types: conditioned (i.e., compounded) and unconditioned. It is the former category that Buddha repeatedly cites as being impermanent. Further, impermanence is a comprehensive process. Even each moment can be subdivided into an origin (utpatti), duration (sthiti), and decay (vināśa), and as such, there is really nothing substantial in the entire phenomenal world to be grasped . . . which has significant import for the nature of Buddhist religious practice. At least for early Buddhism the unconditioned dharmas seem to lie outside the realm of impermanence, a dilemma addressed by Mahāyāna Buddhism through the concept of emptiness (śūnyatā), which they append to the doctrine of the marks of existence as a "fourth mark." The notion of emptiness argues that even unconditioned dharmas have no substantiality or "own-being" (svabhāva), and thus nothing, anywhere, at any time can be justifiably cited as an "object," and therefore worthy of active, experiential pursuit. (See also ANĀTMAN; DUḤKHA; ŚŪNYATĀ.)

⌘ AN SHIH-KAO ⌘

A Parthian monk who traveled to Lo-yang in 148 C.E. and headed a team of (predominantly) Hīnayāna monks who translated Buddhist texts on meditation practice into Chinese. He was one of the earliest translators of Buddhist texts into Chinese, often utlizing Taoist terminology. According to Tao-an (312–385), An Shih-kao was a specialist in dhyāna or meditation practices, and also enumeration of categorized items. He produced at least about three dozen texts in a roughly thirty-year period of activity in China. Little information seems to be available concerning his old age.

⌘ ANURĀDHAPURA ⌘

Capital city of Sri Lanka until around the tenth century, and the location of numerous important Buddhist monasteries and sacred sites. Anurādhapura is reputed in the legends to have had an extremely ancient foundation, and was by the reign of Devānaṃpiya Tissa (247–207 B.C.E.) the capital city of Sri Lanka. When the king was converted to Buddhism by Aśoka's son and other missionaries from India, a great monastery was erected in the capital and known as the Mahāvihāra. Aśoka's daughter even brought a branch of the original Bodhi Tree to the site as well. In the course of time, other great monasteries, most notably Abhayagiri and Jetavana, were established in the city. Great stūpas, some of which were said to enshrine relics of the Buddha, were also erected in the city. Precisely because of its easy accessibility from India, Anurādhapura was subject to periodic plunder from outside the borders of Sri Lanka. Eventually the city was abandoned, not to be reclaimed from the jungle until the nineteenth century. (See also ABHAYAGIRI; JETAVANA; MAHĀVIHĀRA.)

⌘ ANUTTARAYOGA-TANTRA ⌘

The fourth, and last, of the four classes of Buddhist Tantra. In the Tibetan Buddhist canon, the Tantras are located in the seventh subdivision of the Kanjur (bKa'-gyur). They include twenty-two volumes, containing more than three hundred texts. Of the four classes of Tantra, the first two, Kriyā and Caryā, are considered lower than the final two, Yoga and Anuttarayoga. It is the last class of Tantra that designates the ideal types called siddhas or perfected ones. Philosophically, the Anuttarayoga-Tantra is based on the Mādhyamika school, emphasizing emptiness (śūnyatā), the elimination of all subject-object duality, and the union of wisdom (prajñā) and skill-in-means (upāya). Religiously, the Anuttarayoga-Tantra focuses on ritual acts involving meditation, the union of male and female yogic practitioners, eating of sacramental food, and other rites designed to attain powers known as *siddhis*. Two of the most important Buddhist Tantric texts, the Guhyasamāja Tantra and the Hevajra Tantra belong to this class. (See also TANTRA.)

⌘ ĀRĀMA ⌘

Literally, a "pleasure-ground," denoting a type of rainy season dwelling for monks or nuns. In early Buddhism, monks and nuns were allowed to settle in one or another type of dwelling for the rainy season: either a dwelling staked out and built by the individual member (and called an āvāsa) or a property donated by a patron for the use of the monks or nuns (and called an ārāma). Ārāmas were usually located on the outskirts of a town or village and maintained by the patron. Occasionally, ārāmas were donated to the saṃgha on a permanent basis, as with the Veḷuvana donated to the saṃgha by King Bimbisāra. In this latter case, such a donation was called a Saṃghārāma. Unlike the āvāsas, which were clearly temporary and to be torn down at the end of the rainy season, ārāmas were permanent, and some persisted for many years, as was the case with Jetavanārāma, which was still existent during the time of Fa-hien's visit from China to India and Sri Lanka (399–414 C.E.). (See also AVASA; VIHARA.)

⌘ ARHANT ⌘

Technical term derived from the Sanskrit √ arh, meaning "worthy one" and used to identify an enlightened individual who has attained nirvāṇa. The arhant is one who has joined the community of "noble persons" (ārya-pudgalas) by enduring a rigorous series of practices aimed at eliminating all defilements (kleśas) and overcoming all impurities (āsravas). The Visuddhimagga, an extremely important Theravāda Buddhist commentary written by Buddhaghosa identifies three ways of entering the path leading to arhantship: faith, wisdom, and meditation. In the Sarvāstivādin school, only faith and wisdom are mentioned for entry to the path leading to arhantship. Although the goal of arhantship appears to be available to the laity as well as the monastic community in early Buddhism, very few cases of lay members attaining enlightenment are cited, and almost always carry the proviso that upon attaining arhantship, one enters the monastic way of life. It is a goal that does seem to have been open to women as well, as indicated by texts such as the Therīgāthā. There is serious debate in early Buddhism about the status of the arhant, with the Theravāda school maintaining that once nirvāṇa is attained, it can never be lost. The Sarvāstivādin school and others maintain that arhants *can* regress and are capable of falling back in their attainment. With the rise of the Mahāyāna school, and its emphasis on the unfailing compassion of the bodhisattva who seeks complete perfect enlightenment for all sentient beings, the arhant ideal was discredited by Mahāyāna literature to represent a lesser, selfish individual who strives only for personal liberation. Thus, a serious disagreement remains between early Buddhism (i.e., Hīnayāna) and later Buddhism (i.e., Mahāyāna) about the nature, status, and level of attainment of the ideal type. (See also BODHISATTVA; LOHAN.)

⌘ ARNOLD, SIR EDWIN ⌘
(1832–1904)

Nineteenth-century author whose book *The Light of Asia*, published in 1879, popularized Buddhism. Born in England, he went to King's College in London, eventually winning a scholarship to University College, Oxford. He married at age twenty-two, and three years later became principal of Deccan College in Poona, India. He published his first book of verse in 1853, translated texts from Sanskrit, and even compiled a Turkish grammar in 1877. Upon its publication in 1879, *The Light of Asia* became immediately popular. The book inspired many other investigators, and was seen as an antidote to a number of mid-century writers and scholars (such as Eugène Burnouf, Barthélemy Saint-Hilaire, and others) who saw Buddhism as a wholly nihilistic religion. Although never publicly avowing personal commitment to the Buddhist religion, many observers felt that Arnold was a Buddhist at heart. To this end he worked diligently for the restoration of Buddhist sites, especially Bodhgāyā.

⌘ ĀRYADEVA ⌘

The most famous disciple of Nāgārjuna, founder of the Mādhyamika school of Buddhism. There are a variety of sources containing information on Āryadeva, most notably a biographical work translated into Chinese by Kumārajīva, references in the records of the Chinese pilgrim Hsüan-tsang, who visited India between 629–645, and citations in the records of the Tibetan historians Buston and Tāranātha. Āryadeva seems to have been a native of Sri Lanka, living in the third century C.E. He is often cited as having been blind in one eye, and thus also referred to as Kāṇadeva ("One-Eyed Deva"). He is also sometimes listed as one of the twenty-three Indian patriarchs in the Zen lineage. He studied with Nāgārjuna, mastering and championing the Mādhyamika system. He is perhaps best known for his text known as the Catuḥśataka, the first half of which extols the way of the bodhisattva, and the second half of which continues the work of Nāgārjuna's Mūlamadhyamaka-kārikās. His other major work is the Śataśāstra, a polemical treatise which refutes the theories of a number of schools rival to Buddhism. (See also MĀDHYAMIKA; NĀGĀRJUNA.)

⌘ ĀRYA PUDGALA ⌘

A generic term for individuals said to be members of the āryasaṃgha. An ārya pudgala is an individual who has risen beyond status as an "ordinary" person (or pṛthagjana), and attained entry into the path that begins with the stage known as "stream-winner," continues through the "once-returner" and "nonreturner" stages, and culminates with the attainment of arhantship. Entering the stream-winner stage is contingent on totally abandoning (1) belief in a self, (2) doubts about the traditional "three jewels" of Buddha, Dharma, and Saṃgha, and (3) belief in the efficacy of rituals. One progresses through the other developmental stages by eliminating other fetters that bind one to compounded existence. (See also ĀRYA SAṂGHA.)

⌘ ĀRYA SAṂGHA ⌘

Literally the "Saṃgha of Noble Persons," those individuals who have attained status as an ārya pudgala. Although rather widely misunderstood, it is the ārya samgha or saṃgha of noble persons that forms the third of the traditional "three jewels" in Buddhism, and *not* the conventional (or samvṛti) saṃgha of monks, nuns, laymen, and laywomen. (See also ĀRYA PUDGALA.)

⌘ ĀRYA SATYAS ⌘

The famous four noble truths, preached by Buddha in his first sermon and forming the cornerstone doctrine of his Dharma. In his first discourse to his five former ascetic colleagues in a Deer Park in Benares, known as the Dharmacakrapravartana-sūtra or the "Discourse on the Turning of the Wheel of the Law," Buddha revealed his religious vision in terms of four statements that formed the substance of his practical instruction, and which continue to be as meaningful for Buddhists today as then. The first truth boldly stated that all life is *duḥkha*, a word rather badly translated as "pain" or "suffering." Perhaps more appropriately, it suggests that when Buddha argues that all life is duḥkha, he simply means that all of life's experiences, from birth to death, yield an unsatisfactoriness, either through physical pain, change, or conditioned phenomena. The second noble truth, cited as *samudaya*, identifies the cause: craving (tṛṣṇā). Irrespective of precisely what one craves, whether sensual pleasures (kāma-trṣṇā), craving for existence (bhava-tṛsṇā), or craving for nonexistence (vibhava-tṛṣṇā), the net result of craving is rebirth. Moreover, false views (dṛṣṭi) and conceit (māna) are also conducive to the creation of duḥkha. Were Buddha to stop here, a strong case might be made for his Dharma as purely negative, stressing only the vagaries of life. It is in the third and fourth noble truths that Buddha's optimism and pragmatic genius emerge. In the third noble truth, he argues for the cessation of duḥkha, referred to as *nirodha*, through the elimination of craving. The cessation of duḥkha can be achieved by the fourth noble truth, called the *aṣṭāṅgika-mārga* or eightfold path. The path contains clear instructions with regard to the practice of right (1) understanding, (2) thought, (3) speech, (4) action, (5) livelihood, (6) effort, (7) mindfulness, and (8) concentration. Steps 1 and 2 refer to the cultivation of wisdom (prajñā), 3, 4, and 5 to the cultivation of morality (śīla), and 6, 7, and 8 to the cultivation of meditation (samādhi). The famous Theravādin commentator Buddhaghosa is reported to have said that wisdom is the body of Buddhism, while morality and meditation are the legs that support it. With the effective practice of the four noble truths, Buddhist practitioners are reputed to attain nirvāṇa and become "worthy ones," arhants. Upon hearing Buddha's discourse, Ājñāta Kauṇḍinya is said to have attained enlightenment on the spot, becoming the first of Buddha's disciples to do so.

⌘ ASAṂSKṚTA ⌘

Technical term indicating that which is "unconditioned" or which is not produced by cause(s). In the Abhidharma traditions of the early Buddhist schools, the elemental building blocks of experiential reality were referred to as *dharmas,* in this usage not to be confused with the generic term for Buddha's teachings. Dharmas were said to be of two kinds: (1) conditioned (saṃskṛta), or those items which, by their various combinations, produce the compounded world of our ordinary experience, and which adhere to the laws of causality as espoused by traditional Buddhist doctrine, and (2) *unconditioned (asaṃskṛta),* or those items which are beyond conditioned reality, outside ordinary causality, and therefore, not subject to the law of impermanence. For the Theravāda and a number of other early Buddhist schools, there was only one asaṃskṛta dharma: *nirvāṇa.* The Sarvāstivādin school enlarged this number to three: two forms of cessation and space. The Mahāsāṃghikas enlarged the list to nine. Even the Yogācāra, a Mahāyāna school that espouses the emptiness of *all* dharmas, posits a number of asaṃskṛta-dharmas. As such, debate over the number and nature of asaṃskṛta-dharmas was a significant issue in the Abhidharma traditions of the various schools. (See also DHARMA.)

⌘ ASAṄGA ⌘

Famous Buddhist who founded the Yogācāra school of Buddhism. Born to a Brahmin family in Puruṣapura (i.e., modern Peshawar) sometime in the fourth century C.E., Asaṅga was the eldest of three brothers. He was converted to the Mahīśāsaka school of early Buddhism and became a monk in this tradition. Apparently he received teaching, through a vision, directly from the future Buddha Maitreya who provided him with a series of texts that were collected under the name of Maitreyanātha. Quickly converting to Mahāyāna as a result of this interaction, Asaṅga began composing texts in his own name, founded the Yogācāra school of Buddhism, and converted his brother Vasubandhu who, by that time, had developed a reputation as one of the eminent teachers of the Sarvāstivādin school of Buddhism. Asaṅga is identified as the author of the Mahāyānasaṃgraha, Abhidharmasamuccaya, and a major commentary on the Saṃdhinirmocana-sūtra, while Vasubandhu is best known for the Abhidharmakośa, Viṃśatikā, and Triṃśikā. Perhaps more influenced by the Sarvāstivāda school of early Buddhism than Nāgārjuna's dialectic, Asaṅga advocated an idealism that sought to synthesize the various aspects of Mahāyana thought. He developed an eight-membered theory of consciousness, emphasizing a "storehouse consciousness" or ālaya-vijñāna that was a repository for the seeds of past karmic acts, an alternative to Nāgārjuna's notion of two levels of truth resulting in *three natures* called svabhāvas, an emphasis on the *practice* of the bodhisattva, and a doctrine known as the *Tathāgata-garbha* or "Womb of the Buddha" underscoring the potential for all beings to attain Buddhahood. (See also ABHIDHARMASAMUCCAYA; ĀLAYA-VIJÑĀNA; MAHĀYĀNASAṂGRAHA; VASUBANDHU; YOGĀCĀRA.)

⌘ AŚOKA ⌘

Third ruler in the Mauryan Dynasty, reigning from 272–231 B.C.E., and famous for propagating the Dharma as well as erecting rock and pillar edicts throughout his sphere of influence. Grandson of Candragupta Maurya and son of Bindusāra, Aśoka may well have been sympathetic to Buddhism prior to his victory over the Kaliṅga region in 260. However, following the bloody battle of conquest cited above, Aśoka is reputed to have become a Buddhist lay disciple, noted in Rock Edict Number XIII. While attempting to rule as a pious "Dharma-rāja," he emphasized the practice of ahiṃsā (noninjury), respect for religious teachers, and other principles demonstrating a "Reign of Dharma." Aśoka established officers (known as "Superintendents of Dharma" or Dharma-Mahāmātras) to disseminate the religion. He is perhaps best known, though, for two major enterprises during his reign: (1) the convening of a Buddhist council and (2) an extensive missionary activity. Sometime around 250 B.C.E., in response to apparently heretical influences in the saṃgha, Aśoka sponsored a council in his capital city of Pāṭaliputra under the direction of Moggaliputta Tissa (also referred to as Upagupta). Known as the third canonical Buddhist council, it appears to have been a genuine historical event, attended by 1,000 monks, eventually upholding the orthodox or Vibhajyavādin tradition and expelling the proponents of heretical notions (thought by some to be the forerunners of the Sarvāstivādin school). Traditional accounts, to some degree corroborated by epigraphical evidence, also credit Aśoka with a profound missionary enterprise extending, in addition to Sri Lanka (which is rather clearly documented), to an impressive list of sites outside his kingdom. It is during Aśoka's reign that Buddhism became a truly international religion. Whether Aśoka's patronage of Buddhism is as extensive as Buddhist accounts surmise remains a question for discussion, for he also patronized other religious groups in his domain, and may *not have meant Buddhist Dharma* in his use of the term. It is clear, at least, that Aśoka probably ranks as the foremost king in Indian religious history. (See also AŚOKĀVADĀNA; COUNCILS-PĀṬALIPUTRA II; MAURYAN DYNASTY; MISSIONS.)

⌘ AŚOKĀVADĀNA ⌘

The Sanskrit title of a text devoted to the Aśoka legend, embedded in the larger text known as the Divyāvadāna. There are a number of independent versions of the text preserved in Chinese (for example, the A-yü wang chuan and the A-yü wang ching). As a text category, Avadānas relate legends about illustrious Buddhists, and tend to bridge the literary gap between the development of Hīnayāna and Mahāyāna. In the case of the Aśokāvadāna, the text begins with the legend of a monk named Upagupta who eventually played a significant role in Aśoka's reign. Then the text shifts to the actual legends surrounding Aśoka. Critical foci of the legends include Aśoka's conversion of his heretical brother (named Vītāśoka), his building of 84,000 stūpas, Queen Tiṣyarakṣitā's role in the blinding of Prince Kuṇāla, the eventual squandering of Aśoka's wealth, and the death of Aśoka in destitution. The text is our main Sanskrit source for information on King Aśoka, to be used in conjunction with the Pāli materials contained primarily in the Mahāvaṃsa, Dīpavaṃsa, and Buddhaghosa's commentary on the Vinaya. (See also AŚOKA.)

⌘ ĀSRAVA ⌘

Technical term, the translation of which is somewhat problematic, usually (etymologically) rendered as "outflows," but more explicitly intending to indicate defilements, impurities, or, as often presented by early translators, "cankers." They are generally noted to be threefold: (1) the impurity of sensual desire (kāmāsrava), (2) the impurity of desire for continued existence (bhavāsrava), and (3) the impurity of ignorance (avidyāsrava). The elimination of these impurities are requisite for the attainment of nirvāṇa, and historically represent the final impurities eliminated by Siddhārtha prior to his attainment of Buddhahood. To overcome these impurities results in escape from rebirth in the cycle of saṃ sāra.

⌘ AṢṬASĀHASRIKĀ-PRAJÑĀPĀRAMITĀ-SŪTRA ⌘

The Perfection of Wisdom Discourse in 8,000 Lines. The earliest extant text of the Mahāyāna school of Buddhism is the 8,000 line sūtra, reflecting the creation of a new class of literature known as the "Perfection of Wisdom Literature," and dating from the second century B.C.E. It was also the first text of this type translated into Chinese, in the version known as the Tao-hsing Ching, rendered into Chinese by Lokakṣema in 179 C.E. The Prajñāpāramitā sūtras were eventually expanded into versions of varying lengths up to 100,000 lines. By around 300 C.E., summaries were also constructed, including the two most famous: (1) the Vajraccchedikā or "Diamond Sūtra," and (2) the Hṛdaya or "Heart Sūtra." The emphasis of the 8,000 line sūtra, and all the texts of this class, was on the emptiness (śūnyatā) of all dharmas and the practice of perfections (pāramitās) by bodhisattvas. The text is structured as a continuous dialogue between the Buddha and a changing variety of disciples, each of whom reflects a particular level of attainment and insight. (See also PRAJÑĀPĀRAMITĀ LITERATURE.)

⌘ AŚVAGHOṢA ⌘

Buddhist poet best known for his famous epic poem called the Buddhacarita that represents the first complete biography of the Buddha. Information concerning his life is conflicting, but it appears that Aśvaghoṣa was a contemporary of King Kaniṣka (i.e., second century C.E.). He was likely a Brahmin, originally from Śaketa (i.e., Ayodhyā), and probably converted to Buddhism by the Vaibhāṣika master Parśva. There is some speculation that his views are closer to another Buddhist school (known as the Bahuśrutīyas). More than one scholar considers his poetry to be equal to the classical tradition in Indian literature known as kavya or court poetry. He is also the author of a shorter, and less well known epic, titled Saundarananda ("Handsome Nanda"). A famous Mahāyāna text, "The Awakening of Faith in the Mahāyāna" (Mahāyānaśraddhotpāda-śāstra), is attributed to an author of the same name.

⌘ ATĪŚA ⌘

(982–1054)

Famous Bengali Buddhist scholar who arrived in Tibet in 1042, spending the last years of his life there. Atīśa was invited to Tibet from the monastic university of Vikramaśīla on the basis of his vast knowledge of both the exoteric and esoteric Buddhist teachings. He helped Tibetan Buddhism purify the saṃgha, emphasizing celibacy and strict practice, and continued teaching Tantra until his death. His primary writing in this period was the Bodhipaṭhapradīpa or "Lamp for the Way of Enlightenment." Atīśa's chief disciple was 'Brom-ston (1008–1064), a layman, who founded the bKa-gdams sect, representing the first Tibetan Buddhist sect with a *clear* historical record. Atīśa's work also had much influence on later Tibetan Buddhists, especially Tsong-kha-pa and the dGe-lugs-pa school.

⌘ AVALOKITEŚVARA ⌘

"The Lord Who Looks Down," one of the most famous and important of the Celestial Bodhisattvas in Mahāyāna Buddhism. Initially, Avalokiteśvara is a minor figure in such texts as the Vimalakīrtinirdeśa-sūtra and Lotus-sūtra. His first significant role is in the Pure Land Sūtras where he and Mahāsthamaprāpta serve as the chief attendants to Amitābha Buddha. Presumably, Avalokiteśvara has purified himself for countless ages, and accordingly, is the embodiment of compassion (karuṇā) which, along with wisdom (prajñā), are the chief attributes expressive of Buddhahood. He aids all people who call upon him in need, helping them with numerous arms of compassion. In art, Avalokiteśvara is represented in a variety of ways, often as a layman with eleven heads, as many as a thousand arms, and a crown with an image of Amitābha in it. He sometimes holds a blue lotus flower in his hand. In China and Japan, Avalokiteśvara was transformed into a female image, known as Kuan-yin and Kwannon, respectively. In Tibet, he was revered as a patron of the land, known as Chenrezi (sPyan-ras-gzigs).

⌘ ĀVĀSA ⌘

One of two types of rainy season dwellings for monks or nuns. An āvāsa was a monastic dwelling place staked out, constructed, and cared for by the monks and nuns themselves. One entire chapter in the Mahāvagga of the Pāli Vinaya, and in the Varṣāvastu sections of the other extant Vinayas, explains the regulations for construction of the āvāsa, its maintenance, regulations for living within it, and for the appropriate rules of etiquette to be observed. Within each āvāsa, monks and nuns lived in individual houses known as vihāras, and amounting to little more than a hut with a minimum of requisites. Proper boundaries were staked out, care being taken to be sure that no two āvāsas overlapped, and that no colony infringed on another. Āvāsas were generally constructed close enough to villages so as to support the collection of alms, while maintaining sufficient distance to avoid the hustle and bustle of village life. During the rainy season retreat, monks and nuns received their daily support from the laity, and in return offered counsel and Dharma instruction, thus establishing a fine symbiotic relationship. Unlike ārāmas, which represented permanent structures, āvāsas were generally intended to be impermanent units, torn down at rain's end. (See also ĀRĀMA; VIHĀRA.)

⌘ AVATAṂSAKA-SŪTRA ⌘

The "Flower Ornament Sūtra," a Mahāyāna text forming the basis of the Chinese Hua-yen and Japanese Kegon schools of Buddhism. There is little certainty regarding the composition of Avataṃsaka-sūtra. Research indicates that much of the text may have been composed in Central Asia or perhaps even in China. It was presumably translated from Sanskrit into Chinese by Buddhabhadra around 420 C.E. Two very important chapters of the text *do exist in Sanskrit*: (1) the Daśabhūmika, a work on the ten stages of the bodhisattva, and (2) the Gaṇḍavyūha, a work relating the wandering of Sudhana in search of enlightenment, and constituting the concluding portion of the Avataṃsaka-sūtra. The philosophical content of the text focuses on the development of the notion of Dharma-dhātu, the realm where all phenomena interpenetrate, with the whole present in the parts and the parts present in the whole. In keeping with the Mahāyāna ideal, the text argues that the Dharma-dhātu can be identified with emptiness (śūnyatā), suchness (tathatā), and the Womb of the Buddha (Tathāgata-garbha). Based on this text, the Hua-yen school of Buddhism in China was founded by Tu-shun (557–640) and organized by Fa-tsang (643–712). The Kegon school was imported to Japan during the Nara Period (710–794) of its history. (See also HUA-YEN; KEGON.)

— B —

⌘ BARDO THÖDOL (BAR-DO THOS-GROL) ⌘

Text attributed to Padmasambhava and identified as The Tibetan Book of the Dead. It belongs to a category of text known as *Terma (gter-ma)*, or early Buddhist teachings that were hidden in secret places when the Buddhists were persecuted in the early ninth century, to be recovered at later times and expounded by appropriately trained persons known as *Tertöns (gter-ston)*. The text elucidates six kinds of "in-between states" (bar-do), or those conditions that result in the forty-nine days between the time one dies and is reborn into a new form: the (1) birth bardo, (2) dream bardo, (3) meditation bardo, (4) experience of death bardo, (5) supreme reality bardo, and (6) state of becoming bardo. The final three bardos are linked to the Three Bodies of the Buddha (trikāya). The experience of death bardo is associated with the Dharma-kāya or "Ultimate Body," during which time a white light is manifested. The supreme reality bardo is associated with the Saṃbhoga-kāya or "Enjoyment Body," during which time lights in five colors appear, each associated with a maṇḍala representing one of the five "Buddha Families" in Tantric theory. Finally, the state of becoming bardo is associated with the Nirmāṇa-kāya or the "Apparition Body," during which time lesser lights are manifested, associated with the six states of existence (bhavacakra). The strong imagery and rituals associated with the text are designed to help the adept attain liberation. A number of translations of the text are available, beginning with that of W.Y. Evans-Wentz, originally published in 1927. Also significant is a more modern version by Chögyam Trungpa and Francesca Fremantle, published in 1975. (See also TIBETAN BOOK OF THE DEAD.)

⌘ BAREAU, ANDRÉ ⌘

French Buddhologist regarded as perhaps the world's leading authority on Indian Buddhist sectarianism. His classic books *Les premiers conciles bouddhiques* and *Les Sectes bouddhiques du petit Véhicule*, both published in 1955, are still considered the outstanding research volumes in that area. The latter cited volume conclusively demonstrated that the earliest schism in Indian Buddhism *did not* occur at the second Buddhist council of Vaiśālī, as previously thought, but occurred, according to Bareau, thirty-seven years later during the reign of Mahāpadma Nanda, and focused on supposed disciplinary laxity by the future Mahāsāṃghikas and five theses concerning the nature of liberated individuals known as arhants set forth by the notorious monk Mahādeva. Bareau's theory has only been recently questioned in the published research of Charles Prebish and Janice Nattier. Bareau has also published two other major books: (1) *L'Absolu en philosophie bouddhique: Evolution de la notion d'Asaṃskṛta* (1951) and *Recherches sur la biographie du Bouddha dans les Sūtrapiṭaka et les Vinayapiṭaka anciens* (1963, 1971). He was on the initial editorial advisory board of the *Journal of the International Association of Buddhist Studies*.

⌘ BASSUI ZENJI ⌘
(1327–1387)

Zen master associated with the Rinzai school. Motivated by the death of his father at age seven, Bassui came early to a consideration of the key issues of life and death. Although he took monastic ordination at age twenty-nine, he chose not to live in a monastery, searching vigorously until he found a Zen master appropriate for him: Kohō Zenji. He completed his training under Kohō Zenji, attaining enlightenment and receiving confirmation of his achievement. He did not assume the role of abbot of a monastery until his fiftieth year, remaining in that position until his death ten years later. While a number of other Zen masters are well known for their work in the capital of Kyoto, Bassui is perhaps best known for his work in the provinces, working diligently to make Zen doctrine and training understandable in simple language.

⌘ BEAL, SAMUEL ⌘
(1825–1889)

Professor of Chinese at University College, London, who was instrumental in early translations of Chinese Buddhist texts. Although Beal published *A Catena of Buddhist Scriptures from the Chinese* (in 1871), *The Romantic Legend of Sakya Buddha* (in 1875), *Dhammapada, with Accompanying Narratives* (1878), and *The Fo-sho-hing-tsan-king: A Life of Buddha by Asvaghosa Bodhisattva* (in 1883), he is best known for bringing to light the missionary enterprise of the famous Chinese Buddhist pilgrim Hsüan-tsang who traveled to India from 629–645. Hsüan-tsang is famous for bringing back Mahāyāna texts to China, working on Chinese translations of these classics, and for his work with the Fa-hsiang school of Buddhism (i.e., the Chinese version of Yogācāra).

⌘ BECHERT, HEINZ ⌘
(b. 1932)

German Buddhologist at the University of Göttingen, recognized as one of the world's foremost specialists in Theravāda Buddhism. Bechert's chief contribution to scholarship on Buddhism is his masterful three volume work *Buddhismus: Staat und Gesellschaft in den Ländern des Theravāda Buddhismus* (1966, 1967, 1973). He has also recently edited, with Richard Gombrich, a useful anthology titled *The World of Buddhism* (1984) which focuses on Buddhist monastics and their role in society throughout the world. Bechert has also been highly successful in sponsoring a number of international conferences devoted to important topical issues in Buddhist Studies, as well as seeing the collected papers from these conferences into print. He has also been visiting professor at prestigious universities, most notably Yale. He was one of the initial members of the Board of Directors of the International Association of Buddhist Studies.

⌘ BHAIṢAJYAGURU-BUDDHA ⌘

Literally, the "Healing Buddha" or "Medicine Buddha." He is the chief figure in a text called the Bhaiṣajyaguru-sūtra in which he is said to have made twelve vows in a previous life which epitomize the appropriate behavior of healing Buddhas and bodhisattvas, and which become functional upon his own attainment of Buddhahood. The vows include to: (1) illuminate the world by the rays of his body, (2) surpass the brightness of even the sun and moon, (3) offer protection and help to all beings so there will be no deformed beings, (4) lead all beings to the Mahāyāna path, (5) promote self-restraint for all beings, achieving no evil states after hearing his name, (6) cure beings' deformities by hearing his name, (7) cure the illnesses of those too poor to buy medicine by hearing his name, (8) transform women into men (in their next birth) upon uttering his name, (9) promote right views and bodhisattva practices for all beings, (10) alleviate the suffering of beings punished by the king upon hearing his name, (11) provide food for the hungry upon hearing his name, and (12) provide clothing for those destitute upon uttering his name. In iconography, Bhaiṣajyaguru-buddha is often depicted along with Śākyamuni and Amitābha, making the gesture of protection with his left hand. He is associated with *lapis luzuli*, symbolizing purity, and with yellow myrobalam, a healing substance in Buddhist medicine. He was also important in China, Japan, and Tibet.

⌘ BHAVACAKRA ⌘

The so-called "wheel of becoming," representing existence in the cycle of saṃsāra. The wheel is divided into six segments, each of which depicts one of the "destinies" (gatis) of beings. Lowest in the cycle are the hell-beings, animals, and hungry ghosts (pretas), followed by the gods (devas), antigods (asuras), and humans. All of these destinies are united by their common experience of suffering. The entire wheel is held by Yama, god of the netherworld. In the center of the circle are depicted the three causes of the cycle: (1) desire, symbolized by a cock, (2) ignorance, symbolized by a pig, and (3) hatred, symbolized by a snake. On the outer rim of the circle are depicted the twelve links of dependent origination (pratītya-samutpāda).

⌘ BHĀVANĀ ⌘

Sanskrit technical term for meditation. Bhāvanā is as close to a "generic" term referring to meditative practice in general as one can find in Buddhism. Generally speaking, bhāvanā is considered to fall into one or another of two basic categories, each descriptive of the particular practice entertained. First, there is śamatha practice, usually defined as the development of calming, of tranquility. Second, arising out of the first, is vipaśyanā, usually defined as insight. Various Buddhist schools prescribe differing techniques for the attainment of śamatha and vipaśyanā, but they all involve mental cultivation, collectively referred to as bhāvanā. (See also BHĀVANĀKRAMA.)

⌘ BHĀVANĀKRAMA ⌘

Name of three Buddhist meditation texts, written in Sanskrit by Kamalaśīla in the eighth century, and which became the standard approach for much of Mahāyāna Buddhism. The first Bhāvanākrama is roughly divided into two parts, focusing first on the requisites of Mahāyāna practice, and then on a discussion of what develops from study, examination, and meditation. The second Bhāvanākrama retraces the subject area of the first, but from a different perspective illustrating how to turn theoretical items into practice. The third Bhāvanākrama again has two parts, the first of which explains śamatha (or calming) practice, while the second part rejects the viewpoint and meditational method of the Chinese monk Hva-shang as presented at the Council of Lhasa in 792–794. Kamalaśīla's text was carried to its logical conclusion in the classical Tibetan meditation text known as the Lam-rim chen-mo by Tsong-kha-pa and the Chinese Mo-ho chih-kuan by Chih-i, founder of the T'ien-t'ai school. (See also BHĀVANĀ; KAMALAŚĪLA.)

⌘ BHĀVAVIVEKA ⌘
(ca. 490–570)

Southern Indian Buddhist, also known as Bhavya, who founded the Svātantrika school, one of two divisions of Indian Mādhyamika Buddhism. Bhāvaviveka went to Magadha and studied the works of Nāgārjuna, founder of the Mādhyamika school. He was a slightly junior contemporary of another student of Nāgārjuna's work, Buddhapālita (ca. 470–540), who utilized Nāgārjuna's well-known negative dialectic to found the Prāsaṅgika school of Mādhyamika. Bhāvaviveka utilized a positive dialectic in opposing Buddhapālita, in a sense countering those critics who thought Buddhism's dialectic of negation to be counterproductive to expressing a positive goal for the religion. He also differed from Buddhapālita on the nature and relationship of the ultimate (paramārtha) and the relative (saṃvṛti). His writings include a commentary on Nāgārjuna's Mūlamadhyamaka-kārikās known as the Prajñāpradīpa, a refutation of the Yogācāra position known as the Karatalaratna, preserved only in the Chinese version as Chang-chen lun, a verse text refuting rival philosophical systems and known as the Madhyamaka-hṛdaya, and his own personal commentary on the Madhyamaka-hṛdaya referred to as the Tarkajvālā. Bhāvaviveka's work was especially formative for the eighth-century philosophers Śāntirakṣita and Kamalaśīla who extended his work considerably. (See also BUDDHAPĀLITA; MĀDHYAMIKA; SVĀTANTRIKA.)

⌘ BHAVYA ⌘

See BHĀVAVIVEKA

⌘ BHIKṢU ⌘

Technical term for a mendicant monk, a religious professional who has abandoned worldly life to pursue the Buddhist ideal of nirvāṇa. In the earliest tradition, ordination was apparently conferred by the simple formula "Ehi bhikṣu," literally "Come, O Monk!" As the community grew, however, additional procedures came to be required. New requirements included a threefold repetition of the formula known as the triśaraṇa or "Three Jewels" and a responsibility to adhere to ten vows incumbent on all monastic members. Eventually, ordination as a bhikṣu came to be open to all individuals who chose to join freely, had no limiting factors (such as criminal behavior or contagious disease), and had reached a minimum age. Candidates took an initial "going forth" called pravrajyā, became a novice (śrāmaṇera) and were given both a preceptor and a teacher. At age twenty (or older), a novice could ask for full ordination (called upasaṃpadā). The community of bhikṣus was clearly a mendicant order, requiring extensive travel, except during the rainy season, and requiring a life of minimum requisites. Monks were allowed to possess only their robes, an alms bowl, razor, needle, staff, and toothpick. Food was begged, and no fixed residence was permitted. The daily-life routine of the monks was highly regulated with regard to all activities, including meditation. In order to maintain the highest level of respect in the lay community which supported him, and in his personal quest for religious attainment, the moral discipline meticulously outlined in the portion of the Buddhist canon known as the Vinaya Piṭaka was rigorously adhered to and supported. Twice a month, bhikṣus in a given area assembled to celebrate the Poṣadha (or "fast-day") ceremony and recite the offenses contained in the Prātimokṣa-sūtra, a standard disciplinary inventory. In time, the eremitical ideal of the community of monks diminished, and wandering ceased altogether in favor of a *settled, monastic way of life*. While in South Asia, Buddhist monks continue a life that does not permit work nor marriage, Chinese and Japanese monks include work in their daily activity, and monks in particular schools of Tibetan and Japanese Buddhism are permitted to marry. (See also BHIKṢUṆĪ; SAṂGHA.)

⌘ BHIKṢUṆĪ ⌘

Technical term for a female mendicant, a Buddhist nun. A well-known story in Buddhist literature relates how Buddha's foster mother Mahāprajāpatī petitioned him to become a female mendicant or bhikṣuṇī following the death of her husband. Initially, and on several occasions shortly thereafter, he refused her entreaty. Buddha's disciple Ananda intervened on her behalf, eventually convincing Buddha to establish an order of nuns. Buddha then suggested to Ānanda that the establishment of an order of nuns would cause the saṃgha to flourish for only 500 instead of 1,000 years. Legend also reveals that Ānanda was reproved for his conduct in this matter at the first Buddhist council, held in Rajagṛha in the first rainy season following Buddha's demise. The life of a nun is regulated far more comprehensively and severely than that of a monk. Women under twenty years of age or those women who have been married more than twelve years must undergo a probationary stage for two years prior to ordination. Moreover, in addition to those regulations also incumbent on the monks, the nuns' Prātimokṣa-sūtra of offenses contains approximately 100 more rules than that of the monks' text, and nuns must adhere to a severe prohibition known as the *gurudharmas*, eight special rules that essentially establish the nuns' standing to be *lesser* than that of the monks. Although the nuns may have once played a significant role in Buddhist monastic history in various Buddhist countries, that influence has waned considerably today. In most Buddhist countries there are *no Buddhist nuns*, and only a few places exist in the world today where a valid ordination lineage for nuns has been maintained. (See also BHIKṢU; SAṂGHA.)

⌘ BHŪMI ⌘

Technical term, utilized primarily in Mahāyāna, meaning "earth," "level," or most generally, "stage." It is usually applied to the path traversed by the bodhisattva, and describes the various stages attained on the path to complete, perfect enlightenment of Buddhahood. The doctrine of bodhisattva-bhūmis is developed in a series of texts, the best known of which are the Bodhisattvabhūmi-sūtra, the largest section in Asaṅga's massive work called the Yogācārabhūmi, which develops a seven-fold path, and the Daśabhūmika-sūtra, a portion of the larger Avataṃsaka-sūtra, which establishes the now traditional ten-fold path. After a series of preliminaries, in which the Bodhicitta or "Thought of Enlightenment" arises, a Praṇidhāna or "Vow" to gain complete, perfect enlightenment for the sake of all sentient beings is made, and a Vyākaraṇa or "Prediction" received regarding future success, the formal stages of the path are negotiated. These include: the (1) "Joyful Stage" (pramuditā-bhūmi), where the perfection of generosity is practiced, (2) "Immaculate Stage," (vimalā-bhūmi), where moral discipline is perfected, (3) "Radiant Stage," (prabhākarī-bhūmi), where patience is cultivated, (4) "Blazing Stage," (arciṣmatī-bhūmi), where vigor is exerted, (5) "Hard to Conquer Stage," (sudurjayā-bhūmi), where meditation is employed, (6) "Face to Face Stage," (abhimukhī-bhūmi), where wisdom is perfected, (7) "Going Far Beyond Stage," (dūraṅgamā-bhūmi), where skill-in-means is utilized, signifying that the bodhisattva goes far beyond the attainment of an arhant, (8) "Immovable Stage" (acalā-bhūmi), where the vow begins to become manifested, (9) "Good Thought Stage" (sādhumatī-bhūmi), where various powers are employed, and (10) "Cloud of Dharma Stage" (dharmameghā-bhūmi), where absolute knowledge is realized. (See also BODHISATTVA; BODHISATTVA-BHŪMI-SŪTRA; DAŚABHŪMIKA-SŪTRA.)

⌘ BIMBISĀRA ⌘

Famous king of Magadha and royal patron of Buddha, best known for his gift of Veṇuvana ārāma, the first monastic dwelling, to the saṃgha. Bimbisāra was from the Haryaṅka family, reputed to be among the first rulers of Magadha, and ruled for fifty-two years. He became a lay disciple of Buddha at age thirty, following one of Buddha's discourses. It was Bimbisāra who suggested to Buddha the employment of the twice monthly Poṣadha (or confessional) ceremony, modeled after the thrice-monthly practice utilized by other religious groups and designed to increase the number of adherents in the saṃgha. Bimbisāra was eventually thrown in prison by his son Prince Ajātaśatru, where he died of starvation. (See also AJĀTAŚATRU.)

⌘ BKA-GDAMS-PA (KADAMPA) ⌘

Tibetan Buddhist school founded by 'Brom-ston (1008–1064), chief disciple of Atīśa. Apparently the sect received the name bKa-gdams-pa because it held to the authoritative word (bKa-gdams) of Atīśa as embodied in the Bodhipaṭhapradīpa or "Lamp for the Way of Enlightenment." 'Brom-ston and his immediate successors were referred to as the "earlier" bKa-gdams-pa, and although they did not survive for very long, their traditions were later adopted by Tsong-kha-pa. 'Brom-ston eventually founded a monastery which housed Atīśa's relics, and was succeeded there by a series of his own disciples, most notable of whom was Po-to-ba. He established a monastery north of Lhasa near Phan-yul which became the main center of the school. The school carried on Atīṣa's concern for proper monastic practice and Tantric ritual. (See also 'BROM-STON.)

⌘ BKA'-GYUR (KANJUR) ⌘

First portion of the Tibetan Buddhist canon, the name of which is rendered as "Translation of the Word of the Buddha." The first printing of this portion of the canon occurred not in Tibet but in China in 1411. The first Tibetan edition was at sNar-thang in 1731. It contains 13 volumes of Vinaya texts, 21 volumes of Prajñāpāramitā texts, 6 volumes of Avataṃsaka texts, 6 volumes of Ratnakūṭa texts, 30 volumes of sūtras including 270 texts, and 22 volumes of Tantras including more than 300 texts. (See also BSTAN-'GYUR.)

⌘ BKA-RGYUD-PA (KAGYÜPA) ⌘

Tibetan Buddhist school tracing its origins to Marpa (1012–1097) and regarded as one of the four primary schools of Tibetan Buddhism. Mar-pa was a Tibetan Buddhist skilled in Sanskrit who traveled to India, eventually receiving Tantric teaching from Tilopa and Nāropa. Based on the teachings he brought back to Tibet, he laid the ground for the bKa-rgyud-pa school, emphasizing the practice of Mahāmudrā and the "Six Dharmas of Nāropa." Mar-pa passed on his teachings to his closest disciple Milas ras-pa (1040–1123) who became the greatest poet-saint in Tibetan history. Mi-la ras-pa in turn was the spiritual master of sGam-po-pa (1079–1153) who organized the bKa-rgyud-pa school and founded its first monasteries. Following sGam-po-pa, the school subdivided into four major groups: (1) Bri-gung-pa, (2) sTag-lung-pa, (3) Brug-pa, and (4) Karma-pa. In the bKa-rgyud-pa school, much emphasis is placed on the direct transmission of teaching from spiritual master to spiritual heir. (See also MARPA; MI-LAS RAS-PA; SGAM-PO-PA.)

⌘ BODHGAYĀ ⌘

Site of Siddhārtha Gautama's enlightenment experience, and thus, one of the holiest places in Buddhist geography. The legend of Siddhārtha Gautama's life indicates that, following six years of ascetic practices with five companions, he abandoned personal tortures, regained his health, and sat down at the foot of a tree, vowing not to arise until he attained freedom from the suffering of old age, sickness, and death. Of course it was on that occasion that he achieved enlightenment and became the Buddha. As a result, the tree became known as the Bodhi Tree or "Tree of Awakening," and the site became identified as Bodhgayā. A temple still marks the spot, and it remains a major pilgrimage site for world Buddhists. (See also BODHI TREE.)

⌘ BODHI ⌘

Technical term derived from the Sanskrit verb root √ budh, and meaning "to be awakened." In the earliest tradition it is generally applied to those individuals who have realized the efficacy of the four noble truths and attained the results of completing the eightfold path. As such, it could appropriately be applied to an arhant (i.e., "worthy one" who has attained nirvāṇa), pratyeka-buddha (literally, a "private Buddha," who has attained realization but does not embark on a teaching career), or a Buddha (a "fully awakened" one). With the development of Mahāyāna, bodhi took on an expanded meaning insofar as it applied to the realization or wisdom (prajñā) that came from understanding the notion of the emptiness (śūnyatā) of all phenomena and the insight that all beings possessed Buddha-nature. Mahāyāna stressed bodhi not only as a realization for oneself, but for others as well. (See also ENLIGHTENMENT.)

⌘ BODHICARYĀVATĀRA ⌘

Classical text devoted to Mahāyāna ethics and written by Śāntideva (ca. 650–750). That it is intended for the spiritual development of the Mahāyāna bodhisattva is clear from the title of the Tibetan version: Bodhisattvacaryāvatāra. The text is arranged in ten chapters, beginning with the importance of the cultivation of the thought of enlightenment (bodhicitta). He goes on to consider the six traditional perfections (pāramitās), substituting "mindfulness" (smṛti) for the traditional "giving" (dāna) and "awareness" (samprajanyā) for the traditional "morality" (śīla). He also offers two meditations that first note the equality of self and others, and then substitute others for self. Along with Śāntideva's other major text, the Śiksāsamuccaya, this work provides genuine ethical substance to the career of the bodhisattva. (See also ŚĀNTIDEVA; ŚIKṢĀSAMUCCAYA.)

⌘ BODHICITTA ⌘

Technical term in Mahāyāna usually translated as the "thought of enlightenment," and generally considered as a prerequisite to actual entry onto the bodhisattva path. It is essentially regarded as intuitive rather than intellectual, and most often described as having two essential components: (1) the intention to become a Buddha for the sake of all sentient beings, and (2) the actual setting into motion of that intention. One text, the Bodhicaryāvatāra, even suggests that the thought of enlightenment negates the transgressions of a bodhisattva's past lives. It is even said to increase one's spiritual merit, listed as one of the three "roots of merit'' (kuśalamūla). The thought of enlightenment is reinforced by the taking of a formal bodhisattva vow, and by receiving a prediction regarding future attainment.

⌘ BODHIDHARMA ⌘

An Indian meditation master, well known for his knowledge of the Laṅkāvatāra-sūtra, and presumed to be the first *Chinese* patriarch of Ch'an Buddhism. Known in China as P'u-t'i-ta-mo and in Japan as Daruma, he is said to have arrived at Lo-yang in northern China sometime between 516 and 526. Some sources indicate that he may have been in southern China as early as 470. He was reputed to be the twenty-eighth *Indian* patriarch, having received Dharma transmission from his teacher, Prajñādhara. Eventually he transmitted the Dharma to his own student Hui-k'o who became the second patriarch of Chinese Ch'an. Hui-k'o is said to have cut off his arm and offered it to Bodhidharma as a symbol of his seriousness prior to being accepted as a disciple of the master. A number of legends are attributed to Bodhidharma, but especially interesting are two. In the first, Bodhidharma is supposed to have met Emperor Wu of the Liang Dynasty, and when asked by the emperor whether he had accrued much merit through a lifelong effort of building temples, making donations, and so forth, Bodhidharma responded, ''No merit at all!'' In the second, Bodhidharma is said to have sat in meditation at a temple in Lo-yang for nine years, sitting *continuously until his legs fell off*. The Shao-lin temple on Mount Sung-shan is often associated with Bodhidharma. Perhaps the essence of Bodhidharma's message is captured in a verse attributed to him (and cited in Heinrich Dumoulin's *A History of Zen Buddhism*):

> A special tradition outside the scriptures;
> No dependence upon words and letters;
> Direct pointing at the soul of man;
> Seeing into one's own nature, and the attainment of Buddhahood.

(See also CH'AN; HUI-K'O.)

⌘ BODHIRUCI ⌘

Indian monk who arrived in Lo-yang in 508 and convinced T'an-luan (476–542) that devotion to Amitābha resulted in the attainment of everlasting life. Bodhiruci, along with a companion named Ratnamati, is reputed to have translated a commentary on the Daśabhūmika-sūtra known in Chinese as the Shih-ti ching-lun or simply "Ti-lun" for short. As such, he was considered the initiator of the Ti-lun tradition in China. Around 530, he converted T'an-luan to the Pure Land doctrine, and T'an-luan was then generally recognized as the first Chinese Patriarch of Pure Land (Ching-t'u). (See also PURE LAND; T'AN-LUAN.)

⌘ BODHISATTVA ⌘

Literally an "enlightenment being," one who has postponed personal salvation in favor of a compassionate effort to save *all* sentient beings. In early Buddhism the term bodhisattva (or bodhisatta in Pāli) was used to identify Siddhartha Gautama, the historical Buddha, and it was assumed that only future *historical* Buddhas merited this designation prior to their attainment of Buddhahood. In Mahāyāna, this term was given a radical, new interpretation, and used as a designation for *anyone aspiring to complete, perfect enlightenment . . . to Buddhahood*. Motivated by extreme compassion (karuṇā), and tempered by the perfection of wisdom (prajñā), the bodhisattva first completes three basic prerequisites that include generating the thought of enlightenment (bodhicitta), undertaking a formal vow to gain complete, perfect enlightenment for the sake of all sentient beings (praṇidhāna), and receiving a prediction with regard to future attainment (vyākaraṇa). Then, a path known as the bodhisattva path, and including ten stages (bhūmis), is traversed. This path requires rejection of the personal attainment of nirvāṇa, deliberate rebirth in the cycle of saṃsāra, and a sharing of all merit accrued with other sentient beings. In Mahāyāna a number of Celestial Bodhisattvas became extremely important, most notably Avalokiteśvara, Mañjuśrī, Mahāsthāmaprāpta, and Samantabhadra. They served as ideal models for their earthly counterparts by exhibiting extreme compassion and wisdom. The entire Mahāyāna notion of the bodhisattva was a clear antithesis to the ideal type in early Buddhism, the arhant, whose effort was found by Mahāyānists to be self-centered and ego-based. An enormous literature developed focusing on the bodhisattva and the bodhisattva path, including such famous texts as the Bodhisattvabhūmi-sūtra, Daśabhūmika-sūtra, and others. (See also ARHANT; BODHISATTVA-YĀNA.)

⌘ BODHISATTVABHŪMI-SŪTRA ⌘

Mahāyāna Buddhist text attributed to Asaṅga, outlining the stages (bhūmis) of the path of the bodhisattva. It is embedded in the voluminous text known as the Yogācārabhūmi, and represents the fifteenth and largest section. A popular text, it was translated into Chinese on several occasions by Dharmarakṣa (between 414 and 418), Guṇavarman (in 431), and Hsüan-tsang (647). It was also translated into Tibetan by Prajñāvarman. The text is divided into three parts. The first expounds the basic spiritual practices of the bodhisattva, along with the incumbent attainments. The second deals with ancillary practices. The third discusses the final attainments of a bodhisattva. This text treats the bodhisattva path in seven stages. (See also BHŪMI; BODHISATTVA.)

⌘ BODHISATTVA-ŚĪLA ⌘

Moral discipline of the bodhisattva. The daily conduct of monks and nuns in early Buddhism is carefully regulated by the monastic code embedded in the Vinaya Piṭaka. In Mahāyāna, the general ethical conduct of its ideal type, the bodhisattva, is addressed in a variety of ways. While some bodhisattvas also lived the monastic life, and were thus subject to the traditional monastic rules, *others did not choose a monastic vocation*. Consequently, a series of Mahāyāna texts emerged that dealt with ethical concerns fully and completely. Quite possibly the most famous of these are Śāntideva's Bodhicaryāvatāra and Śikṣāsamuccaya. However, there is also a well-known text called the Bodhisattva-prātimoksa-sūtra, presumably accomplishing for Mahāyāna adherents what its Hīnayāna counterpart does for its disciples. More importantly, there is a Mahāyāna text called the Brahmajāla-bodhisattva-śīla-sūtra that outlines ten major and forty-eight minor rules for bodhisattvas. All of these texts might well be categorized under the heading "Mahāyāna Vinaya." (See also ETHICS; MAHĀYĀNA VINAYA.)

⌘ BODHISATTVA-YĀNA ⌘

The "Vehicle of the Bodhisattva." Bodhisattva-yāna is another means of referring to the Mahāyāna or so-called Greater Vehicle school of Buddhism. Mahāyāna of course coined a pejorative phrase to describe the entirety of early Buddhism: "Hīnayāna" or "Lesser Vehicle." Within this Hīnayāna appelation, however, Mahāyāna identified two individual paths: (1) the Vehicle of the Srāvaka, or Srāvaka-yāna, literally "hearers," the immediate disciples of the Buddha (and their spiritual descendants), and (2) the Vehicle of the Pratyeka-buddhas, or Pratyeka-buddha-yāna, those who attained enlightenment on their own and who did not embark on a teaching career. In light of the above, it was only logical to also refer to the Mahāyāna path as the Bodhisattva-yāna, the "Vehicle of the Bodhisattvas."

⌘ BODHI TREE ⌘

The "Tree of Awakening," under which Siddhārtha Gautama sat on the occasion of his attaining complete, perfect enlightenment, Buddhahood. It is classified in botanical terms as *ficus religiosa*. The tree has remained important throughout history as a symbol of attainment, despite the fact that the original Bodhi Tree was destroyed in the seventh century. Nonetheless, in the Mahābodhi Temple in Bodhgayā, a Bodhi Tree remains, taken from the shoot exported to Sri Lanka by King Aśoka in the third century B.C.E.

⌘ BOROBUḌUR ⌘

Famous Javanese stūpa, built around the ninth century. It is probably the most important, and extravagant, stūpa in Buddhist history. Built by rulers of the Śailendra Dynasty, the stupa was constructed as a giant maṇḍala or sacred diagram. It is comprised of five terraces, the walls of which are decorated with bas-reliefs. On the first four terraces, the traditional Buddhas of the various directions are represented: Akṣobhya (East), Ratnasambhava (South), Amitābha (West), and Amoghasiddhi (North). On the fifth terrace Vairocana adorns all sides. Circumambulating the stūpa reveals scenes from Śākyamuni Buddha's life, Jātaka tales, and Mahāyāna sūtras. The vertical ascent to the top of the stūpa is a symbolic journey from saṃsāra to nirvāṇa (from the world of desire, through the realm of form, to the formless realm). An important pilgrimage site for Buddhists worldwide, it has become (from the nineteenth century onward) a meaningful site for

Buddhist scholarship, particularly that devoted to cosmology. It has generated a significant amount of scholarly literature, including Paul Mus's two-volume masterpiece *Barabuḍur: Esquisse d'une histoire du Bouddhisme fondée sur la critique archéologique des textes.* In 1974 the University of Michigan sponsored an "International Conference on Borobuḍur," resulting in an important research volume titled *Barabuḍur: History and Significance of a Buddhist Monument,* edited by Luis O. Gómez and Hiram W. Woodward, Jr. (See also STŪPA.)

⌘ BRAHMĀ-VIHĀRAS ⌘

The "divine abodes," including love (maitrī), compassion (karuṇā), sympathetic joy (muditā), and equanimity (upekṣā). They are generally associated with early Buddhism, reflecting a high ethical import, and generally emerging as one's Buddhist practice deepens and matures. They are sometimes compared to the Mahāyāna doctrine of perfections (pāramitās) in terms of their intent and function, and often *wrongly* associated with detachment in a negative sense, suggesting that detachment includes the destruction of all emotions. On the contrary, while fully liberated beings have destroyed the traditional "three poisons" of greed, hatred, and delusion, they have not eliminated *all* emotion. As such, a whole range of emotions are available, of which the divine abodes are representative. It has also been suggested by some writers on Buddhism that these four approaches to Buddhist practice hold the key by which a new, and effective *modern* Buddhist ethics might be generated that is operatively both transcultural and transtemporal. (See also DIVINE ABODES.)

⌘ 'BROG-MI (DROK-MI) ⌘

Founder of the Sa-skya monastery in 1073, and consequently, the Sa-skya-pa school of Tibetan Buddhism. He was a contemporary of Atīśa, and studied at Vikramaśīla monastery in India for eight years. He emphasized the "new" Tantras, those translated by Atīśa and Rin-chen bzang-po, as opposed to the older texts accepted by the rNying-ma-pa school. He was the main teacher of dKon-mchog rgyal-po of the Khon family, important because of the traditional belief that Mañjuśrī would appear in seven reincarnations in dKon-mchog rgyal-po's line. Sa-skya-pa abbots were permitted to marry. Thus 'Brog-mi passed on his office to his son, and thereafter it was usual to pass on the lineage from an uncle to a nephew. As one of the four major schools of Tibetan Buddhism, the Sa-skya-pa tradition remains important today. (See also SA-SKYA-PA.)

⌘ 'BROM-STON (DROM-TÖN) ⌘

(1008–1064)

Atīśa's chief disciple and founder of the bKa-gdams-pa school of Tibetan Buddhism. Following his teacher's death, he founded a monastery which housed Atisa's relics. A number of his own disciples succeeded him, the most significant of which was Po-to-ba. 'Brom-ston's followers adhered to a rigorous moral practice, and regarded seven elements as basic to their doctrine: the three baskets of the Tripiṭaka, Buddha Śākyamuni, Avalotikeśvara, his female counterpart Tārā, and as their protective deity Acala. (See also BKA-GDAMS-PA.)

⌘ BSAM-YAS ⌘

The first Buddhist monastery built in Tibet, probably completed around 787 during the reign of King Khri-srong-lde-btsan. It is located about thirty miles from Lhasa. Presumably founded by Padmasambhava and Śāntirakṣita, and modeled on the Indian Buddhist temple of Otantapurī in Bengal, a Sarvāstivādin ordination lineage was established at bSam-yas, and it became a lively place for religious discussion and debate. It was the site of a famous debate between Śāntirakṣita's pupil Kamalaśīla and a Chinese monk known as Hva-shang over the issue of sudden versus gradual enlightenment. In spirited debate, Kamalaśīla successfully defended the Indian position, thus establishing the efficacy of the Indian standpoint for Tibetan Buddhism. (See also COUNCILS-LHASA.)

⌘ BSTAN-'GYUR (TENJUR) ⌘

Second portion of the Tibetan Buddhist canon, the name of which is rendered "Translation of Teachings." Because this portion of the collection contains works attributed to individuals other than the Buddha, it is considered only semi-canonical. The sNar-thang edition of the bStan-'gyur appeared in 1742. It contains 1 volume of Stotras including 64 texts, 86 volumes of Commentaries on the Tantras including 3,055 texts, and 137 volumes of Commentaries on the Sūtras including 567 texts. (See also BKA'-GYUR.)

⌘ BUDDHA ⌘

Derived from the Sanskrit verb root √ budh, the title of one who has become awakened. It describes an individual who "sees the world as it really is" (yathābhūtam) and "does what needs to be done." He has achieved nirvāṇa through the eradication of craving (tṛṣṇā), eliminated all impurities (āsravas), and will no longer be reborn in the cycle of saṃsāra. He is considered to be omniscient with regard to matters of Dharma or "Teaching." In the Hīnayāna tradition there seems to be one historical Buddha per world cycle, with Siddhārtha Gautama being identified as the Buddha for the current era. In the Pāli literature it is noted that he was a disciple of a still earlier Buddha named Dīpaṅkara while in an earlier existence as a young man named Sumedha. Additionally, Hīnayāna literature mentions six previous Buddhas: Vipaśyin, Śikhin, Viśvabhū, Krakucchanda, Kanakamuni, and Kāśyapa, as well as a future Buddha, known as Maitreya. In the Mahāyāna tradition, where the term *Buddha* comes to be identified *not* with an historical person, but rather with a *symbolic representation of ultimate reality* (called Dharma-kāya), Buddha's are presented in physical form *only as apparitions* (called Nirmāṇa-kāya), such as Siddhārtha Gautama, to address wholly common worldlings, and in quasi-physical forms known as *enjoyment bodies* (called Saṃbhoga-kāya) to address those already on the bodhisattva path. In this latter case, a series of so-called Celestial Buddhas are mentioned, including Akṣobhya, Amitābha, Amoghasiddhi, Ratnasambhava, and Vairocana. (See also SIDDHĀRTHA GAUTAMA; TRIKĀYA.)

⌘ BUDDHABHADRA ⌘
(359–429)

Sarvāstivādin monk from Kaśmīr who went to China in 409, translating a number of Buddhist texts and conversing with Buddhist masters. Regarded as a meditation master, upon arriving in China, he first lived at Ch'ang-an with the renowned translator

Kumārajīva. He apparently left Ch'ang-an due to the lifestyle of Kumārajīva's community and their excessive involvement with the royal court. From Ch'ang-an he went south, living for a while with Hui-yüan at Lu-shan. Eventually he reached the capital city of Chien-k'ang, where he was able to continue his work in meditation and translation. He translated the Avataṃsaka-sūtra, the basic text of the Hua-yen school of Buddhism, into Chinese in sixty books.

⌘ BUDDHADATTA ⌘

Important Theravāda commentator who was the first of Buddhaghosa's successors. Very little historical data is available on Buddhadatta. However, the colophon of the Vinaya-vinicchaya notes that he was born in Uragapura, a city in southern India, and that he entered the saṃgha at the Mahāvihāra in Anurādhapura, Sri Lanka. Most likely, he lived in the late fourth to early fifth cen turies. His most famous works include the Vinaya-vinicchaya and the Abhidhammāvatāra. There is some similarity between this latter work and Buddhaghosa's critically important text, the Visuddhimagga. While one account indicates that Buddhadatta and Buddhaghosa may have met while shipbound on separate boats, Buddhadatta's writing is perhaps clearer and less ambiguous than Buddhaghosa's. As such, his very clear expositions of Abhidhamma are both significant and useful for Theravāda scholarship.

⌘ BUDDHADHARMA ⌘

Literally, "Buddha-Doctrine." This is a general way to refer to the teachings of the Buddha. It is useful in that it can be applied in a nondenominational fashion to Buddhist notions accepted by all Buddhist schools, while still being used in a case-specific manner by individual Buddhist groups. As a techincal term, it has become extremely commonplace in modern Buddhism, especially among Western Buddhist groups.

⌘ BUDDHAGHOSA ⌘

Fourth-fifth century, exegete considered to be the greatest Theravādin commentator. Less is known about his life than is desirable, primarily because the chief account of his life's history, the Buddhaghosuppatti, is a rather quixotic work with little historical value. In the Mahāvaṃsa we learn that he was born a Brahmin near Bodhgayā in Magadha. He was converted to Buddhism by a monk named Revata and given the name Buddhaghosa ("The Voice of the Buddha"). He then traveled to Sri Lanka, took up residence at the Mahāvihāra in Anurādhapura, and set about translating the Sinhalese Buddhist commentaries into Pāli. More than a dozen commentarial works are credited to Buddhaghosa, spanning the Vinaya Piṭaka, Sūtra Piṭaka, and Abhidhamma Piṭaka. Whenever Buddhaghosa introduced his own opinions into his compilations, he acknowledged this fact by indicating so with the Pāli phrase *ayaṃ pana me attano mati*, "now this is my opinion." No doubt his great masterpiece is the text known as Visuddhimagga or "Path of Purity," a voluminous explanation of the entire Theravāda path. It is divided into three parts: (1) the "purification of virtue" (sīla), (2) the "purification of concentration" (samādhi), and (3) the "purification of wisdom" (paññā). Through the years, the first part has developed into a clear guide to proper morality, while the second part is regarded as the foremost Theravādin meditational handbook, and the third part reveals the philosophic insight that emerges from proper cultivation of the first two parts. It has become standard reading for Buddhists and students of Buddhism alike. (See also VISUDDHIMAGGA.)

⌘ BUDDHAHOOD ⌘

Quite simply, the state of being Buddha. It is an expression of complete, perfect enlightenment (samyak sambodhi) or that beyond which it is impossible to go. As such, it is the highest goal and attainment. Precisely because Mahāyāna philosophy presumes that all beings are *already* Buddha, this term reflects the concern to *manifest* that perfectness in everyday life. (See also BUDDHA-NATURE.)

⌘ BUDDHAKṢETRA ⌘

Cosmological term, usually translated as "Buddha-Land," and referring to each place where a Celestial Buddha resides. In the Pāli tradition, the term *khetta* seems *not* to have been used in quite the cosmological sense that we find in Mahāyāna. Nor does the term *Buddhakhetta,* as used in the Visuddhimagga of Buddhaghosa, convey the sense of a cosmological realm. This is because one who has gained complete, perfect enlightenment, in that tradition, is said to be a Tathāgata and attains nibbāṇa, a state that is "undetermined" (avyākata). In Mahāyāna a fully enlightened being inhabits a *Buddhakṣetra,* a Buddha-Land. As the Pure Land tradition, especially, developed within Mahāyāna, it was presumed that, based on the experience of Buddha Śākyamuni who inhabited our own world system, and Amitābha who inhabited the Pure Land of Sukhāvatī, other world systems possessed Buddhas as well in their own appropriate Buddha-Lands. In consequence of the above, a number of practices were suggested to facilitate birth into one of the Buddha-Lands. These practices included such endeavors as repeating a Buddha's name while reflecting upon him, worshipping a Buddha, expressing one's faith that a particular Buddha has vowed to save those who are faithful, leading a pure life, and the like.

⌘ BUDDHA-LANDS ⌘

See BUDDHAKŚETRA

⌘ BUDDHA-NATURE ⌘

Mahāyāna notion that all sentient beings possess an inherently pure nature identical to that of the Buddhas, worldly or cosmic. This Buddha-ness (tathatā) is one of the issues that clearly differentiates Mahāyāna from Hīnayāna, for in the latter there is no notion suggesting that all beings can become Buddhas. This notion is taken to its logical conclusion in Japanese Zen, where the idea of Buddha-nature (busshō) is not something to be *attained,* but rather to become *aware of* and lived experientially.

⌘ BUDDHAPĀLITA ⌘

(ca. 470–540)

Contemporary of Bhavaviveka who, after studying the works of Nāgārjuna, founded the Prāsaṅgika school, one of two divisions of Indian Mādhyamika Buddhism. His work, embodied in texts like the Mūlamadhyamakavṛtti, utilized a negative dialectic in establishing his position. He was opposed by Bhāvavivekeka who utilized a positive dialectic and founded the Svātantrika school. The seventh-century figure Candrakīrti regarded himself as Buddhapālita's successor and advanced the Prāsaṅgika school significantly. (See also BHĀVAVIVEKA; CANDRAKĪRTI; MĀDHYAMIKA; PRĀSAṄGIKA.)

⌘ BUDDHIST CANON ⌘

See TRIPIṬAKA

⌘ BUDDHIST CHURCHES OF AMERICA ⌘

The western hemisphere representative of the Japanese Jōdo Shinshū ("True Pure Land") tradition. In 1898 two informal missionaries from Hompa Honganji in Kyoto were sent to San Francisco on a fact-finding tour. Their report resulted in the arrival, the following year, of Reverend Shuei Sonoda and Reverend Kakuryo Nishijima who founded the (then called) Buddhist Mission of North America. Their organization ministered to the Japanese community in and around San Francisco. Complicated by the Japanese Immigration Exclusion Act of 1924, and the Second World War, the organization grew only gradually until the late 1940s when, as the renamed Buddhist Churches of America, it began to expand its programs both geographically and financially. It now boasts centers across the United States, has an extensive educational program as well as a study institute in Berkeley, California, an aggressive publication program, and a membership in excess of 100,000 members. It remains one of the most stable organizations in the development of American Buddhism.

⌘ BUDDHO-TAOISTS ⌘

Informal title given to the three generations of Chinese intellectual monks from Tao-an to Kumārajīva. They were referred to as Buddho-Taoists because they utilized Taoist vocabulary to present and discuss Buddhist ideas. Consequently, wu-wei, for example, came to represent nirvāṇa. Included in this group were Tao-an (312–385), Hui-yüan (334–416), Kumārajīva (344–413), and Seng-chao (374–414). (See also HUI-YÜAN; KUMĀRAJĪVA; SENG-CHAO; TAO-AN.)

⌘ BUSSHO ⌘

See BUDDHA-NATURE

⌘ BU-STON ⌘
(1290–1364)

Tibetan historian who collected and edited the Tibetan Buddhist canon. His works were instrumental for providing information about Indian Buddhist sectarianism and the various textual traditions of the sects, the development of the various schools of Buddhist thought, and for cross-referencing the work of other historians of Indian Buddhism.

— C —

⌘ CAITYA ⌘

A religious monument or stūpa where the relics of the Buddha or another famous individual are housed. These structures were often located within the confines of vihāras or monasteries that grew up in various Buddhist countries, sometimes housed in special structures called caitya-halls. A cult, apparently short-lived, grew up around the devotional worship of these caityas. Additionally, one Hīnayāna Buddhist sect even took the name Caitikas.

⌘ CAKRA ⌘

Sanskrit technical term meaning "wheel" or "circle." It is a prominent symbol in early Buddhism, often associated with the Dharma, in which case it is represented as eight-spoked with each spoke being identified with a member of the eightfold path. It is also utilized to symbolize the twelve-spoked wheel of "dependent origination," the Buddhist theory of causality. In later Buddhism it came to be associated with a physiological framework prominent in Tantra (and similar to that of Kuṇḍalinī-yoga). In this case, the cakras represent a series of seven energy centers connected by a series of channels called nādīs. The seven cakras include the (1) Mūlādhāra-cakra, a root center located in the perineum, (2) Svādhiṣṭhāna-cakra, another lower center located at or below the navel, (3) Maṇipūra-cakra, located near the navel, (4) Anāhata-cakra, located near the heart, (5) Viśuddha-cakra, located near the bottom of the throat, (6) Ājñā-cakra, located in the space between the eyebrows, and (7) Sahasrāra-cakra, located *above* the crown of the head. There is an extensive iconography associated with the cakras as well as a physiological function identified with each and a thorough series of religious attainments associated with each cakra.

⌘ CAKRAVARTIN ⌘

Literally a "wheel-turner." In the life story of Siddhārtha Gautama, the historical Buddha, it is said that a sage was called in by Śuddhodana shortly after the birth of the child in order to better understand the circumstances of the child's birth. The sage examined both the child and the stories surrounding his conception, gestation, and birth, and responded that the child would become a cakravartin, a wheel-turner. Further, he remarked that if the child were to remain in secular life he would become a universal monarch, uniting all of India under his rule, while if he abandoned the secular life in favor of a sacred profession, he would become a "Buddha," an "Awakened One" who would turn the wheel of the religious law. In view of the anticipated success of the child irrespective of whichever choice of vocation emerged, he was named Siddhārtha, or "he who will accomplish his goal." From that time onward, Cakravartin was utilized as one of the several most prominent epithets of Buddha.

⌘ CANDRAGUPTA MAURYA ⌘

Founder of the Mauryan Dynasty, said to have reigned over Magadha for twenty-four years, likely from 324–300 B.C.E. He was highly imperialistic, expanding his domain throughout his reign. He seemed unsympathetic to Buddhism, as evidenced in the Commentary to the Theragāthā, and was succeeded by his son Bindusāra, who ruled from 300–272, after which Aśoka became king. (See also MAURYAN DYNASTY.)

⌘ CANDRAKĪRTI ⌘

Mahāyāna philosopher (ca. 650) who championed the Prāsaṅgika school of Mādhyamika. He saw himself as the successor to Buddhapālita, and as such, clearly the rival of Bhāvaviveka's Svāntantrika-Mādhyamika school. He argued strongly against the positive dialectic utilized by Bhavaviveka, and sought to uphold the approach and intent of Nāgārjuna. He is credited with the composition of a number of extremely important philosophical treatises, most notably the Prasannapadā or "Clear Worded" and the Madhyamakāvatāra. In some respects, Candrakīrti was able to move beyond Nāgārjuna because of his formal training in logic, and his ability to utilize the work of Dignāga. His exposition of the two levels of truth, ultimate (paramārtha-satya) and worldly (saṃvṛti-satya), is extremely important in the Prāsaṅgika school. (See also BHĀVAVIVEKA; MĀDHYAMIKA; PRĀSAṄGIKA.)

⌘ CARUS, PAUL ⌘

(1852–1919)

Editor, author, and philosopher, born in Ilsenburg, Germany, the son of Dr. Gustav Carus and Laura Krueger Carus. He earned a Ph.D. from Tübingen in 1876. His first professional position was as an educator at the military academy in Dresden, an appointment he soon resigned due to conflicts over his liberal religious views. He then lived briefly in England (1881–1884) before traveling to the United States, settling in LaSalle, Illinois, where he lived for the remainder of his life. At the outset of his literary career in America, Carus published several articles in a new journal called *Open Court*. Shortly thereafter, Carus became editor of *Open Court*, a position he maintained from 1887 until his death in 1919. He also edited *The Monist*, a somewhat more technical quarterly, from 1890–1919. In addition, he was instrumental in founding the Open Court Publishing Company in LaSalle, Illinois. It must also be noted that Carus was instrumental in bringing a variety of Asian Buddhists to America, including such individuals as Anagarika Dharmapala, Soyen Shaku, and D.T. Suzuki. He was fortunate to meet most of these individuals at the World Parliament of Religions, held in Chicago in 1893 as part of the Columbian Exposition. While living in Carus's home, D. T. Suzuki began work on his famous *Outlines of Mahayana Buddhism*, his first English-language book. Along with his tasks as editor of *Open Court* and *The Monist*, Carus was a prolific author with more than fifty titles to his credit, a number of which continue to be widely read today. The combination of all aspects of Carus's work seems to reflect an overarching attempt to bring Buddhism to the West in a fashion that was meaningful, understandable, and in keeping with Buddha's original intent, which Carus felt had diminished in Asia.

⌘ CAUSALITY ⌘

See PRATĪTYA-SAMUTPĀDA

⌘ CAVES ⌘

Beginning with the Āndhran dynasties in India, the geographical road map was regularly dotted with Buddhist cave temples. The most famous cave temples are located at Ajaṇṭā, Bhajā, Nāsik, Kārlī, and Ellora, and are usually of two types: either (1) monastic housing for monks or nuns or (2) units housing a stūpa. When the caves house a stūpa, they are generally referred to as caitya-ghara or "caitya-halls." When the caves are utilized for housing, they are referred to by the generic term for dwelling or cell, vihāra. Cave temples are not distinct to India, however. One can find significant cave temples in Sri Lanka, China, Korea, Japan, and Tibet. The caves at Tun-huang, in China, have produced some of the most treasured manuscript collections yet to be unearthed. (See also AJAṆṬĀ.)

⌘ CHADŌ ⌘

Japanese term meaning the "way of tea." The tea ceremony, as it is more commonly known, has long been associated with the Zen tradition, dating at least as far back as the Kamakura Period, and possibly going back to Eisai, the founder of Rinzai Zen. The ceremony itself is a simple and elegant occasion in which the participants can be fully present in an act of sharing both an aesthetic experience and a drink designed to help them stay fresh and alert. The drinking of tea was part of the ceremony honoring Bodhidharma, the first Ch'an (Zen) patriarch in China. Additionally, it has become an art form that brings with its experience an enjoyment of pottery, an appreciation for ritual, and an exercise in grace.

⌘ CH'AN ⌘

Buddhist school in China whose name is presumably a transliteration of the Sanskrit term dhyāna, meaning meditation, and thus identifying the major thrust of the school. The Ch'an school traces its beginnings to Bodhidharma, an Indian meditation master who arrived in north China sometime between 516 and 526 and is reckoned to be the first Chinese patriarch (and twenty-eighth Indian patriarch) of the school. Bodhidharma passed on his teaching lineage to his disciple Hui-k'o, and a line of transmission was thus established in China. The history of the school is not without controversy in that the identity of the sixth patriarch was questioned, with one group arguing for Shen-hsui (606–706) and another for Hui-nêng (638–713). Eventually Hui-nêng wins out by offering a better poetic response demonstrating his qualifications. Hui-nêng's Ch'an is thoroughly Mahāyāna, emphasizing emptiness (śūnyatā) and the suddenness of the enlightenment experience (wu). Eventually, a monastic tradition for Ch'an emerged based on the rules of Po-chang Huai-hai (720–814) and geared to a Chinese lifestyle that was different from that of Indian Buddhism. During the T'ang Dynasty, Ch'an divided into five "houses," only two of which survived (eventually merging during the Ming Dynasty): (1) Lin-chi, founded by Lin-ch I-hsüan, and (2) Ts'ao-tung, founded by Tung-shan Liang-chieh (807–869) and Ts'ao-shan Pên-chi (840–901). Lin-chi was taken to Japan by Eisai as Rinzai Zen, while Ts'ao-tung was taken to Japan as Sōtō by Dōgen. Ch'an practice emphasizes meditation, and, depending on the school, may require enigmatic sayings called kung-an (kōan in Japanese), reflection on which is designed to bring to mind beyond logic to direct experience of reality. Great emphasis is put on the relationship between the master and the disciple, with the master urging the student on through skillful means and great compassion. (See also BODHIDHARMA; ZEN.)

⌘ CH'ANG-AN ⌘

Major early Chinese Buddhist center in northern China, eventually becoming capital during the Sui and T'ang dynasties. It was the major center of Kumārajīva's translation enterprises, and a Pure Land stronghold in the seventh century.

⌘ CHAO-CHOU TS'UNG-SHEN ⌘

(778–897)

Great Ch'an master of the T'ang Dynasty in China and Dharma-heir to Nan-ch'üan P'u-yüan. He is reputed to have gained enlightenment while still in his late teens, but continued to study for over forty years with his master. He wandered for many years following his master's death, settling down only when he reached the age of eighty. He continued teaching until his death at an advanced age. He is mentioned repeatedly in the two famous collections of Ch'an dialogues, the Pi-yên Lu or "Blue Cliff Records," and the Wu-mên Kuan or "Gateless Barrier."

⌘ CH'EN, KENNETH K.S. ⌘

Distinguished scholar of Buddhist studies, and specialist in Chinese Buddhism. He was born in Hawaii in 1907, studied at a variety of major universities, and earned his doctorate at Harvard University. His teaching career included posts at the University of Hawaii, Yenching University, Harvard University, and finally, Princeton University. He was awarded both a Guggenheim Fellowship and a Fulbright Fellowship, was an active member of the Association for Asian Studies and American Oriental Society, and contributed continuously to the scholarly literature devoted to the study of Buddhism. His *Buddhism in China: A Historical Survey*, published in 1964, remains a classic, and *Buddhism: The Light of Asia*, published in 1968, is still a highly readable textbook for introductory classes.

⌘ CHÊN-YEN. ⌘

Buddhist Tantric school, introduced into China during the eighth century. It was probably introduced around 720 by Śubhakarasiṃha, where it was popular at the T'ang Dynasty court. Its name means true or efficient word, corresponding to the Sanskrit term mantra, and represents the clearest form of Vajrayāna Buddhism in China. As an independent Buddhist school, it was popular only for a short time, probably no more than two centuries. It was, nonetheless, brought back to Japan by Kūkai (774–835), where it was known as the Shingon school. (See also SHINGON; TANTRA; VAJRAYĀNA.)

⌘ CHICAGO COLUMBIAN EXPOSITION ⌘

Major event hosting the World Parliament of Religions in 1893. This conference was one of the first occasions in which Asian religions were presented to the American public in an organized fashion. In addition to a number of famous Hindu representatives, a series of venerable Buddhists were in attendance: Anagārika Dharmapāla and Sōyen Shaku most notable among them. Virtually all of the major Buddhist schools, however, were represented in the proceedings. During the Parliament, a fortuitous meeting took place between Paul Carus, editor of *The Monist* and Open Court Press, and Sōyen Shaku that paved the way for D. T. Suzuki to come to the United States. In the aftermath of the Parliament, the American Buddhist movement began its first small steps toward catching the American eye and interest. (See also WORLD PARLIAMENT OF RELIGIONS.)

⌘ CHIH-I ⌘

(538–597)

Disciple of Hui-ssū and organizer of the T'ien-t'ai school of Buddhism. Chih-i entered the Buddhist order in his teens, becoming a disciple of Hui-ssŭ (515–576), founder of T'ien-t'ai Buddhism. He was particularly interested in the Lotus-sūtra, and regarded it as the essence of Buddhist teaching. He was also appointed to lecture on the Prajñāpāramitā-sūtras by Hui-ssŭ, and left in charge of the community when the master moved south. Chih-i was also renowned as a great meditator, especially adept at the practice referred to as chih-kuan (śamatha-vipaśyanā) or calming and insight. His voluminous work Mo-ho chih-kuan remains a classic text on this topic in Chinese Buddhism. After continuing for eight more years at Nanking, Chih-i moved to Mount T'ien-t'ai, from which the school of Buddhism he organized took its name, remaining there until his death. He stressed meditation and doctrinal matters equally, providing a great syncretism within Chinese Buddhism. (See also T'IEN-T'AI.)

⌘ CHIH-KUAN ⌘

Meditative practice especially popular in the T'ien-t'ai school of Buddhism. As elucidated in the Chih-i's text Mo-ho chih-kuan, both traditional practices of early Buddhism, calming and insight, are practiced. Chih represents calming (śamatha). The practice of chih involves overcoming the traditional hindrances to meditation, cultivating ethical practices (śīla), and engaging in concentration methods designed to bring the meditator to the realization that all dharmas, the elemental building blocks of experiential reality, are empty of own-being (śūytatā). Kuan, or insight, extends the meditation practice inward to an even deeper realization of the emptiness of all phenomena, stripping away the final bondage to ego. (See also ŚAMATHA; VIPAŚYANĀ.)

⌘ CHIH-KUAN-TA-TSO ⌘

Technical term usually rendered as "aiming at nothing except sitting." It was extensively utilized in the Ts'ao-tung school of Ch'an in China, and its Japanese counterpart Sōtō Zen, where it is referred to as shikantaza. It does not involve a *specific* meditational assignment, nor does it utilize the enigmatic riddles of Linchi Ch'an (corresponding to Rinzai Zen in Japan). There is to be no "trying" and no distraction from simply sitting, confident and faithful that realization will occur. It functions on the premise that *sitting in meditation itself* is the actualization of the Buddha nature inherent in all sentient beings. (See also SHIKANTAZA.)

⌘ CHING-T'U ⌘

Chinese technical term for "Pure Land." It corresponds to the Sanskrit term Sukhāvatī, and reflects the traditional Mahāyāna cosmology, asserting that there are countless Buddha-Lands inhabited by countless Buddhas. In this case, specific reference is made to the Western Paradise, ruled over by Amitābha Buddha. Rebirth in the Pure Land is highly desired among sentient beings because of the many splendors of this paradise, and due to the improved circumstances for attaining complete, perfect enlightenment. Pursuit of rebirth in this paradise developed into an independent Buddhist school, especially popular in China and Japan. (See also JŌDO SHINSHŪ; JŌDO SHŪ; PURE LAND; SUKHĀVATĪ.)

⌘ CHING-T'U TSUNG ⌘

Formal title of the "Pure Land School" in China (corresponding to the Jōdo Shū in Japanese Buddhism). Devotion to Amitābha Buddha was, prior to Hui-yüan (344–416), an optional practice within Buddhism. Hui-yüan established this enterprise as an *independent* activity, and developed a new Buddhist school around the practice by forming the White Lotus Society in 402. His disciple T'an-luan (476–542) organized the school, and is claimed as the first Chinese patriarch of the Ching-t'u Tsung. They emphasize Amitābha's (shortened to Amita and rendered A-mi-t'o in Chinese) vow to cause all faithful beings to be reborn in his paradise, focusing religious practice on repetition of the phrase known as the Nien-fo: "Nan-mo A-mi-t'o Fo," literally meaning, "Homage to Amita Buddha." This practice is also used in the Japanese version of the Pure Land school, where it is called the "Nembutsu" ("Namu Amida Butsu"). Because the school relies on the saving grace of Amitābha Buddha, it is often referred to as the "easy path," of dependence on outside help (t'zŭ-li in Chinese; tariki in Japanese). Textually, the school utilizes the Sukhāvatī sūtras and the Amitāyurdhyāna-sūtra. The school was passed down through a succession of masters including Tao-cho (562–645), Shan-tao (613–681), and Tz'u-min (680–748). Due to its simplicity of practice, it was better able to survive periods of decline (mo-fa in Chinese; mappō in Japanese), and thus weathered the anti-Buddhist persecution of 845 better than virtually all other Buddhist schools. It was founded in Japan by Hōnen (1133–1212), where it remains among the most popular Buddhist schools. (See also JŌDO SHINSHŪ; JŌDO SHŪ; PURE LAND.)

⌘ CHI-TSANG ⌘

(549–623)

Greatest master of the San-lun school of Chinese Buddhism. Following the death of Kumārajīva and his immediate successors, the San-lun school lost the interest of Chinese Buddhists. With the appearance of Chi-tsang, the "Three Treatise School," as it was called, was revived. He clarified the doctrines of Nāgārjuna, founder of the Indian Mādhyamika school (which served as the basis for San-lun), and rebuilt the reputation of the school sufficiently that he was invited to the capital of Chang-an to present the teachings to the Buddhist community assembled there. After Chi-tsang, the school lost its influence in China. (See also SAN-LUN.)

⌘ CHRONICLES ⌘

Chronicles are historical texts that describe events and circumstances in a given time frame and location, usually based on more or less accurate data available to the author. Chronicles are often enhanced by the use of traditional legends and amplified by mythological references. In Buddhist context, they are most often written in prose, although not exclusively so. Additionally, we can find useful chronicles in virtually every country where Buddhism has existed for any duration. With regard to the Indian Buddhist tradition, the most meaningful chronicles can be found within the Tripiṭaka. For example, in Pāli, the Vinaya Piṭaka records events surrounding Buddha's enlightenment, ministry, and death, as well as the first two councils following Buddha's death. Also instrumental for our knowledge on Indian Buddhism are the Sanskrit chronicles, including much of the Avadāna literature, and especially the Aśokāvadāna, Divyāvadāna, and Mahāvastvāvadāna. Chronicles written by later Mahāyāna authors such as Bhāvaviveka are also useful for unraveling complicated issues in Indian Buddhist history. We are especially fortunate with regard to chronicles relative to Sri Lankan history, having at our disposal the Dīpavaṃsa or "Island Chronicle," Mahāvaṃsa or "Great Chronicle," and Mahābodhivaṃsa, to mention a few. From Burma comes a wealth of chronicles including the "Glass Palace Chronicle," the "Celebrated Chronicle," and a host of recent works. Tibet offers the "Red Annals" from the fourteenth century, the "Blue Annals" approximately one hundred years later, and historical texts by the great Tibetan authors Bu-ston (fourteenth century) and Tāranātha (seventeenth century). Thailand has the Jinakāmālī, written in the sixteenth century, and China and Japan also have a series of useful texts in this category. By reading selectively and carefully, much can be learned from this literature, not only pertinent to the culture in which each respective text was composed but also spanning the whole of Buddhist history. It is a critical literature for understanding Buddhism as a *world religion*.

⌘ CITTA ⌘

Derived from the Sanskrit verb root √ cit, to think, a technical term that is usually translated as "mind" or "thought."

In early Buddhism, the term was often used synonymously with two other technical terms, manas ("mind organ") and vijñāna ("consciousness"). It was extremely interesting to Abhidharma philosophers insofar as it was concerned with the chief object of their psychological concern. It was categorized by the Sarvāstivādins as one of their seventy-five "dharmas," the building blocks of experiential reality. In Yogācāra thought, the meaning of citta is clarified. It is used as a synonym for the ālaya-vijñāna or "storehouse consciousness" which serves as a repository for the seeds resulting from all karmic acts. As such, the word is sometimes compounded with another term to form the conjunct "citta-mātra," or "mind-only." The concept appears in several texts and represents a response to the problem of what exists in the world if all experiential phenomena are empty; the world is simply a product of mind. When meditative practice enabled one to eliminate the false distinction of subject and objects, then ultimate reality is reached, variously called tathatā, Tathāgata-garbha, and other terms by the Yogācārins.

⌘ CĪVARA ⌘

The generic term for robes worn by the monastic community. Indian Buddhist monks generally wore three robes: (1) an inner robe extending below the knee and likened perhaps to an undergarment, (2) an upper robe worn as a covering over both shoulders, and (3) a double robe worn as an overgarment. Indian Buddhist nuns added two further robes: (4) a loose vest which covers the upper body, and (5) a bathing robe. During the period of rain-retreat, monastic dwellers usually received new robe material in a ceremony known as the kaṭhina-rite, held at the culmination of the rainy season. Colors for the robes seem to vary from tradition to tradition. In early Buddhism the robes were generally yellow. In Chinese Buddhism, robes may be brown or blue. Tibetan Buddhists wear red robes. Japanese monks wear black.

⌘ COMMENTARIES ⌘

Commentarial literature in Buddhism is that which augments, explains, and expands upon primary texts. In each Buddhist tradition, the primary literature, agreed to be the teaching (or "speaking") of Buddha, was *fixed and closed* at a relatively early date in the history of each tradition. In this way, each tradition generated its own "canonical literature." Several of these are summarized in "The Buddhist Scriptures" portion of the introductory materials to this volume. Nonetheless, Buddhism was at its inception and has remained throughout its history a growing, spreading, reflecting religion, changing and adapting to new cultures and changing times. Precisely because the canon was *fixed and closed,* new ways had to be developed to cope with infusing new meanings and interpretations into Buddha's sermons and disciplinary discourses if Buddhism hoped to remain a vital, meaningful religious tradition. The vehicle that emerged to meet that need was the creation of an extensive commentarial tradition. By writing new commentaries on old texts, the tradition was able to revitalize itself, to remain current, and to address needs that have become transcultural and transtemporal. In the course of Buddhist history additional texts appeared in virtually every Buddhist culture and tradition that were clearly not "the word of Buddha," identified with individual authors, but nevertheless of critical importance for the understanding and practice of Buddhism. Many of these texts have also generated commentaries, some of them even auto-commentaries, and, in the process, kept Buddhism fresh, creative, and facing an increasingly changing definition of modernity.

⌘ COMMUNITY ⌘

See SAṂGHA

⌘ COMPASSION ⌘

See KARUṆĀ

⌘ CONSCIOUSNESS ⌘

See VIJÑĀNA

⌘ CONZE, EDWARD ⌘
(1904–1979)

World-famous Buddhologist primarily known for his landmark work on the Prajñāpāramitā or "Perfection of Wisdom" literature. If a single individual had to be identified who had advanced the general understanding of Mahāyāna Buddhism in the scholarly community more than anyone else, it would be Edward Conze. With more than twenty books, over one hundred articles, and well over one hundred reviews to his credit, he must be counted among the world's most erudite and prolific scholars of Buddhism. Born in London in 1904, he earned his Ph.D. in philosophy (in Germany) in 1928. To use Conze's own word, he "rediscovered" Buddhism in the 1930s, primarily through the writings of D. T. Suzuki and Har Dayal, each of whom produced scholarly writings on Buddhism. The ongoing events of his life have been published in a lively autobiography, *The Memoirs of a Modern Gnostic*. Teaching often in the United States, he returned to Europe shortly before his death in 1979. His translations of various Prajñāpāramitā-sūtras are too numerous to mention, but his *Buddhism: Its Essence and Development* (1951), *Buddhist Thought in India* (1962), and *The Prajñāpāramitā Literature* (1960) still make interesting and important reading.

⌘ COSMOLOGY ⌘

A number of cosmological schemata are present in Buddhism, possibly the earliest of which emerges from the Pāli Canon, in which the universe is divided into three realms, the Kāmadhātu or "Realm of Desire," Rūpadhātu or "Realm of Forms," and Ārūpyadhātu or "Formless Realms." Hell beings, hungry ghosts, animals, men, antigods, and six classes of gods dwell in the first realm (desire). In the second realm (forms) dwell gods who have practiced certain dhyānas or meditations. In the final realm (formless) dwell those beings who have attained the four stages of formlessness. A variation on this pattern can be found in Vasubandhu's famous Abhidharmakośa. In this framework, the earth sits atop six cold and six hot hells. A huge mountain called Sumeru is located in the center of the earth, circumscribed by four continents. An enormous mountain range surrounds the entire system, thus maintaining the oceans in their integrity. Above the world, gods and other heavenly beings dwell in two categories of heavens: desire heavens and form heavens. When Mahāyāna developed, opening up the cosmos with its theory of various Buddha-Lands, each ruled by a Celestial Buddha and housing Celestial Bodhisattvas, the Buddhist picture of the universe expanded as if derived from a Robert Heinlein novel or an episode from *Star Trek*. Vajrayāna further expanded the horizon. In the new schemata, the Eastern Paradise is known as Abhirati, ruled over by

Akṣobhya Buddha, who is associated with Vajrapāṇi Bodhisattva. The Western Paradise, known as Sukhāvatī, is ruled over by Amitābha Buddha, who is associated with Avalokiteśvara Bodhisattva. Amoghasiddhi Buddha rules the Northern Paradise and is associated with Viśvapāṇi Bodhisattva. Ratnasambhava Buddha rules the Southern Paradise, and is associated with Ratnapāṇi Bodhisattva. Finally, the center of the cosmic maṇḍala is occupied by Vairocana Buddha, associated with Samantabhadra Bodhisattva.

⌘ COUNCILS-ANURĀDHAPURA ⌘

Theravāda council held in 25 B.C.E. under King Vaṭṭagāmaṇī. During the first century B.C.E., the Buddhist community of Sri Lanka was threatened by an invasion of Tamils from southern India, forcing King Vattagāmaṇī to abandon the throne for fourteen years (43–29 B.C.E.). Upon resuming his rule in 29 B.C.E., the king found the land overcome by famine and in the midst of schismatic waves in the Buddhist community. To resolve the religious unrest, he convened a conference in the capital city of Anurādhapura in 25 B.C.E., to be held at the Mahāvihāra. The expedient occasion for the meeting was to commit the Buddhist scriptures to writing in Pāli, thus "closing" the three baskets of scriptures in the Theravāda tradition. Such an act provided an institutional base for the community, and a means with which to develop the Theravāda tradition more fully. This site was significant, for it provided the Mahāvihāra with a canonical orthodoxy in its rivalry with the residents of Abhayagiri. (See also MAHĀVIHĀRA.)

⌘ COUNCILS-GANDHĀRA ⌘

Council held around 100 C.E. under the reign of the Indian king Kaniṣka, probably in Gandhāra. Near the end of the first century C.E. when Kaniṣka assumed the throne of the Kuṣāṇa Dynasty, he tried to imitate the style of the great Indian ruler Aśoka, while supporting the Sarvāstivādin school of Buddhism. It was suggested to Kaniṣka by the Sarvāstivādin monk Pārśva that invitations be sent to all the learned Buddhists of the era to attend a council to be convened in Gandhāra. A great scholar named Vasumitra was made president of the council, consisting of 499 monks, and he was assisted by the learned Aśvaghoṣa. In addition to compiling a new Vinaya, they prepared a commentary called the Mahāvibhāṣā on the Abhidharma text Jñānaprasthāna. This work was to become the standard reference work for all Sarvastivadin Abhidharma issues. It can be said that this council fulfilled the same role in Sarvastivadin history that Aśoka's council did for Theravādin (or Vibhajyavādin) history. (See also AŚVAGHOṢA; VASUMITRA.)

⌘ COUNCILS-LHASA ⌘

Council held in Lhasa under the reign of King Khri-srong-lde-btsan in 792–794. Tibetan Buddhism in the sixth century was complicated by the fact that the king, Srong-btsan-sgam-po, was married to both Nepalese and Chinese wives, thus affording a dual input of information and practice relative to Buddhism. Following the completion of the great monastery at bSam-yas in 787, a council was convened there to resolve the differences between the Tantric notions of Padmasambhava, the earlier Indian Buddhist ideals of Śāntirakṣita, and the Chinese viewpoints present. The council took the form of a debate between Śāntarikṣita and a Chinese monk generally called Hva-shang in the literature. The Chinese monk argued for the notion of "sudden" enlightenment while Śāntirakṣita argued for "gradual" enlightenment. Śānti rakṣita also stressed the efficacy of meritorious action which Hva-shang refuted. The Chinese position was soundly defeated, continuing an Indian basis for the development of Tibetan Buddhism. After the debate, the Chinese participants left the country. (See also ŚĀNTIKRAKṢITA.)

⌘ COUNCILS-MANDALAY ⌘

Council held in Burma in 1871, sometimes referred to as the fifth Theravāda council (following those held at Rājagṛha, Vaiśālī, Pāṭaliputra, and Anurādhapura). Convened during the reign of King Mindon Min who had prior religious training in the monastic order, this council was charged with an explicit purpose: to revise the Pāli texts. The revised texts were inscribed on 729 marble tablets, and entombed in stūpas to ensure their survival.

⌘ COUNCILS-PĀṬALIPUTRA I ⌘

Noncanonical council, quite possibly held during the reign of the Indian king Mahāpadma the Nandin in 137 A.N. (i.e., after nirvāṇa of the Buddha), and resulting in the initial schism in Indian Buddhism. There is no doubt whatsoever that by the reign of King Aśoka (272–231), Buddhism was already sectarian. Until the last fifty years, it was virtually impossible to determine precisely when and where the Indian Buddhist sectarian movement began. Largely through the work of the French Buddhologist André Bareau, but with input from Marcel Hofinger, Paul Demiéville, and Nalinaksha Dutt, an hypothesis was pieced together that traced the origins of Buddhist sectarianism to a noncanonical council mentioned in a wide variety of secondary literature, dating from quite early times. Presumably, King Mahāpadma was asked to mediate a dispute between rival groups in the *still unified* Buddhist community that centered around laxity in disciplinary proceedings and five theses regarding the nature of an arhant voiced by a monk named Mahādeva. The king simply assembled the parties and took a vote. The majority party took a name consistent with its position: "Great Group-ists" (Mahāsāṃghikas). The minority party, in affirming their assumed status as the "orthodox" disciplinary and doctrinal party, called themslves "Elders" (Sthaviras). The Mahāsāṃghikas were associated with liberal disciplinary policies, and with Mahādeva, while the Sthaviras were considered conservative on all accounts. Each group began to subdivide internally within a short period of time. A second hypothesis regarding the initial sectarian split in Indian Buddhism argues that both the time and circumstance of the council are contrary to Bareau's findings, agreeing only on the site. This latter position, utilizing the same textual materials as Bareau and advocated by Janice Nattier and Charles Prebish, suggests that the date of the council was 116 A.N., with the sole cause focusing on unwarranted Vinaya expansion on the part of the future Sthaviras. The Nattier and Prebish hypothesis considers the future Mahāsāṃghikas neither lax in disciplinary matters nor philosophically critical of the status of the arhant. The matter remains unresolved. (See also MAHĀSĀṂGHIKA; STHAVIRA.)

⌘ COUNCILS-PĀṬALIPUTRA II ⌘

Canonical council held during the reign of the Indian king Aśoka, intending to establish Buddhist orthodoxy. Although the Mahāvaṃsa and Dīpavaṃsa provide slightly difffering dates for the council, it appears to have occurred around 250 B.C.E. So-called "heretics" had been entering the Buddhist community for some time, so King Aśoka decided to convene a council under the directorship of the learned monk Moggaliputta Tissa in order to reestablish the Dharma properly. A thousand monks were assembled, and under Tissa's guidance, the various unacceptable viewpoints were considered and rejected, with their proponents being expelled from the capital of Pāṭaliputra. The council concluded that Buddha was a "distinctionist" or Vibhajyavādin, thus establishing this position as officially orthodox and therefore, the precursor of the Theravāda sect. The viewpoints discussed were collected and recorded in the Pāli Abhidharma text known as the Kathāvatthu. It also appears that those individuals expelled from the capital were the Sarvāstivādins, destined to become one of the most important groups in Indian Buddhist religious and philosophical history. The council is only mentioned in the Pāli records, and for this reason it is often referred to as the third Theravāda council. (See also AŚOKA.)

⌘ COUNCILS-RĀJAGṚHA ⌘

Council thought to be the first of its kind in Indian Buddhist history, convened in the year of Buddha's death to establish the Dharma and Vinaya. Fearful that the community would dissolve through uncertainty over Buddha's teachings, the saṃgha decided to hold a council, generally thought to have occurred in 483 B.C.E., to preclude that possibility. King Bimbisāra, one of Buddha's royal patrons, donated the site in his capital city of Rājagṛha, thus accounting for the name of the council. Kāśyapa, a senior, leading monk of the time was appointed president of the council, selecting 500 arhant monks to participate in the proceedings. Buddha's disciple Upāli recited all of the disciplinary rules, known as the Vinaya Piṭaka, fixing that portion of the Buddhist canon. Ānanda, Buddha's personal attendant, who became enlightened only the night prior to the convocation of the council, recited all Buddha's discourses, establishing the Sūtra Piṭaka. Other business was conducted as well, with the council referring to itself as the "Chanting of the Vinaya" or Vinayasaṃgīti. Functionally, it marks an important event in the history of the community, for it establishes *authority* for the group in the absence of its charismatic leader, while at the same time reinforcing communal solidarity. Scholarly research suggests that the canonical accounts of the council may be greatly exaggerated.

⌘ COUNCILS-RANGOON ⌘

Reckoned to be the sixth Theravāda council, held in Rangoon in 1954 to recite and confirm the whole Pāli Canon. This council was convened so as to coincide in proximity with the celebration of the twenty-five hundredth anniversary of Buddha's death. The prime minister of Burma, U Nu, delivered the opening address for the meeting to 2,500 monks in attendance. These monks edited and recited texts for two years, concluding on the anniversary date of Buddha's death according to the Burmese tradition. It was a national festival in Burma, but additionally established solidarity for Theravāda Buddhists throughout the world.

⌘ COUNCILS-VAIŚĀLĪ ⌘

Deemed the second Indian Buddhist council in all accounts, it dates one hundred years following Buddha's death, having been convened to resolve a dispute in the community over supposedly illicit monastic behavior. The story associated with the council explains that a Buddhist monk known as Yaśas wanders into Vaiśālī and observes a group of monks identified as the Vṛjiputraka monks engaging in ten practices that he believes to be inappropriate monastic behavior. In speaking out against the monks, Yaśas is punished by the community, requiring him to beg the pardon of the apparently offended monks. He chooses *not* to do so, is banished from the community, and journeys on to Kauśāmbī to seek support for his position. In order to resolve the conflict between Yaśas and the Vaiṣālī monks, a council is convened in Vaśālī with 700 monks in attendance. A well-respected monk named Revata was made president of the council, and an elder monk known as Sarvagāmin (who was a direct disciple of Buddha's servant Ānanda) was questioned on the ten points. Each point was *rejected* by Sarvagāmin, the offending practices outlawed, and concord reestablished. Although a reconciliation was effected, the proceeding of the council does suggest rather dramatically that *within one hundred years of Buddha's demise,* significant tensions and disagreements had begun to appear in the still unified Buddhist community. These would shortly ferment into the first sectarian split in Indian Buddhism.

⌘ CRAVING ⌘

See TṚṢṆĀ

— D —

⌘ DAIMOKU ⌘

Chant recited by members of the Japanese Sōkagakkai Buddhist sect, known in America as Nichiren Shōshū of America. The chant involves the repetition of the phrase Nam Myōhō Renge Kyō, literally "Homage to the Lotus-sūtra." The sect takes its doctrinal basis from Nichiren's (1222–1282) supposition that the Lotus-sūtra was the most complete Buddhist text, as such utilizing the daimoku as an expression of faith and practice. Proper recitation of the daimoku represents the highest practical expression of the law of simultaneous cause and effect, establishing harmony with the universe for its reciters, and also yields benefits in the secular world. (See also NICHIREN.)

⌘ DAITOKU-JI ⌘

Famous Zen monastery in Kyoto, Japan, built in 1319 by Akamatsu Norimura to accommodate students of its first abbot who was known as Myōchō, but sometimes referred to as Daitō Kokushi (1283–1337). He was trained by his master Jōmyō (sometimes referred to as Daiō Kokushi, 1236–1308) following the Chinese Ch'an tradition of the Yang-chi sect (a subsect of Lin-chi Ch'an). For some time it was counted among the "Five Mountains" of Zen in Kyoto, eventually assuming a special position as the monastery at which to pray for the emperor's health. It became a cultural center as well, attracting many tea-masters, and finally developed into a great monastic complex, housing a number of subsidiary monasteries.

⌘ DALAI LAMA ⌘

Honorary title afforded to successive reincarnations of Avaloiteśvara, chosen from within the dGe-lugs-pa sect of Tibetan

Buddhism, and considered to be both the political and religious leader of Tibet. The lineage started in the dGe-lug-pa sect begun by Tsong-kha-pa (1357–1419). Tsong-kha-pa's nephew was his third successor in the lineage of this school, and was given the honorary title Dalai Lama (dalai bla-ma) by the Mongolian ruler of the time (Altan Khan). It denoted one whose wisdom was as great as the ocean, and elevated the dGe-lugs-pa sect to a political prominence higher than that of the other Tibetan Buddhist sects. With the passing of each Dalai Lama, a new reincarnation (called a tulku) is sought after, providing much intrigue in the selection process. Additionally, the histories of the various Dalai Lamas are enormously interesting, demonstrating much complexity and literacy of Tibetan Buddhism. To date, there have been fourteen Dalai Lamas, the current one being Tenzin Gyatso (born in 1935). He recently was awarded the Nobel Peace Prize in recognition of his work in the aftermath of the Tibetan Holocaust. Although based at the Tibetan refugee community in Dharamsala, India, he is a constant world traveler, promoting issues relative to the plight of the Tibetan people and world peace in general. (See also DGE-LUGS-PA; PANCHEN-LAMA.)

⌘ DĀNA ⌘

Technical term generally translated as "giving," quite often considered in texts dealing with ethical issues. In the early tradition it was frequently associated with the laity providing goods and/or services to the monastic community. The generosity associated with dāna was considered sufficient to generate a stock of good merit that would bring fruit in a future life. It established the saṃgha as a "field of merit" which the laity pursued through such activities as alms-giving. It was a reciprocal arrangement, however, for a verse in the Dhammapada (354) suggests that the gift of Dharma is the highest of all gifts. As such, the monks and nuns returned a gift to the laity at least equal to what they received in support. In modern Theravāda countries, the practice of dāna remains extensive. In Mahāyāna, the practice of giving was established as a perfection (pāramitā) associated with the first stage of the bodhisattva path. In addition to correlation with love (maitrī) and compassion (karuṇā), the bodhisattva is encouraged to manifest the highest expression of giving possible: to give oneself wholly and completely, nothing held back. In so doing, the ego is overcome absolutely, and the bodhisattva's activities are viewed as truly selfless, carried out for the sake of all sentient beings.

⌘ DAŚABHUMIKA-SUTRA ⌘

Mahāyāna text, the title of which translates to the "Sūtra on the Ten Stages." It is a chapter of a longer work known as the Avataṃsaka-sūtra, but broke free and became an independent text, circulating in its own right. It is highly important in Mahāyāna practice because it clearly and thoroughly establishes the ten stages of the bodhisattva path. It designates ten bhūmis or "stages" that the bodhisattva must traverse on the path to complete, perfect enlightenment. These include: the (1) "Joyful Stage" (pramuditā-bhūmi), (2) "Immaculate Stage" (vimalā-bhūmi), (3) "Radiant Stage" (prabhākarī-bhūmi), (4) "Blazing Stage" (arciṣmatī-bhūmi), (5) "Hard to Conquer Stage" (sudurjayā-bhūmi), (6) "Face-to-Face Stage" (abhimukhī-bhūmi), (7) "Going Far Beyond Stage" (dūraṅgamā-bhūmi), (8) "Immovable Stage" (acalā-bhūmi), (9) "Good Thought Stage" (sādhumatī-bhūmi), and (10) "Cloud of Dharma Stage" (dharmameghā-bhūmi). Other Buddhist texts, such as the Mahāvastu in Sanskrit and the P'u-sa-pen-yeh ching in Chinese, present a tenfold path for bodhisattva practice, but none has attained the status and importance of the Daśabhūmika-sūtra. (See also BHŪMI; BODHISATTVA; BODHISATTVA-BHŪMI-SŪTRA.)

⌘ DENGYŌ DAISHI ⌘

See SAICHŌ

⌘ DENKŌ-ROKU ⌘

"Book of Transmission," containing the specific kōan and its solution in *each* of the fifty-two transmissions of Dharma from Śākyamuni Buddha to Dōgen Zenji (1200–1253), the founder of Sōtō Zen. The text is the work of Keizan Zenji (1268–1325), a young man who entered Eiheiji monastery at age twelve and was instrumental in advancing the Sōtō Zen tradition dramatically. Along with Dōgen's Shōbōgenzō, it is one of the most important texts in this Zen lineage. It is rather poetic in style and intuitive in content. The text captures the actual circumstance and frame of mind of the particular individual associated with the solution of each kōan. (See also KEIZAN JŌKIN ZENJI.)

⌘ DEPENDENT ORIGINATION ⌘

See PRATĪTYA-SAMUTPĀDA

⌘ DEVADATTA ⌘

Cousin of Buddha who tried to usurp Buddha's authority and displace him as head of the saṃgha, eventually resorting to a failed attempt on Buddha's life. Having entered the order as a young man, Devadatta became an influential monk in the Buddhist saṃgha. Discontent with his role, and blinded by personal ambition, Devadatta entered into a plot with Prince Ajātaśatru of Magadha whereby they intended to displace both Buddha and King Bimbisāra, Ajātaśatru's father. Devadatta utilized hired assassins to eliminate Buddha, and when their attempts failed, he even resorted to his own abortive attempt. During the last years of Buddha's life, Devadatta tried to create a schism in the saṃgha by proposing five new rules that would establish greater austerity on the part of the monks. While initially successful in beginning a new community with five hundred newly ordained monks, Devadatta's followers were led back into the orthodox saṃgha by Śāriputra and Maudgalyāyana. At his death, it is apparent that Devadatta would reap much karmic retribution for his evil activity. (See also AJĀTAŚATRU.)

⌘ DEVĀNAṂPIYA TISSA ⌘

King who ruled Sri Lanka from 247–207 B.C.E. and was responsible for the introduction of Buddhism to the island. Although Devānaṃpiya Tissa already knew about Buddhism from King Aśoka, his first real occasion for receiving Buddhist teaching came from Mahinda, Aśoka's missionary to Sri Lanka. After meeting, quite possibly in Mihintalē, Mahinda and his associates were invited to the capital of Anurādhapura. The king offered Mahāmeghavana Park to the saṃgha, on the site that eventually became the Mahāvihāra monastery. Within a short period, young men from Sri Lanka were initiated into the saṃgha, thus establishing a valid ordination lineage on the island, a branch of the

Bodhi Tree was brought from India, the Vinaya was recited, and an order of nuns established. By the end of Devānaṃpiya Tissa's reign, Buddhism in Sri Lanka was firmly entrenched.

⌘ DEVOTION ⌘

Although it is clear that devotion was not unknown in early Buddhism, particularly as expressed in the formula of the "Three Refuges" and the reverence exemplified in the rise of stūpa worship, the notion of a formally devotional Buddhism is largely a product of a series of Mahāyāna texts known as the Pure Land Sūtras. Including such texts as the Larger and Smaller Sukhāvatī-vyūha-sūtras and the Amitāyurdhyāna-sūtra, the worship of Celestial Buddhas emerged as a valid means of attainment of progress on the spiritual path. Thus the meaning of *faith* was radically transformed in Buddhist doctrine, elevated in status as a means worthy of generating rebirth in the Pure Land. Along with the profound philosophical implications of such a transformation, the validity of devotional practice altered community life as well, affording a new potential for the Buddhist laity. While Mahāyāna in general ascribed a greater status to the laity than in Hīnayāna, the notion of actualizing favorable rebirth in the Pure Land by reciting an appropriate mantra properly was a new and utterly radical conception, breeding Buddhist schools in East Asia based entirely on this new presumption, schools which remain the most popular today. (See also AMITĀBHA; AMITĀYURDHYĀNA-SŪTRA; LARGER SUKHĀVATĪVYŪHA-SŪTRA; SMALLER SUKHĀVATĪVYŪHA-SŪTRA; PURE LAND.)

⌘ DGE-LUGS-PA ⌘

Tibetan Buddhist school founded by Tsong-kha-pa (1357–1419). Tsong-kha-pa, the founder of the school, not only joined the order as a young boy, and had extensive training in both the exoteric and esoteric Buddhist traditions, but also was profoundly influenced by the bKa-gdams-pa school. Consequently, the dGe-lugs-pa school that Tsong-kha-pa founded "literally means "School of the Virtuous," and reflects *both* an emphasis on the Vinaya *and* systematic study of the doctrinal texts. The school is sometimes referred to as the "Yellow Hat School" because they rejected the traditional red hat of the prior Buddhist schools in favor of the yellow hat now traditional in their group. They became the most influential of the Tibetan Buddhist schools, and once the line of the Dalai Lamas was established within this school, the dGe-lugs-pa school was afforded political leadership as well. Like all other surviving Tibetan Buddhist schools, they pursue their activity in exile in the aftermath of the Tibetan Holocaust. (See also TSONG-KHA-PA.)

⌘ DHAMMAPADA ⌘

One of the books of the Khuddaka Nikāya, the fifth major division of the Sutta Piṭaka in the Pāli Canon. The text title translates as "Stanzas on the Teaching" or "Verses of Dhamma," and represents a series of 423 verses arranged in 26 chapters. Throughout Buddhist religious history, this text has been one of the most popular in all Buddhist literature, primarily because of its simple edifying verses of highly ethical content. Versions of this text appear also in Sanskrit and Prakrit. A number of texts in the Chinese canon utilize this text name, and the Udānavarga in Tibetan translation contains nearly four hundred verses corresponding to those in the Dhammapada. (See also KHUDDAKA NIKĀYA.)

⌘ DHARMA ⌘

Generic term most generally utilized to represent the teaching of the Buddha. Derived from the Sanskrit verb root √ dhṛ, which has an enormous number of meanings, Dharma refers to the totality of Buddha's teaching, and as such, is identified as one of the "Three Jewels" in the formula of the "Three Refuges," the others being Buddha and Saṃgha. It is an inclusive term which can be used to include the Hīnayāna, Mahāyāna, and Vajrayāna, as well as the doctrine of any sect or school listed under one of the above categories. It is also utilized in Buddhist philosophy to indicate the so-called building blocks of experiential reality, the elements of existence. It is this latter usage, often written in all lowercase letters (as "dharma"), that Hīnayāna sects affirm as real existents governed by the law of dependent origination, while being rejected by Mahāyāna sects as empty (śūnyatā) of reality in their own right (called svabhāva). In either of these two critical forms, the term is one of the most important in all of Buddhism. (See also ASAṂSKṚTA; SAṂSKṚTA)

⌘ DHARMACAKRA ⌘

Literally, the "Wheel of the Teaching." The Dharmacakra is a Buddhist symbol utilized to represent the Buddha's teaching, usually depicted as an eight-spoked wheel with each spoke representing one member of the eightfold path (the fourth of the noble truths). Later Buddhist traditions have also argued that the Wheel of the Teaching was turned on three occasions: (1) with the preaching of Buddha's first sermon, (2) with the rise of Mahāyāna and its new emphases, and (3) with the development of Vajrayāna or esoteric Buddhism.

⌘ DHARMACAKRAPRAVARTANA-SŪTRA ⌘

Title of Buddha's first sermon, the translation of which is often rendered "Sermon on the Turning of the Wheel of the Law." Buddhist history informs us that Siddhārtha Gautama, the historical Buddha, preached his first sermon in a Deer Park outside Benares to his five former ascetic colleagues. In so doing, he fulfilled the prophecy of his youth in which it was determined that he would turn the wheel of either the secular or religious law depending on his choice of vocation. As such, the first sermon is appropriately named. The substance of this text focuses on the futility of the two extremes of life (i.e., pleasure seeking and asceticism) as well as espousing the cornerstone doctrine of Buddha's Dharma, the Four Noble Truths. Upon hearing the sermon, one of the four ascetics, Ajñāta Kauṇḍinya, becomes enlightened and is enjoined to go forth into the homeless, mendicant life with the formula, "Ehi bhikṣu," "Come, O Monk." Thus, in a single stroke, the Buddha launches his ministry of preaching (Dharma) and begins a community of like-minded followers (Saṃgha).

⌘ DHARMAGUPTAKA ⌘

One of the early Indian Buddhist sects, probably in existence by the time of King Aśoka. Its members broke off from the Mahīśāsakas who emerged out of the Sthavira lineage and may have been the forerunners of the Theravāda school. Their name means "Protectors of the Dharma." The Dharmaguptakas were extremely important with regard to the development of the Vinaya or disciplinary tradition in China in that their Vinaya texts were most revered of all the Hīnayāna schools. It is singularly important that of all the Vinayas studied by modern scholars, the Dharmaguptaka school alone has significant regulations (twenty-six in number) concerning behavior at a stūpa. This, coupled with additional information concerning the nature of their ritual function texts, suggests that the Dharmaguptakas may have been "professional ritualists."

⌘ DHARMĀKARA ⌘

Central figure in the Larger Sukhāvatīvyūha-sūtra, associated with having made forty-eight vows, each regarding the nature of existence when he becomes a Buddha. Dharmākara was a monk eons ago who, upon hearing the Dharma from a Buddha known as Lokeśvararāja, becomes instilled with the desire to gain complete, perfect enlightenment. He requests not only instruction from Lokeśvararāja, but also seeks to learn the qualities of a pure Buddha-Land. After countless lifetimes Dharmākara is able to actualize the teaching given him by Lokeśvararāja, thus becoming the Buddha Amitābha, and the forty-eight vows taken by Dharmākara reflect the qualities of life in his Buddha-Land of The Western Paradise, the Pure Land of Sukhāvatī. (See also AMITĀBHA; LARGER SUKHĀVATĪVYŪHA-SŪTRA.)

⌘ DHARMA-KĀYA ⌘

"Dharma-Body," third of the three bodies of the Buddha in Mahāyāna, and used as a synonym for ultimate reality. Although present in earlier Mahāyāna thought, later texts like the Laṅkāvatāra-sūtra developed the notion of three bodies of the Buddha more fully, with the concept coming to maturity in the Yogācāra school. There, the historical body of Buddha was referred to as an "apparitional body" (nirmāṇa-kāya) visible to ordinary, common worldlings as an inspiration to begin the (Mahāyāna) Buddhist path. Once on path, as a bodhisattva, one relates to a Buddha in another form: "enjoyment body" (saṃbhoga-kāya), a quasi-physical preacher of Mahāyāna sūtras. Finally, at the completion of the path, one attains the "Dharma body" (Dharma-kāya), the true nature of Buddhahood, described in a variety of technical terms, all used virtually synonymously: Tathatā (Suchness), Tathāgata-garbha (Womb of the Tathāgata), Buddhatā (State of Buddhahood), and so forth. In other words, each of the three bodies of the Buddha speaks to an individual at a different level of spiritual development, with Dharma-kāya representing the true, ultimate reality. (See also TRIKĀYA.)

⌘ DHARMAKĪRTI ⌘

Indian Buddhist logician (ca. 650) who was regarded in some circles as the classic, representative Buddhist philosopher. Dharmakīrti studied at Nālandā University, and elaborated on the logic and epistemology set forth by an earlier great Buddhist logician, Dignāga. He is especially well known for his text called the Pramāṇavārttika, purportedly a commentary on Dignāga's Pramāṇasamuccaya, but more accurately a reworking and supplement to Dignāga's treatise. In this text, he was especially interested in inference, direct perception, and a general theory of knowledge. Dharmakīrti was also the author of a highly regarded logic text known as the Nyāyabindu, and exerted much influence on the later Buddhist logicians.

⌘ DHARMAPĀLA ⌘

(530–561)

Yogacara philosopher, disciple of Dignāga, and his successor as abbot of Nālandā University. His most famous work is a text known as the Vijñaptimātratā-siddhi, preserved in Chinese, and representing a commentary on Vasubandhu's famous Triṃśikā. It was translated into Chinese by the Chinese pilgrim Hsüan-tsang, and became the fundamental text of the Fa-hsiang school of Chinese Buddhism (which also developed in Japan as the Hossō school). Dharmapāla is primarily identified with an eightfold theory of consciousness, and with the notion that while external things are empty of any reality in their own right, consciousness itself exists. As such, his philosophy is called the "consciousness only" theory. (See also FA-HSIANG.)

⌘ DHARMAPĀLA, ANAGĀRIKA ⌘

(1864–1933)

Former Sri Lankan Christian named Don David Hewavitarne who founded the Mahābodhi Society. Inspired by Colonel Henry Steele Olcott (1832–1907), a theosophist, he took the name Anagārika Dharmapāla in 1881, and devoted the remainder of his life to championing Sri Lankan Buddhism. After visiting Bodhgayā in 1891, he founded the Mahābodhi Society, hoping to regain control of that site for Buddhists worldwide. He attended the World Parliament of Religions at the Chicago Columbian Exposition in 1893, returning again in 1896 at the invitation of Paul Carus, and in 1902–1904. A British branch of the Mahābodhi Society was formed in 1925. (See also MAHĀBODHI SOCIETY.)

⌘ DHYĀNA ⌘

Sanskrit technical term, possibly from the verb root √ dhyai, and meaning "meditation." In its Pāli counterpart, jhāna, it refers to four meditative states in the Theravāda tradition, sometimes called trances or absorptions, that lead to the eradication of one's āsravas, "outflows" or defilements, and therefore, to salvation. Each jhāna is characterized by a series of characteristics, with successively higher jhānas being attained by the elimination of limiting factors. In Mahāyāna, dhyāna is listed as the fifth perfection (pāramitā), and refers to meditation as a more general practice designed to eliminate ego involvement. It was in this broad context that the practice moved into China, referred to as Ch'an (or Ch'an-na) a reasonably close transliteration of the term. In Japan, it became Zen (or Zen-na), again an attempt at close transliteration.

⌘ DIAMOND-SŪTRA ⌘

Famous Mahāyāna text that is much more readily known by its English title as "Diamond-Sūtra" than by its formal Sanskrit name: Vajracchedikā-prajñāpāramitā-sūtra. The text is a short work in thirty-two chapters, representing a dialogue between Buddha and his disciple Subhūti. It reflects that Mahāyāna philosophy as espoused by all texts of the prajñāpāramitā or "perfection of wisdom" variety, namely, that all phenomena are but empty projections of one's own mind. The text's name, "Diamond-Sūtra," suggests that it cuts like a diamond, that is to say, because it possesses so little entropy, or disorder, it is able to incise all other theories and, accordingly, dispatch them. Nonetheless, because it essentially represents a condensation of a much longer and elaborate philosophical form, it is puzzling, confusing, and often difficult to follow. One of its most ardent translators, Edward Conze, remarks in his introductory note to *Buddhist Wisdom Books*, that the meaning of the text is so difficult to elicit because its particulars are "(1) Buddhist technical terms, (2) in Sanskrit, (3) *used by sages*, and (4) *for the purpose of spiritual emancipation*." The last two italics are mine, but they are used to highlight the fact that for Conze, these last two points reveal that the text "discloses itself not to erudition but to meditation." (See also PRAJÑĀPĀRAMITĀ LITERATURE.)

⌘ DĪGHA NIKĀYA ⌘

The first collection in the Sutta Piṭaka of the Pāli Canon, and composed of thirty-four long discourses. It corresponds to the Dīrgha Āgama of the Sanskrit Buddhist canon (the most famous version of which was translated into Chinese by Buddhayaśas in 413, containing thirty discourses, twenty-seven of which are common to both versions). The discourses are arranged in three series. The first series, including discourses 1–13, treats mostly moral issues categorized under the general heading sīla. These texts discuss the training of the monk, moving on to a consideration of concentration (samādhi) and wisdom (paññā). The second series, including discourses 14–23, presents a series of texts dealing with legendary matters. Most important here is the Mahāparinibbāna-sutta, the discourse relating the last events in the life of the historical Buddha. The third series, including discourses 24–34, is a miscellany. Of special note in this section is the Sigālovāda-sutta, a text considering the proper mode of conduct in various types of social relationships. (See also ĀGAMA; TRIPIṬAKA.)

⌘ DIGNĀGA ⌘

Important Buddhist logician responsible for abandoning the old logic of the so-called Nyāya school and founding the New Buddhist Logic. Dignāga lived in the fifth-sixth century (dates of 400–485 or 480–540 are suggested as possibilities), and is best known for his two famous logic treatises: the Pramāṇasamuccaya (preserved in Tibetan) and the Nyāyamukha (preserved in Chinese). He replaced the five-membered syllogism of the older logic with a new, three-membered variety. He spent much time at Nālandā University, had Dharmakīrti as his chief disciple, and falls under the general approach of Yogācāra idealism. (See also DHARMAKĪRTI.)

⌘ DĪPAṄKARA ⌘

In the early Buddhist tradition, considered to be the first of twenty-four Buddhas immediately prior to Śākyamuni Buddha. Dīpaṅkara is presumed to have preached, in a prior world cycle, to a young man named Sumedha, who upon hearing the words of Dīpaṅkara, roused the thought of enlightenment (bodhicitta), and took the vow of the bodhisattva. Dīpaṅkara then offered a prediction regarding the actualization of Sumedha's vow which, it turns out, is coincident with Śākyamuni's attainment of Buddhahood. Thus, Sumedha becomes the forerunner of the current historical Buddha, having perfected himself through countless rebirths, eventually taking birth as Siddhārtha Gautama and attaining Buddhahood.

⌘ DĪPAVAṂSA ⌘

The "Island Chronicle," dating from the fourth century C.E., and dealing primarily with the establishment of Buddhism in Sri Lanka. The Dīpavaṃsa is not associated with any particular author, and probably represents the work of several writers, but chronicles the early history of Buddhism, beginning from its origins, and continuing to the reign of King Mahāsena 334–361 C.E. It is extremely valuable for the historical glimpse of ancient Buddhism that it provides.

⌘ DIVYĀVADĀNA ⌘

Sanskrit text, the title of which translates to "The Heavenly Avadāna," from which the famous Aśokāvadāna is extracted. Like all Avadānas, the Divyāvadāna relates much legendary material about early Buddhism. It opens with a Mahāyāna salutation, "Oṃ, respect to all the Buddhas and Bodhisattvas," but for the most part is Hīnayāna (perhaps of the Mūlasarvāstivādin sect) in content. It makes a number of references to other Sanskrit Buddhist texts, and it, in turn, is equally cited in a variety of sources. It is possible that it represents a montage, with various legends gleaned from across a rather wide time frame in Indian Buddhist history. Further, portions of it, at least, were translated into Chinese as early as 265 C.E. As such, it still represents something of an enigma in Buddhist literature.

⌘ DŌGEN ZENJI ⌘
(1200–1253)

Zen master who traveled to China and returned with the tradition identified as Sōtō Zen in Japan. He became a Buddhist priest at age 12, and studied Tendai Buddhism on Mt. Hiei. Finding this tradition unsatisfying, he studied Rinzai Zen with Eisai (1141–1215) and Eisai's student Myōzen Ryōnen (1184–1225). In 1223, Dōgen and Myōzen went to China in search of new and more effective teaching. Myōzen died in China, but Dōgen experienced enlightenment under the Ch'an master T'ien-t'ung Ju-ching (1163–1228), and received Dharma transmission from him. Returning to Japan, he lived at Kennin-ji monastery in Kyoto, but eventually moved on to become abbot of Kōshō-ji monastery. About a decade later he was given the opportunity to found Daibutsu-ji monastery, later referred to as Eihei-ji, where he died. Dōgen's principal text is known as the Shōbōgenzō, literally, "The Treasury-Eye of the True Teaching." It is a collection of writings gleaned from the last two decades of his life, and is regarded as perhaps the foremost text in all of Zen literature. Unlike Rinzai Zen, which utilizes enigmatic sayings called kōan, Dōgen emphasizes a practice known as shikantaza or "just sitting." It presumes that *sitting in meditation itself* (zazen) is the actualization of Buddha nature. As a result Dōgen's Sōtō Zen is sometimes called, in Heinrich Dumoulin's words, "silent illumination Zen" (mokushō-zen), as opposed to the Rinzai approach, referred to as "kōan gazing Zen" (kanna-zen). Dōgen is certainly to be considered one of Japanese Buddhism's greatest figures. (See also SHŌBŌGENZŌ; SŌTŌ ZEN; ZAZEN.)

⌘ DOKUSAN ⌘

Private, formal meeting between Zen student and master. One of the critical aspects of a Zen student's training, this meeting provides the occasion for the student to discuss his particular meditation problems with the master, and in the process, demonstrate the depth and degree of his attainment. Equally, it provides the master with an opportunity to deal with *each* student individually, probing those areas where the student may be struggling. It was originally traditional in *all* Zen schools, but seems to be functioning today primarily in the Rinzai tradition. In the Rinzai tradition, it is often the occasion for each student to be questioned on his progress in solving kōans given to him by the master. (See also SANZEN.)

⌘ DUḤKHA ⌘

First of the famous Four Noble Truths, cornerstone of Buddha's Dharma or "Teaching." In his first sermon, Buddha is reputed to have said, "Birth is suffering, old age is suffering, disease is suffering, death is suffering, association is suffering, separation from what is pleasant is suffering, not obtaining what one desires is suffering." To translate the first of the Noble Truths, duḥkha, simply as suffering is perhaps to miss the point of Buddha's message. More appropriately, Buddha is stating that all life's experiences are transient, that they yield an unsatisfactoriness, either through purely physical pain, change, or conditioned phenomena. It is usually identified with its cause, craving, the elimination of which stops suffering. Duḥkha is also listed as one of the three marks of existence. (See also ĀRYA SATYAS.)

⌘ DWELLING ⌘

See ĀRĀMA; ĀVĀSA; VIHĀRA

— E —

⌘ EIGHTFOLD PATH ⌘

Fourth of the Four Noble Truths preached in Buddha's first sermon to the five ascetics in Benares. Following his evaluation of the human condition, namely, that all life is duḥkha or suffering caused by craving (tṛṣṇā), and his prognosis: that there can be a cessation of suffering, Buddha outlined a clear-cut path to the attainment of that goal. The eightfold path (aṣṭāṅgika-mārga) begins with (1) right understanding (samyak dṛṣṭi). This step suggests that one affirms corrects views, i.e., Buddhist views. Next, one cultivates (2) right thought (samyak saṃkalpa), or thought that is free from lust, ill-will, and cruelty. It is a proper "shaping together" of mental activity. These first two steps refer to the cultivation of wisdom (prajñā). The following three stages deal with the cultivation of morality (śīla). Initially one practices (3) right speech (samyak vācā), refraining from falsehood, malicious speech, and harsh or frivolous talk. This is followed by (4) right action (samyak karmānta), in which one avoids killing, stealing, and general misconduct. Finally, one practices (5) right livelihood (samyak ājīva), or shunning any vocation that utilizes astrology, magic spells, acting as a religious official, interpreting dreams and/or omens, functioning as a go-between, or engages in careers that are harmful to other living beings. The third portion of the eightfold path concerns the cultivation of meditation (samādhi). One first practices (6) right effort (samyak vyāyāma), in which one eliminates existing evil thoughts from one's mind, prevents further evil thoughts from arising, and replaces evil thoughts with good thoughts. Then, (7) right mindfulness (samyak smṛti) is pursued, where one begins to establish mindfulness as a meditative exercise, according to a specified methodology. This stage leads to (8) right concentration (samyak samādhi), the generation of the four trance states which eventually lead to the attainment of nirvāṇa. The effectiveness of the eightfold path as part of a soteriological methodology in Buddhism is attested to continually throughout Buddhist literature, but nowhere more impressively than in the case of Ājñāta Kauṇḍinya who, upon hearing Buddha's first discourse, achieves nirvāṇa *immediately on the spot!* (See also ĀRYA SATYAS.)

⌘ EIHAI-JI ⌘

One of two major monasteries of the Sōtō Zen tradition in Japan. It was founded in 1243 by Dōgen Zenji who began the Sōtō lineage in Japan. Initially called Daibutsu-ji, its name was later changed to Eihai-ji. It is located in Fukui province, in a portion of Japan known for difficult winter seasons. Dōgen remained there until his death in 1253. With Sōjī-ji, it is a major training monastery for Sōtō Zen. (See also DŌGEN ZENJI.)

⌘ EISAI ZENJI ⌘
(1141–1215)

Zen master who traveled to China and returned with the tradition identified as Rinzai Zen in Japan. As a young man Eisai, who is also called Zenkō Kokushi, became a Buddhist monk in the Tendai tradition, studying on Mt. Hiei. He first went to China in 1168, visiting the T'ien-t'ai centers, but had some contact with Ch'an centers as well. He set out again in 1187, originally intending to trace Buddhism to its Indian origins, but the plan failed, and his journey was limited to exploring China once more. He received the seal of enlightenment in the Huang-lung lineage of the Lin-chi Ch'an tradition, known as the Ōryō school in Japanese. When he returned to Japan, he built the first Rinzai Zen temple, known as Shōfuku-ji, at Hakata in Kyūshu in 1191. In his writings and discussions, he proclaimed Zen's superiority to Tendai, incurring much opposition from the Tendai establishment as a result. Eisai was supported, however, by the Shōgun Minamoto Yoriie, who appointed him head of the new monastery of Kennin-ji in Kyoto in 1204. He also founded Jūfuku-ji in Kyoto in 1215 as the third temple of Rinzai. His major writings include the Kōzen gokuku-ron or "The Spread of Zen for the Protection of the Country" and the Kissa yōjō-ki or "Drink Tea to Improve Health and Prolong Life." He was also the initial Zen teacher of Dōgen, founder of the Sōtō Zen lineage. (See also RINZAI ZEN.)

⌘ EKAYĀNA ⌘

Sanskrit technical term which is generally translated as "One Vehicle," and is generally applied to a Mahāyāna idea referred to as the Buddha Vehicle. The various paths to enlightenment are sometimes called by the generic term Triyāna or "Three Vehicles," and refer to the Śrāvaka-yāna or way of the solitary hearer, Pratyekabuddha-yāna or way of the private Buddha, and Bodhisattva-yāna or way of the compassionate future Buddha. In a Mahāyāna text known as the Saddharmapuṇḍarīka-sūtra, the Discourse on the Lotus of the Good Teaching, it is suggested that all three traditional vehicles are relative expressions of an ultimate truth, and that there is only *one vehicle* that results in complete perfect enlightenment, a vehicle called the Ekayāna or "One Vehicle." This One Vehicle, or Buddha Vehicle, is the most perfect teaching of Buddhism, and as such, is ultimate reality itself and therefore beyond reasoning.

⌘ EMPTINESS ⌘

See ŚŪNYATĀ

⌘ ENGAKU-JI ⌘

Main monastery of the Engaku-ji lineage of Rinzai Zen. Founded in the Kamakura Period (in 1282) by the Chinese Ch'an Master Wu-hsüeh Tsu-yüan (Mugaku Sogen in Japanese) under the patronage of Shōgun Hōjō Tokimune, it was considered one of five major Rinzai temples of the time, and continues today as an active Zen temple, responsible for the administration of a number of smaller temples. It was designated as an official place of prayer by the Kamakura government.

⌘ ENLIGHTENMENT ⌘

Traditional "cover" term in Buddhism for one who has become awakened. As Buddhism developed into a religious tradition, the term took on meanings that were distinct to each Buddhist culture and tradition. In the early Indian tradition, the term was a gloss for the Sanskrit word *bodhi,* and referred to the individual, either Buddha or arhant, who had eliminated their impurities, cultivated the eightfold path, and attained nirvāṇa. In Indian Mahāyāna, the meaning of the term came to be extended so as to include an experiential realization of emptiness (śūnyatā). Since Mahāyāna predicates a path in which there can be no ultimate realization of *complete perfect* enlightenment until all sentient beings are free, the general sense of the term enlightenment is dramatically altered. Nowhere is this change more explicitly encountered than in the class of literature known as Prajñāpāramitā, focusing on the "Perfection of Wisdom." Since the basic intellectual content of Chinese and Japanese Buddhism reflects its predominantly Mahāyāna orientation, enlightenment as a technical term is captured by its rendering as *wu* in Chinese and *kenshō* (or *satori*) in Japanese. (See also BODHI; KENSHŌ; SATORI; WU.)

⌘ ENNIN ⌘
(794–864)

Major figure of the Tendai school of Japanese Buddhism who spent nine years in China, later compiling his experiences in a journal. Born in Shimotsuke Province, Ennin entered the monastery on Mt. Hiei at age fifteen, where he studied with and served the school's master, Saichō (also known as Dengyō Daishi). Following Saichō's death in 822, Ennin traveled in China from 838–847, studying T'ien-t'ai, Chên-yen, and Ch'an, but suffering through the anti-Buddhist persecution of 845, returning with hundreds of volumes of sūtras and commentaries. He became the third chief priest of the Tendai school, carrying on the work of Saichō, and augmenting the popularity of the school. His journal, translated by Edwin O. Reischauer as *Ennin's Diary,* is valuable for its insight into the conditions in T'ang China in the middle of the ninth century. Ennin was posthumously named Jikaku Daishi. (See also TENDAI.)

⌘ ETHICS ⌘

General moral framework in Buddhism captured by two essential kinds of literature: that devoted to (1) Vinaya, the formal rules of conduct for the saṃgha, and (2) śīla, the noncodified general maxims for proper human conduct. Like most religious systems, Buddhism argued that proper human conduct was a necessary requisite for spiritual progress, and as such, outlined specific codes and guidelines to regulate behavior. On a formal level, the canonical codes of the Vinaya Piṭaka addressed the needs of individual members of the saṃgha as well as concerns for proper functioning of the saṃgha as a collective unit. The specifics were considered in hundreds of rules, procedures, and the like, and amplified by a commentarial literature designed to keep the Vinaya tradition current. While the Vinaya Piṭaka furnished an externally enforced ethical code, a need existed for an internally enforced set of guidelines as well, and this was met by the notion of śīla. At various points in a number of Buddhist scriptures, sūtras were preached that outlined the proper mode of conduct in human relationships. Collectively, these preserved the tradition of śīla. Commentaries on these scriptures kept them current, too. With the rise of Mahāyāna, a new ethical literature developed, reflecting the Mahāyāna philosophy without compromising the rigorous standards required by both religious professionals and serious lay practitioners. As Buddhism moved out of its Indian homeland, and throughout Asia and the world, its aggressive ethical tradition made it an attractive choice for potential adherents. In each new geographic locale, Buddhist ethics was shaped to fit the cultural norms of that place and time. Additionally, in the modern world, the Buddhist insistence on (1) respect for life, (2) nontheft, (3) proper conduct in sexual matters, (4) abstention from false speech, and (5) abstention from substance abuse has required a redefinition of and rededication to those principles in the context of transtemporal and translocational circumstances that are utterly challenging. (See also BODHISATTVA-ŚĪLA; MAHĀYĀNA VINAYA; PAÑCA-ŚĪLA; ŚĪLA; VINAYA PIṬAKA.)

⌘ EVANS-WENTZ, WALTER YEELING ⌘
(1878–1965)

Scholar of Buddhism most famous for his work on the Tibetan tradition, and particularly on the Tibetan Book of the Dead. Following an M.A. degree from Stanford, he traveled to Europe, eventually earning a B.Sc. degree from Jesus College, Oxford, and a Ph.D. from the University of Rennes, France. He journeyed East, first to Egypt, and then to India and Sri Lanka. In 1919 he met Kazi Dawa-Samdup, and the two collaborated on an English translation of the Tibetan Book of the Dead, a task in which Evans-Wentz was clearly more a facilitator than a collaborator. Nonetheless, Evans-Wentz's work was of pioneering importance in bringing to Western scholarship the previously unavailable texts of the Tantric Buddhist tradition, and although his primary resource person (Kazi Dawa-Samdup) died in 1922, he was able to carry on with other scholars. In addition to *The Tibetan Book of the Dead*, published in 1927, he published *Tibet's Great Yogi Milarepa* (1928), *Tibetan Yoga and Secret Doctrines* (1935), and *The Tibetan Book of the Great Liberation* (1954). After returning to Oxford in 1931, he received the D.Sc. degree in Comparative Religion. He died in Encinitas, California at the age of 88.

— F —

⌘ FA-HIEN ⌘
(337–422)

Chinese Buddhist monk who traveled to India in 399 and returned in 414. Fa-hien's importance for the study of Buddhism can be measured by the fact that he was the first Chinese pilgrim to travel to India, study there for an extended period, and then actually return to China with scriptures. He left Ch'ang-an in 399, attempting to reach India by traveling overland through Tun-huang, Khotan, and the Himalayas. He studied Sanskrit and collected scriptures, most notably a version of the Mahāsāṃghika Vinaya from Pāṭaliputra and the Mahāparinirvāṇa-sūtra which he and Buddhabhadra eventually translated into Chinese, and the Sarvāstivādin Vinaya. Prior to his return, he spent two years in Sri Lanka where he collected fragments of the Sarvāstivādin canon and the Mahīśāsaka Vinaya. In 414 he returned home by sea, arriving after being blown off course to Java, and being under sail for over two hundred days. His travel account has been translated by a number of individuals. An especially readable version by James Legge is cited in the bibliography.

⌘ FA-HSIANG ⌘

Chinese Buddhist school organized by Hsüan-tsang (596–664) and his disciple K'uei-chi (632–682) from the Shê-lun school begun by Paramārtha. The school name is a Chinese rendering of the Sanskrit term dharma-lakṣaṇa which means "marks of the dharmas." It is based on the writings of Asaṅga and Vasubandhu, and corresponds to the Indian Yogācāra school. The major text of the school is Hsüan-tsang's Ch'eng wei-shih lun (Vijñaptimātratā-siddhi in Sanskrit). Consistent with the basic Yogācāra ideology, the central concept of the school is a development of Vasubandhu's notion that "everything is ideation only" (idam sarvam vijñaptimātrakam). It upholds the theory of eight consciousnesses, with seeds of karmic experiences being stored in the ālaya-vijñāna or storehouse consciousness. It classifies all apparently existent reality into 100 dharmas organized in five categories, and affirms *three* levels of truth (as opposed to the Mādhyamika school's notion of *two* levels). The school did not fare well after Hsüan-tsang and K'uei-chi, and was severely undermined by the anti-Buddhist persecution of 845. It was known as the Hossō school in Japanese Buddhism. (See also HOSSŌ; YOGĀCĀRA.)

⌘ FAITH ⌘

Tradition in Buddhism beginning with the Pure Land Sūtras, and developing into formal traditions in virtually all Buddhist cultures in East Asia. Upon the development of the Larger and Smaller Sukhāvatīvyūha-sūtras, and the Amitāyurdhyāna-sūtra, the notion of putting one's confidence, or more precisely, *faith*, in the saving grace of Amitābha Buddha became important in Indian Buddhism. This faith is expressed by the Sanskrit formula Namo Amitābhāya Buddha, literally, "Homage to Amitābha Buddha." As the Buddhist tradition moved into China, this practice of placing faith in Amitābha Buddha became even more popular, and the ritual formula was translated into Chinese as Namo A-mi-t'o Fo, forming the basis of religious practice in the Chinese Pure Land school (known as Ching-t'u). In Japan, too, the formula of proclaiming faith in Amitābha Buddha (Namu Amida Butsu, in Japanese) became critical in the Pure Land schools of Jōdo Shū and Jōdo Shinshū. The way of faith, referred to as tariki in Japanese, is sometimes called the "easy way," as contrasted with the "difficult way" (jiriki) of the meditative schools. In sheer numbers, the Buddhist schools that have developed in the "faith" tradition far outnumber the practitioners in the various other schools, thus making a critical impact on the development of Buddhist history throughout the world.

FA-TSANG
(643–712)

Third patriarch and organizer of the Chinese Hua-yen school of Buddhism. Born into a Central Asian (Sogdian) family, he became a Buddhist layman and began to study Buddhist scriptures, eventually becoming a monk in 670. He studied Hua-yen doctrine under Chih-yen (602–668), the second patriarch of the school, who himself was a disciple of the first patriarch Tu-shun (557–640). He was famous for building Hua-yen temples in Lo-yang and Ch'ang-an as well as other places. Additionally, at the request of Empress Wu Tse-t'ien, he assisted Śikṣānanda in translating an eighty-chapter version of the basic text of the school, the Avatamsaka-sūtra. Fa-tsang is also well known for his "Essay on the Golden Lion," written to help the Empress Wu Tse-t'ien better understand the Hua-yen notion of the interpenetration of all phenomena by comparing the golden color to noumenon and the lion to phenomenon—with each part being inseparable from the other. Fa-tsang was succeeded by a number of other significant teachers in this lineage, most notably Ch'eng-kuan (737–820) and Tsung-mi (780–841). (See also HUA-YEN.)

⌘ FESTIVALS ⌘

Activities in Buddhism designed primarily to commemorate an auspicious person or event, to provide an occasion for merit-making, or both. Although initially not concerned with ritual endeavors, early in its history festivals began to appear, thus providing the occasion for Buddhists to reaffirm their commitment to the tradition, acknowledge communal solidarity, and in the process, develop a seasonal calendar of religious events. Although all traditions seem to recognize the birth, enlightenment, and death of Buddha as occasions worthy of recognition and celebration, other festivals tend to be case specific to Hīnayāna, Mahāyāna, or Vajrayāna Buddhism. In countries populated by the one surviving Hīnayāna sect, Theravāda, generally but not exclusively in South Asia, traditional New Year celebrations are popular. Additionally, the rain-retreat period is celebrated, as is the ceremony ending the rain-retreat. The robe receiving ceremony, known as kaṭhina, is also popular. Religious ceremonies tend to emphasize the monastic tradition rather than the secular. In the Mahāyāna countries of East Asia, Confucian, Taoist, and Shintō traditions are often woven into Buddhist events. There is a highly popular "hungry ghost" festival in China, corresponding to a "feast for the dead" ceremony in Japan. In Vajrayāna northern Asia, the death of Tsong-kha-pa is celebrated in the Fall, as well as a New Year festival, somewhat symbolic of Buddhism's victory over the indigenous Bön tradition. Of course within the specific schools of Buddhism in the various countries, festivals particular to that group and tradition are celebrated.

⌘ FIRST SERMON ⌘

See DHARMACAKRAPRAVARTANA-SŪTRA

⌘ FIVE DEGREES OF ENLIGHTENMENT ⌘

Step-wise scale of the depth of enlightenment in the Ch'an and Zen tradition. Initially postulated by the Chinese Ch'an master Tung-shan Liang-chieh (807–869), one of the two founders of the Ts'ao-tung sect, this schemata measured the degree of enlightenment in five increasingly more profound stages of depth. Also referred to as the "five ranks," they include (1) Sho-chu-hen, the absolute within the relative, (2) Hen-chu-sho, the relative within the absolute, (3) Sho-chu-rai, the absolute alone, (4) Ken-chu-shi, the relative-phenomenal alone, and (5) Ken-chu-to, the absolute and the relative-phenomenal together. Although Tung-shan, known in Japanese as Tōzan Ryōkai, was the spiritual forerunner of Dōgen and the Sōtō school of Japanese Zen, the notion of the five degrees of enlightenment also had influence on other Ch'an schools. (See also TUNG-SHAN LIANG-CHIEH.)

⌘ FIVE HOUSES OF ZEN ⌘

See GOKE-SHICHISHŪ

⌘ FO-T'U-TENG ⌘

(232–348)

Kuchean who arrived in China around 310, becoming a mentor to Shih Lo of the Later Chao. He built a center in Lo-yang, where he served as court advisor for more than two decades. He is credited with starting the order of nuns in Chinese Buddhism, as well as training Buddhist monks. Notorious for his ability to perform magic, he was instrumental in involving monks in politics. He had a number of influential disciples, including Tao-an (312–385).

⌘ FOUR NOBLE TRUTHS ⌘

See ĀRYA SATYAS

⌘ FRAUWALLNER, ERICH ⌘

(1898–1974)

German Buddhologist well known for his work on the Vinaya tradition and Abhidharma. In 1956 Frauwallner published his famous *The Earliest Vinaya and the Beginnings of Buddhist Literature* which has remained one of the most important and revolutionary books on literature relative to the Buddhist community. His theories address not only the regulation of monastic life, but also shed much light on the history of the Buddhist councils, the relationship between a number of the early sects, and early Buddhism's place in Indian religious history. His work on Abhidharma includes the suggestion that there may have been *two* philosophers named Vasubandhu: (1) Asaṅga's younger brother, living around 320–380, and (2) the author of the Abhidharmakośa, living around 400–480. This theory has never gained wide acceptance among scholars despite its ingenuity.

⌘ FRIENDS OF THE WESTERN BUDDHIST ORDER ⌘

Lay Buddhist organization, emphasizing Mahāyāna, founded by the Venerable Sangharakshita in 1967. Sangharakshita is a British-born Buddhist who became a monk in 1950. After spending nearly two decades in India, working for about half of that time with Ambedkar Buddhists, he returned to England and founded Friends of the Western Buddhist Order. His movement now includes centers in various parts of Europe, New Zealand, Australia, the United States of America, and India. His major emphasis is on four basic kinds of structures: (1) urban centers, (2) living communities, (3) local groups, and (4) cooperative units. A wide range of activities is sponsored by the Friends of the Western Buddhist Order, including an emphasis on meditational training, study of Buddhism, and commitment to living within a Buddhist ethical framework.

⌘ FUKASETSU ⌘

Japanese term literally meaning "the unspeakable," and referring to the content of enlightening experience. Within the context of Mahāyāna Buddhism, of which Zen is a part, it has always been argued that the experience of one's Buddha-nature cannot be explained in words or concepts because it is empty of any contextual basis by which it might be expressed. Buddhism in general, and the Zen tradition in particular, is filled with stories reflecting the manner in which enlightenment is experienced: dramatically outside of "orthodox" teaching, beyond scripture, directly revealing each sentient being's inherent Buddha-nature. Fukasetsu, as an expression of that experience, summarizes the ineffability of the enlightenment.

— G —

⌘ GAṆḌAVYŪHA-SŪTRA ⌘

The "Flower-Array Sūtra," a portion of the Avataṃsaka-sūtra focusing on the development of a young disciple named Sudhana. The Gaṇḍavyūha-sūtra, along with the Daśabhūmika-sūtra, is one of two major fragments of the Avatamsaka-sūtra that broke off from the parent text and became an independent discourse. Although it is more widely available in Chinese translation (as the Ju fa-chieh p'in), several Sanskrit versions are available. The text is closely related to southern India where Sudhana traveled on a pilgrimage in search of Dharma instruction. Upon hearing the preaching of the bodhisattva Mañjuśrı, Sudhana experiences the thought of enlightenment (bodhicitta), traveling thereafter to hear the teaching of fifty-three teachers, including Maitreya, the future Buddha. Upon meeting Samantabhadra, in the last section of the text, he attains enlightenment. The text is one of the fundamental treatises of the Chinese Hua-yen school of Buddhism (Japanese: Kegon). (See also HUA-YEN; KEGON.)

⌘ GANDHĀRA ⌘

Region of northwest India once considered a significant area of Buddhist culture. It is best known not only for its art, but as the home (along with Kaśmīr) of the Sarvāstivādin school of Buddhism. The portion of the school housed in Gandhāra was likely more progressive than that of Kaśmīr, eventually giving rise to the Sautrāntika school. By the second century B.C.E., the first figures of Buddha began to appear in the art work of the region. Gandhāran art was strongly influenced by the Greeks and is sometimes referred to as "Greco-Buddhist" in style. Because Buddha is depicted as a person in the art work, contrary to the prevailing trend of the period, it has been argued that Gandhāran art reflects the initial influence of Mahāyāna (which was gestating at this time period). Such a suggestion is both interesting *and problematic,* for it would have been unusual to see Mahāyāna influence in an area so dominated by the Hīnayāna thought of the Sarvastivādins. By the time of the Chinese pilgrim Hsüan-tsang's visit (629–645), Gandhāran Buddhism was essentially on the wane or extinct.

⌘ GATI ⌘

Literally "destiny," and usually referring to six modes of existence in the three realms (triloka). The destinies refer to the various rebirths that are possible within the traditional cycle known as saṃsāra. The individual destinies include (1) hell-beings, (2) animals, (3) hungry ghosts (pretas), (4) gods (devas), (5) antigods (asuras), and humans. The first three destinies are considered low or "bad," while the latter three destinies are considered "good." All six destinies are united by their common experience of suffering.

⌘ GEDATSU ⌘

Japanese term for liberation. It is a synonym for enlightenment (nirvāṇa), presumed to be the focal point of meditation practice or zazen.

⌘ GENJO-KŌAN ⌘

Chapter of Dōgen Zenji's Shōbōgenzō, often translated as "Enlightenment in Everyday Life" or "The Problem of Everyday Life." This particular chapter in Dōgen's famous text is especially important because it addresses the relationship between delusion and enlightenment, and, necessarily, between oneself and Buddhism. It demonstrates that true Buddhahood is exhibited in daily life, in everyday experiences.

⌘ GENSHIN ⌘

(942–1017)

Tendai priest whose writings were influential in the development of Pure Land Buddhism (Jōdo Shū) in Japan. He entered the great monastic complex on Mt. Hiei before his tenth birthday, was ordained at age thirteen, and eventually became the eighteenth chief priest of Enryaku-ji. He wrote a famous text known as Ōjōyōshū ("Compendium on the Essence of Rebirth") that contrasted the agonies of hell with the splendor of the Pure Land, thus influencing Hōnen (1133–1212), the founder of the Japanese Pure Land school.

⌘ GE-SAR (GESAR) ⌘

Mythical hero in Tibetan Buddhism who inspired a series of legends in which Ge-sar (literally "Lotus Temple") battles against evil. The legends surrounding Ge-sar, beginning in about the eleventh century, constitute a kind of Tibetan national epic. The story represented in the legends is an allegorical account in which

Ge-sar, regarded as the embodiment of Avalokiteśvara, symbolizes the qualities of Buddhism in the struggle against the indigenous Bön religion, symbolized as evil. The Ge-sar legends spawned an interesting iconography and even a cult in Tibet. Later legends suggest the conquering of other countries with Ge-sar being represented as a warrior god.

⌘ GIVING ⌘

See DĀNA

⌘ GOHONZON ⌘

Japanese Buddhist term for an object of worship. More specifically, it refers to a maṇḍala-like form, scrolled on paper, with the words inscribed by Nichiren (1222–1282): Nam Myōhō Renge Kyō ("Homage to the Scripture of the Lotus of the Good Teaching"), at the center. Nichiren was convinced that Buddhist methods of the time were not sufficient for the attainment of salvation, but was persuaded that the Lotus-sūtra contained the true essence of Buddhism and was the one vehicle (ekayāna) by which salvation could be attained. He believed that enlightenment could be attained by chanting the phrase Nam Myōhō Renge Kyō, known as the daimoku, while gazing at the gohonzon. In addition to the daimoku at its center, the gohonzon contained names of various Buddhas and bodhisattvas, as well as other symbolic figures. The gohonzon became extremely important, not only in the school of Buddhism founded by Nichiren but also in the modern school known as Sōkagakkai. (See also NICHIREN; SŌKAGAKKAI.)

⌘ GOKE-SHICHISHŪ ⌘

Japanese term for the "five houses" and "seven schools" of Ch'an (Zen) Buddhism during the T'ang Dynasty in Chinese Buddhist history, first used by Fa-yen Wen-i (885–958). One of the most significant sources of information on the five houses comes from the Ninden Gammoku (Chinese: Jen-t'ien yen-mu), compiled by Hui-yen Chih-chao, a monk from the Lin-chi tradition who specialized in this aspect of Ch'an (Zen) history. The five houses include: (1) Kuei-yang (Japanese: Igyō), founded by Kuei-shan Ling-yu (771–853), (2) Lin-chi (Japanese: Rinzai), founded by Lin-chi I-hsüan (d. 866), (3) Ts'ao-tung (Japanese: Sōtō), founded by Tung-shan Liang-chieh (807–869) and Ts'ao-shan Pen-chi (840–901), (4) Yün-men (Japanese: Ummon), founded by Yün-men Wen-yen (864–949), and (5) Fa-yen (Japanese: Hōgen), founded by Fa-yen Wen-i (885–958). The seven schools include the above five plus two additional schools resulting from an internal split in the Rinzai school: (6) Yōgi, founded by Yang-ch'i Fang-hui (992–1049), and (7) Ōryō, founded by Huang-lung Hui-nan (1001–1069).

⌘ GOMBRICH, RICHARD F. ⌘

Boden Professor of Sanskrit at Oxford University and Professorial Fellow of Balliol College since 1976. Richard Gombrich has been one of the world's foremost authorities on Theravāda Buddhism for over twenty-five years. He has published many books, most notably including *Buddhism Transformed: Religious Change in Sri Lanka*, *Buddhist Precept and Practice: Traditional Buddhism in the Rural Highlands of Ceylon*, and *Theravāda Buddhism: A Social History from Ancient Benares to Modern Columbo* (with Gananath Obeyesekere). He has also served as European secretary for the International Association of Buddhist Studies and as honorary secretary and treasurer of the Pāli Text Society.

⌘ GOSAN-BUNGAKU ⌘

Literature collection of Zen masters' writings from five of the most famous monasteries in Kyoto during the Ashikaga Period of Japanese history (1338–1573). The collection was presumably founded by the Chinese Ch'an master I-shan I-ning, who came to Japan around 1299, and one of his Japanese students. This "Five Mountain Literature" was instrumental in bringing Chinese culture, and especially science and art, to Japan.

⌘ GOVINDA, LAMA ANĀGĀRIKA ⌘
(1898–1985)

German Buddhist scholar who took initiation in a Tibetan Buddhist sect and was an important source of information on Tibetan Buddhist philosophy and practice. Originally named E. L. Hoffmann, Lama Govinda was initiated into the 'Brug-pa branch of the bKa-rgyud-pa sect of Tibetan Buddhism. Nonetheless, he considered himself part of the "nonaligned" (Ris-med) movement of the rNying-ma-pa sect. He founded a layman's organization known as the Arya Maitreya Mandala in the West. His best-known books, *The Way of the White Clouds* and *Foundations of Tibetan Mysticism* are widely read by Western students of Buddhism. In the years prior to his death, he made a number of visits to leading Western centers of Buddhism where he was a highly sought after lecturer.

⌘ GREATER VEHICLE ⌘

See MAHĀYĀNA

⌘ GUHYASAMĀJA-TANTRA ⌘

Important Vajryāna Buddhist text belonging to the Anuttara-yoga-Tantra class. Along with the Cakrasaṃvara-tantra, Hevajra-tantra, and Kālacakra-tantra, it is included among the most important texts in Tantric literature. It was almost certainly written before 750, and possibly as early as the sixth century. It is composed of two parts, a Mūla-tantra of seventeen sections, and an Uttara-tantra comprising the eighteenth section. It is sometimes called the Tathāgata-guhyaka. In its meditational framework, it presents a visualization of the Buddha, depicted as Vairocana, and an accompaniment of four female bodhisattvas: Locanā, Māmakī, Pāṇḍarā, and Tārā. All dualities and distinctions are denied in the text, using the term vajra or "diamond" to symbolize ultimate reality. It also offers a unique rendering of the technical term bodhicitta (usually translated as "thought of enlightenment") as the unity of emptiness (śūnyatā) and compassion (karuṇā). (See also TANTRA.)

⌘ GURU ⌘

Sanskrit term most often rendered as "teacher." In some Buddhist traditions, the guru represents the spiritual teacher who guides the adept on the Buddhist path. As a spiritual teacher, it is presumed that the guru is thoroughly conversant with and skilled in the path that he or she teaches. In this way, the guru is able to help the student overcome obstacles that block progress on the spiritual path. Precisely because of the significance of the role of the guru in helping the student make spiritual progress, the student must place *complete* confidence in the guru's knowledge, and thus obediently follow the guru's instructions, however unusual or eccentric they may appear. The trust required in the guru's guidance has raised curious questions, especially in modern Buddhism, about the authenticity of some rather "colorful" and unorthodox teachers who have appeared on the Buddhist landscape.

⌘ GYŌGI ⌘

(668–749)

Japanese Buddhist monk important during the Nara Period of Japanese history. Possibly of Korean origin, Gyōgi was ordained at Yakushu-ji temple at age fifteen, studying Hossō (i.e., Yogācāra) doctrine. He traveled extensively as a teacher and propagator of Buddhism, eventually gaining the confidence of Emperor Shōmu. In 745 he was appointed as an administrator of monks (daisōjō). When the emperor decided to construct a large image of Vairocana Buddha, Gyōgi was vital in soliciting financial support for the project. Additionally, due to his previous background in civil engineering, Gyōgi was able to help in building bridges, roads, and assisting in a wide variety of public assistance activities. Because of his great efforts on behalf of the populace, he was often referred to as Gyōgi Bosatsu or "Gyōgi Bodhisattva."

— H —

⌘ HAIKU ⌘

Japanese poetic form composed of seventeen syllables arranged in a 5-7-5 sequence. It became important in Zen largely through the effort of a layman named Matsuo Bashō (1644–1694) who was one of Japan's most famous poets. He composed his first *Zen* Haiku in response to a question posed by his meditation master. Rather than trying to *describe* reality, which is really nothing more than a conceptual exercise, Zen Haiku poems *express* reality simply and fully. In so doing, they capture the *nondual, experiential* quality of living, everyday experiences.

⌘ HAKUIN ZENJI ⌘

(1685–1768)

Important Rinzai Zen master who revitalized the tradition of kōans or "public case" riddle-like questions designed to stop the conceptual activity of the mind. Hakuin expressed the desire to become a monk at a very early age following a discourse by a Buddhist monk, but deferred in respect to his parents' opposition. At age fifteen he entered the monastery with a firm resolve to study diligently. In his early twenties he had his first enlightenment experience, thereafter working even harder than previously. Hakuin never received Dharma transmission from his master, Dōkyō, but today is considered his Dharma heir. Hakuin became abbot of several Zen monasteries, including the still important Ryūtaku-ji. As abbot, he emphasized work as part of the meditational tradition, along with zazen. Hakuin noted three essential components of zazen practice: (1) great faith, (2) great doubt, and (3) great resolve. To facilitate this practice he utilized the kōan practice which is standard in Rinzai Zen. He is perhaps best known for his famous kōan: "What is the sound of one hand clapping?" Also known as an artist and sculptor, Hakuin wrote as well, with much of his work now available in English translation. (See also KŌAN.)

⌘ HAN DYNASTY ⌘

Period in Chinese history (206 B.C.E.-220 C.E.) during which Buddhism entered China. In the first century C.E. the Han Dynasty began to extend its sphere of influence into Central Asia, an area that was filled with Buddhist groups from a variety of traditions. Thanks to the Silk Route, merchants moved freely back and forth between areas and cultures, creating an atmosphere in which Buddhism was able to make its first inroads into China. Although there are a variety of accounts of Buddhism's first entry to China in the Han Dynasty, it met with a Chinese environment dominated by Confucian and Taoist culture. Buddhism made gains in Lo-yang where a translation center was organized by foreign monks. The first Chinese converts joined the Buddhist community, and Buddhist ideas were being circulated by the time of the downfall of the Han Dynasty in 220 C.E.

⌘ HAN-SHAN ⌘

Buddhist layman in T'ang Dynasty China, best known as a sort of enlightened vagabond. Along with his friend Shih-te, he lived on Mt. Han-Shan or "Cold Mountain," leading a rather unusual lifestyle outside the traditional Ch'an orthodoxy. His poems were collected into an anthology that reflect a keen sense of insight into the true nature of reality. Han-shan was often the subject of art work that eventually was transmitted to Japan where he also became popular (known as Kanzan).

⌘ HARA ⌘

Technical term in Zen to indicate one's spiritual center. The hara is said to be located in the lower abdomen area, and is supposed to be the focus or source of one's breathing in zazen practice. It is also called the kikai tanden.

⌘ HASSU ⌘

Zen technical term to indicate the Dharma heir or successor to a Zen master. In order to be considered hassu or "transmitted," the student must have received inka-shōmei or the seal of authentication from the master. Once a disciple has been so empowered, that individual is charged to carry on the Dharma mission of the master. What complicates the matter, however, is the fact that Zen presumably cannot "be taught," and that one does not actually "receive" anything in the transmission process. As such, a variety of ways to designate Dharma successors have appeared in Zen, some of which appear as rather eccentric to the general populace. (See also ZEN.)

⌘ HEALING BUDDHA ⌘

See BHAIṢAJYAGURU-BUDDHA

⌘ HEART SŪTRA ⌘

Famous Mahāyāna text that is much more readily known by its English title as "Heart Sūtra" than by its formal Sanskrit name: Prajñāpāramitā-hṛdaya-sūtra. It is essentially a one-page condensation of Mahāyāna philosophy, especially emphasizing the doctrine of emptiness (śūnyatā), and particularly the relationship between form and emptiness. The text ends with an extremely puzzling verse: "Gone, gone, gone beyond, gone completely beyond, O what an Awakening!" Because the text of the sūtra is so terse and difficult to understand, it cannot be unpacked without considerable commentary. One of the best attempts at commentary is that provided by the foremost modern scholar of Prajñāpāramitā literature, Edward Conze, in his important study *Buddhist Wisdom Books*. (See also PRAJÑĀPĀRAMITĀ LITERATURE.)

⌘ HEAVEN ⌘

Cosmological realms designated as places of rebirth for devas or "gods." Buddhist cosmology has been both interesting and important in virtually all Buddhist countries and cultures. Nonetheless, there is especially significant disagreement as to the number, location, and function of the various heavens elucidated by the various traditions. One early tradition identifies twenty-six heavens grouped according to a classification schema for rebirth. The lowest six heavens are included in the sphere of sense-desire (kāmāvacara). The next sixteen heavens are located in the sphere of pure form (rūpāvacara). The final four heavens constitute the sphere of the formless (arūpāvacara). Various characteristics are attached to each of these heavens. In the third chapter of Vasubandhu's Abhidharmakośa another schema is presented focusing on two "sets" of heavens: (1) six "desire" heavens and (2) seventeen "form" heavens. Variations on both the number and characteristics of the heavens exist in the Hīnayāna sects. With the development of Mahāyāna, the cosmos expanded greatly into a much wider variety of "Buddha-Lands," such as the Pure Land of Sukhāvatī, inhabited by celestial beings, complicating the issue of heavens greatly. What is most important to consider is that, in any case, Buddhism affirms the law of impermanence (anitya), and accordingly, residence in any heaven is transitory. Invariably, the emphasis in Buddhist practice must be *to end rebirth altogether, irrespective of location*. As such, pursuit of the attainment of heavenly rebirth must not be grasped after as a *permanent* situation in any form of Buddhist endeavor. (See also HELL.)

⌘ HEIAN PERIOD ⌘

Period in Japanese history (794–1185) when the Emperor Kammu moved the capital from Nara to Heian, site of modern-day Kyoto. The Heian Period was exceedingly important for the development of Japanese Buddhism and perhaps its zenith. Two new Buddhist schools were imported from China: the Tendai (Chinese: T'ien-t'ai) brought to Japan by Saichō, and the Shingon (Chinese: Chên-yen), brought to Japan by Kūkai. Saichō instituted a new Mahāyāna ordination lineage on Mt. Hiei, but by the late Heian Period, some Buddhist thinkers thought a period of decline was immanent. There was continued growth of the Amida cult during the period, aided by the personal charisma of figures such as Genshin (942–1017). Nevertheless, by the end of the period there was a corrupt relationship between government and the saṃgha, setting the stage for the development of the Kamakura Period.

⌘ HEKIGAN ROKU ⌘

See PI-YÊN LU

⌘ HELL ⌘

Cosmological realms designated as places of rebirth characterized as negative. Generally referred to by the Sanskrit terms naraka and niraya, they are places located under the earth that are typified by extreme physiological and/or psychological suffering. The best known of the hells are a series of eight hot hells and eight cold hells. Various Buddhist texts are filled with dramatic, chilling descriptions of the horrors that await the inhabitants of these rebirths. It is hoped that these lurid descriptions will serve as encouragement for beings to traverse the proper path of conduct, escaping the devastation depicted in the hells. It is important to emphasize that, like the heavens, these hell existences represent only temporary residences. In the destruction of the world in each successive kalpa, the process begins with the hells. (See also HEAVEN.)

⌘ HEVAJRA-TANTRA ⌘

Important Vajrayāna Buddhist text belonging to the Anuttarayoga-tantra class. It has been preserved in Sanskrit, Chinese, and Tibetan versions, all of which seem to be later than around 700. It is a complicated text opening with a dialogue between the Buddha as Vajrasattva and a bodhisattva named Vajragarbha. Although the text contains much philosophical material, it focuses mainly on religious practice and ritual, described in detail. The text is fraught with seemingly contradictory material, as well as sexual concern, the resolution of which is critical for an accurate understanding of the Vajrayāna path. (See also TANTRA.)

⌘ HĪNAYĀNA ⌘

Pejorative Sanskrit term, literally meaning "Lesser Vehicle" or "Small Vehicle," used by the newly formed Mahāyānists (literally, the "Greater Vehicle") to designate all Buddhist sectarian groups and Buddhists of early Buddhism. By the time of the beginnings of the Mahāyāna movement, around 200 B.C.E., early Buddhism had already witnessed an extensive sectarian development of almost two hundred years duration. Although traditional records claim the existence of eighteen of these early sects, actually many more existed, with some passing out of existence quite quickly, by 200 B.C.E. Many of these early sects, now generally referred to as *nikāyas*, or *"groups,"* are very well known, having left a significant historical, textual, and doctrinal legacy. The best known of these early nikāyas include the (1) Mahāsāṃghikas, who internally divided to produce the Ekavyāvahārikas, Lokottaravādins, Gokulikas, Bahuśrutīyas, Prajñaptivādins, Caitikas, and perhaps several others; and (2) Sthaviras, who internally subdivided into the Vatsiputriyas, Sarvastivadins, and Vibhajyavādins. The Vātsīputrīyas then internally divided, producing at least four other nikāyas. Equally, the Sarvāstivādins internally divided, producing the Sautrāntikas. Finally, the Vibhajyavādins subdivided as well, producing the Mahīśāsakas, Kāśypaīyas, and Theravādins. To date, only the Theravādin nikāya survives, primarily in modern South and Southeast Asia. The so-called Hīnayānists all emphasized rules of disciplinary deportment contained in the Vinaya Piṭaka as the core of their social system. Philosophically, these Hīnayāna groups share a common, realistic worldview, as espoused in the Sūtra and Abhidharma Piṭakas, emphasizing the three marks of existence, four noble truths, dependent origination, and five aggregates, as well as belief in the efficacy of individual salvation through the attainment of nirvāṇa. It is this latter emphasis that is severely attacked by the Mahāyāna movement, arguing for the attainment of Buddhahood for all sentient beings. (See also MAHĀYĀNA; VAJRAYĀNA.)

⌘ HINDRANCES ⌘

Obstructions to spiritual progress, usually listed as five in number, which must be overcome in order to make meditational advancement (i.e., attaining upacāra-samādhi). The hindrances are technically referred to as nīvaraṇas and include (according to the Abhidharmakośa): (1) sensual desire (kāmacchanda), (2) ill will (vyāpāda), (3) sloth and torpor (styāna-middha), (4) restlessness and worry (auddhatya-kaukṛtya), and (5) doubt (vicikitsā).

⌘ HIRAKAWA, AKIRA ⌘
(b. 1915)

Japanese Buddhologist regarded as one of the world's greatest authorities on Indian Buddhism in general and the Vinaya tradition in particular. Hirakawa is professor emeritus of Indian Philosophy at Tokyo University. He was elected president of the Japanese Association of Indian and Buddhist Studies in 1983. In addition to more than 200 professional articles, he is best known for a number of extremely important books: *Ritsuzō no kenkyū* (A study of the Vinaya-piṭaka), *Genshi Bukkyō no kenkyū* (A study of early Buddhism), *Shoki Daijō no kenkyū* (Studies in early Mahāyāna Buddhism), and *Indo Bukkyōshi* (A history of Indian Buddhism, 2 volumes). His work on the Vinaya tradition is regarded as the most comprehensive and sophisticated study in print in any Buddhist research language.

⌘ HOMELESSNESS ⌘

The state of the wanderer in early Buddhism. In the earliest tradition it was argued that the clearest path to the attainment of enlightenment (nirvāṇa) was that of renouncing worldly life in favor of a simpler, less encumbered, more focused approach to spiritual practice. That simpler life, pursued by Buddhist mendicants of both genders, was generically referred to as "homelessness." The advantages of the homeless state are praised throughout the early literature, and individuals were constantly encouraged by Buddha and his retinue to "go forth into homelessness," or in technical terms, to take the initial ordination called pravrajyā. In so doing, they became (male) śrāmaṇera or (female) śrāmaṇerī novices.

⌘ HŌNEN ⌘

(1133–1212)

Founder of the Pure Land school (Jōdo Shū) in Japanese Buddhism. Hōnen became a monk at age fifteen, entering the Tendai tradition and studying on Mt. Hiei. Within a decade he was highly regarded for his scholarship. At age forty-three, he became concerned that practitioners were not able to achieve enlightenment through the Tendai path, and turned to the Pure Land teachings of Shan-tao and Genshin, convinced that reliance on Amida Buddha was the certain path to salvation. Hōnen's writings on the Pure Land were seized and burned, but he continued to preach his Pure Land message of the repetition of Amida's name in the formula of the nembutsu to all listeners. In 1206 Hōnen was exiled by his rivals, returning to the capital in 1211, only a year prior to his death. (See also JŌDO SHŪ.)

⌘ HOSSEN ⌘

Japanese technical term indicating a Dharma contest. Hossen is a Zen method for demonstrating reality directly. Although it may consist of an exchange of words or gestures, it is neither a debate nor a philosophical enterprise. It is simply an occasion for two enlightened individuals to reveal their experience directly in a dramatic fashion, thus advancing the depth of their training.

⌘ HOSSŌ ⌘

Name of the Japanese version of the Chinese Fa-hsiang (Sanskrit: Yogācāra) school of Buddhism. The teachings were introduced to Japan on at least four separate occasions by: (1) Dōshō, who went to China in 653 and studied under Hsüan-tsang, (2) Chitsū and Chidatsu, who went to China in 658 also studying under Hsüan-tsang, (3) Chihō, Chiran, and Chiyū, who went to China in 703 studying under Chih-chou, and (4) Gembō, who went to China in 716 and studied under Chih-chou. Dōshō's lineage, passed on through the famous monk Gyōgi (668–749), is referred to as the Southern Temple, while Gembō's lineage is called the Northern Temple. (See also FA-HSIANG; YOGĀCĀRA.)

⌘ HṚDAYA-SŪTRA ⌘

See HEART SŪTRA

⌘ HSÜAN-TSANG ⌘

(596–664)

Famous Chinese pilgrim who traveled to India from 629–645, returning with many texts and teachings. Hsüan-tsang left China in 629, traveling overland to India through Central Asia. He entered India at Gandhāra, studied in Kaśmīr for two years, and then sailed down the Ganges to visit many Buddhist sacred sites, including Kapilavastu and Bodhgayā. He moved on to Nālandā University where he studied Yogācāra with Śīlabhadra for over a year. After further travel in southern India, he returned to Nālandā prior to his return home. He returned to the capital of Ch'ang-an in 645, receiving a hero's welcome. Eventually he wrote an acount of his travels, known as the Ta-T'ang Hsi-yü chi (Records of the Western regions). He is reputed to have brought back more than 650 Buddhist texts, the study and translation of which occupied the rest of his life. In addition to his translations, Hsüang-tsang wrote the Ch'eng wei-shih lun (Sanskrit: Vijñaptimātratā-siddhi). Along with his disciple K'uei-chi (632–682), he is credited with organizing the Fa-hsiang Buddhist school from the Shê-lun school begun by Paramārtha. Hsüan-tsang was so venerated in China that upon the occasion of his death in 664, the emperor canceled his audiences for three days.

⌘ HUANG-PO HSI-YÜN ⌘

(d. 850)

Great Ch'an master (known as Ōbaku Kiun in Japanese), one of the forefather's of the Lin-chi sect (Japanese: Rinzai) of Buddhism. He was a student and Dharma heir to Pai-chang Huai-hai, and had thirteen Dharma heirs himself, one of whom was Lin-chi I-hsüan, founder of the Lin-chi school of Ch'an.

⌘ HUA-YEN ⌘

School of Chinese Buddhism derived from the Hua-yen Ching or "Flower Ornament Sūtra" (Sanskrit: Avataṃsaka-sūtra) and playing an important role in T'ang Dynasty history. The text from which the school takes its origin was presumably translated into Chinese by Buddhabhadra around 420 C.E. The school itself was founded by Tu-shun (557–640) and organized by Fa-tsang (643–712). Its fundamental tenet is sometimes referred to as the "Buddhist teaching of totality" because of the school's emphasis on the interpenetration of all phenomena. This idea is expressed through the doctrine of Dharma-dhātu or mutual causality, and the notion that principle (li) and phenomena (shih) are interdependent. Like other Mahāyāna schools, it affirms the idea of emptiness (śūnyatā), identifying the ideal realization as suchness (tathatā). Like other Chinese scholastic schools, it did not fare well in the aftermath of the anti-Buddhist persecution of 845. It was taken to Japan in the eighth century, becoming known as the Kegon school. (See also AVATAṂSAKA-SŪTRA; KEGON.)

⌘ HUI-K'O ⌘

(487–593)

Second patriarch of Ch'an in China. Although he studied Confucian classics and Taoism as a young man, he entered the Buddhist order and studied in a number of places. At age forty, he traveled to Shao-lin monastery to study with Bodhidharma, the first patriarch of Ch'an in China. When several attempts to prove his earnestness as a disciple failed to rouse Bodhidharma from his meditation in front of his cave's wall, Hui-k'o is reputed to have cut off his arm and presented it to Bodhidharma. Following six years of meditation practice with Bodhidharma, Hui-k'o was confirmed as his Dharma heir. Upon Bodhidharma's death, Hui-k'o went to Yeh, the capital of the Eastern Wei Dynasty. Later, Emperor Wu of the Northern Chou Dynasty sponsored an anti-Buddhist persecution, forcing Hui-k'o into exile, where he met Seng-ts'an, his own Dharma heir and the third patriarch of Chinese Ch'an. (See also BODHIDHARMA.)

⌘ HUI-NÊNG ⌘

(638–713)

Sixth patriarch of Ch'an in China. Hui-nêng is considered the Dharma heir of the fifth patriarch Hung-jen, although there is considerable controversy surrounding that choice. When Hung-jen was old, as a prelude to selecting a Dharma heir, he requested that monks in his charge write stanzas depicting their understanding of the teaching. His brightest student, Shen-hsui, wrote the following verse (in Richard Robinson's translation):

> The Body is the Bodhi Tree,
> The mind is like a bright mirror-and-stand.
> At all times wipe it diligently,
> Don't let there be any dust.

Hui-nêng, although having little education, upon seeing Shen-hsui's verse, wrote (again in Robinson's translation):

> Bodhi really has no tree,
> The bright mirror also has no stand.
> Buddha-nature is forever pure (or: Really no thing exists);
> Where is there any room for dust?

Hung-jen, fearing Shen-hsui's jealousy, installed Hui-nêng in the middle of the night, giving him a robe as a sign of his installation, but sent him into hiding in southern China. Shen-hsiu proclaimed himself the sixth patriarch and became head of what was known as the "Northern School." Eventually, Hui-nêng was recognized as the true sixth patriarch, beginning what was known as the "Southern School." His text of the T'an-ching (Platform Sūtra of the Sixth Patriarch) is now quite famous. Hui-nêng was ordained at Fa-hsin monastery, moved on to the Pao-lin monastery near Ts'ao-ch'i, and began to acquire students, some of whom became important in Ch'an. (See also SHEN-HSUI.)

⌘ HUI-YÜAN ⌘
(334–416)

Student of Tao-an (312–385), inspiration of the White Lotus Society, and also father of the Chinese Pure Land school of Buddhism. Although schooled in the Confucian and Taoist classics, Hui-yüan ran a school for monks and scholars. He went to Mt. Lu in 381, established a monastery, and developed it into an important center for Buddhism. In 402, along with 123 of his disciples, he established the White Lotus Society, a group devoted to meditation on the figure of Amitābha and attaining rebirth in the Pure Land of Sukhāvatī. As such, he is considered the founder of Chinese Pure Land Buddhism. He also seems to have carried on a correspondence with Kumārajīva (344–413), a Kuchean translator largely responsible for rendering Indian Buddhist texts into Chinese and, with Hui-yüan, famous for utilizing Taoist terms to make Buddhism more readily understandable to its initial Chinese audience. (See also BUDDHO-TAOISTS.)

⌘ HUMPHREYS, CHRISTMAS ⌘
(1901–1983)

British barrister, largely responsible for the development of Buddhism in England. He became a Buddhist as early as age seventeen, and in 1924 founded the Buddhist Lodge of the Theosophical Society, absorbing the remnants of the then-failing Buddhist Society of Great Britain and Ireland. In 1943 the Buddhist Lodge changed its name to the Buddhist Society. It continues to publish a journal known as *The Middle Way*. Humphreys published more than a dozen books, the best known of which still remains *Buddhism*, first published in 1951. His autobiography *Both Sides of the Circle*, published in 1978, is wonderfully engaging reading.

— I —

⌘ I-CHING ⌘
(635–713)

Famous Chinese pilgrim who traveled to India to study Buddhism. I-ching left for India in 671, visited many Buddhist sites, and eventually studied both Hīnayāna and Mahayana at Nalanda University. After more than twenty years in India, he returned to China in 695 with over 400 Sanskrit Buddhist texts. At home in Lo-yang, he translated the Avataṃsaka-sūtra and Mūlasarvāstivādin Vinaya Piṭaka with Śikṣānanda. Altogether, he is reported to have translated fifty-six Buddhist texts into Chinese. Like other Chinese Buddhist pilgrims who preceded him, he also wrote an account of his travels.

⌘ IKEDA, DAISAKU ⌘
(b. 1928)

Third president of Nichiren Shōshū Sōkagakkai, militant wing of the Japanese Buddhist school founded by Nichiren. Daisaku

Ikeda was the closest disciple of Josei Toda (1900–1958), second president of the organization and immediate successor to the founder Tsunesaburo Makiguchi. He was inaugurated on May 3, 1960, the same year that he visited the United States. The "Value Creation Society," as it is called, boasts more than several million adherents in Japan, organized into a highly functional, aggressively missionary, astutely political religious unit. Under Ikeda, it has become a world religion, presumably best categorized as one of the "new religions" (shinkō shūkyō) of Japan. (See also NICHIREN SHŌSHŪ SŌKAGAKKAI.)

⌘ IMAGES ⌘

Statues of Buddha or other famous individuals in Buddhism utilized as a symbol of respect and/or an object of devotion for Buddhist disciples. In the earliest tradition, *no figures of Buddha* were crafted for fear that such a gesture would develop into a cult of personality at best or a clear deification of Buddha at worst. Such a position is consistent with Buddha's repeated statements that he was *just a man*. In time, perhaps as early as the reign of King Kaniṣka, as Buddha's absence was felt deeply, and in similarity with other Indian religious traditions, Buddha-figures gradually began to appear, in both Hīnayāna and Mahāyāna art. With the development of the Vajrayāna tradition, an even greater emphasis developed around various Buddhist images, reflecting the significant role of their symbolism in the Tantric tradition. Within several hundred years, images could be found extensively in cave temples, monasteries, and other sites. Additionally, the creation of images was not distinct to Buddhism's Indian homeland. There is virtually no Buddhist country today without an extensive heritage of Buddhist images. By no means do images mean the *same* thing in each Buddhist group, as each responds to them in a fashion consistent with its own doctrinal position. Nonetheless, they represent part of the heritage of Buddhist art that continues to shape Buddhism as a living world religion.

⌘ IMPERMANENCE ⌘

See ANITYA

⌘ INKA-SHŌMEI ⌘

Japanese technical term indicating the "seal of proof" that a disciple has been confirmed as a Dharma heir to a Buddhist master. Although Inka-shōmei officially establishes one as an individual's Dharma successor, it by no means implies that training in the tradition is over. It simply authorizes one to teach other students, to continue the work of one's own master, and in appropriate occasions to be addressed as rōshi (i.e., master). It generally means that the individual conferring Inka-shōmei is satisfied with the disciple's mastery of the training, however it was specifically applied.

⌘ INSIGHT ⌘

See VIPAŚYANA

— J —

⌘ 'JAM MGON KON SPRUL (JAMGÖN KONGTRÜL) ⌘ *(1813–1899)*

Major Tibetan teacher of the nineteenth century, famous for promoting religious tolerance. He was recognized as a "tulku" or incarnate lama at age thirty-six. He received monastic ordination in both the rNying-ma-pa and bKa-rgyud-pa traditions, having an especially close relationship with a subsect of the latter group called the Kar-ma bKa-rgyud-pa lineage. During his life, he collected much of the so-called hidden literature (gter-ma). He manifested various incarnations after his death.

⌘ JĀTAKA ⌘

Pāli title of a category of literature devoted to stories of Buddha's previous existences. The Jātaka tales are part of the canonical writings of the Theravāda school, contained in the Khuddaka Nikāya or fifth portion of the Sūtra Piṭaka. Most of the stories contained in the collection are intended to provide edifying tales designed to illustrate values and morals to be sought by all Buddhist disciples. They are simple in format, resembling folk tales in Western literature, and clearly demonstrate the benefits of achieving an ever increasing stock of good merit, derived from propitious karmic acts. Many of the stories focus on rather universal themes of propriety, and both Sanskrit and Chinese Jātaka texts exist today. (See also KHUDDAKA NIKĀYA.)

⌘ JETAVANA (INDIA) ⌘

Famous Buddhist monastery in Śrāvastī. This monastery was donated to the saṃgha by Anāthapiṇḍika, a wealthy banker of Śrāvastī in Kośala. He was a Buddhist lay disciple (upāsaka) who sought to share his wealth with the religious community. The site for the monastery was selected by Buddha's close disciple Śāriputra, and Buddha is reported to have spent the last twenty-five rain retreats of his ministry at Jetavana.

⌘ JETAVANA (SRI LANKA) ⌘

Famous Buddhist monastery in Sri Lanka built by King Mahāsena (334–362) and donated to Mahāyāna monks on the island. During the next several centuries, Jetavana vied for supremacy with the two other major Buddhist monasteries of Anurādhapura: Mahāvihāra and Abhayagiri. In times of threat of invasion, it was common for the Sri Lankan kings to support the Mahāvihāra while championing all three vihāras in tranquil times. (See also ABHAYAGIRI; ANURADHĀPURA; MAHĀVIHĀRA.)

⌘ JHĀNA ⌘

See DHYĀNA

⌘ JINA ⌘

Sanskrit term literally meaning "conqueror" or "victorious one," and often used an an epithet of Buddha. Subsequent to his attainment of enlightenment and his establishment as a Buddha, Siddhārtha Gautama was identified by a number of epithets in various Buddhist literary texts. Most frequent among these honorific titles were Tathāgata, rendered as "Thus-Come," Śākyamuni, "Sage of the Śākya Clan", and Jina. He is also referred to as an Arhant (worthy one), and as Samyak Sambuddha (Completely and Perfectly Enlightened One).

⌘ JIRIKI ⌘

Japanese technical term, most often translated as "own-power," indicating a religious attainment achieved through one's own striving through a particular means (such as zazen). Jiriki (Chinese: tzŭ-li) is almost always played off against tariki or "other-power," a term readily utilized in the Pure Land tradition to indicate a religious attainment, such as rebirth in the Pure Land, achieved through another's effort, in this case the saving grace of Amida Buddha. As such, jiriki is most often associated with the Zen tradition since it insists on a rigorous path of religious training involving sitting meditation and perhaps other activities as well. Jiriki is also called the "difficult path," again contrasted with tariki, the "easy path." (See also TARIKI.)

⌘ JIZO ⌘

A Bodhisattva whose name means "Earth Respository," and who was entrusted by Śākyamuni Buddha with the task of saving beings in all the traditional six realms of existence until the next earthly Buddha appeared. This Bodhisattva is known as Kṣitigarbha in the Sanskritic tradition, and Ti-ts'ang in Chinese, but seems to have reached his highest point of development in Japanese Buddhism. The figure was probably introduced to Japan during the Nara Period from T'ang China, developing quickly in the Heian and Kamakura periods. He is most often depicted as a monk with a staff in his right hand and a jewel in his left. He is especially regarded as a protector of children who have been killed, assuring them of a favorable rebirth.

⌘ JÑĀNA ⌘

Sanskrit technical term, most often translated as "knowledge." Derived from the Sanskrit verb root √jñā, to know, it is regularly utilized to designate knowledge that is associated with the *intellectual* process. Consequently, it is sometimes contrasted with prajñā, also derived from √jñā, but associated with an *intuitive* process. Like prajñā, jñāna is considered one of the ten perfections (pāramitās) in Mahāyāna, listed as the tenth, and linked to the stage (bhūmi) called the "Cloud of Dharma" (Dharmameghā).

⌘ JŌDŌ SHINSHŪ ⌘

"True Pure Land School," of Japanese Buddhism, founded by Shinran (1173–1263), and based on the Jōdo Shū of Hōnen (1133–1212) that preceded it. The school is based on the Pure Land texts which emphasize the saving grace of Amida (Sanskrit: Amitābha)

Buddha. Shinran's religious practice focuses on the recitation of the formula known as the Nembutsu, precisely stated as Namu Amida Butsu ("Homage to Amida Buddha"). This formula is an expression of complete trust in Amida, recitation of which presumably guarantees the disciple's rebirth in the Pure Land. Since it is *Amida's* effort that results in the religious advancement of the disciple, this school falls under the designation of tariki, the "other-power" or "easy path" tradition in Japanese Buddhism. Unlike many other schools of Japanese Buddhism, Jōdo Shinshū is an exclusively lay organization with no formally monastic tradition. Nonetheless, it has an extensive series of temples and functioning clergy. The head of the organization is known as the abbot, located at the main temple, with the position being maintained on a *hereditary* basis. Today Jōdo Shinshū has two main divisions (Ōtani and Honganji), both having their main centers in Kyoto. Collectively, the school maintains the largest membership of all Japanese Buddhist schools. (See also CHING-T'U; JŌDO SHŪ; PURE LAND; SHINRAN; SUKHĀVATĪ.)

⌘ JŌDO SHŪ ⌘

"Pure Land School" of Japanese Buddhism, founded by Hōnen (1133–1212). Although originally a Tendai monk, Hōnen embraced the Pure Land ideal primarily through the teachings of Shan-tao and Genshin after having become convinced that the Tendai path was becoming increasingly unworkable as a means for attaining salvation. Of course Pure Land teachings had been in Japan at least since the time of Ennin (794–864), who had studied it and other traditions while in China, but Hōnen is regarded as the "founder" of the school in Japan. The textual basis of the school remained the Larger and Smaller Sukhāvatīvyūha-sūtras, as well as the Amitāyurdhyāna-sūtra, and the religious practice focused on the Nembutsu, thus identifying it as an "other-power" or "easy path" approach to salvation. For Hōnen, the formula "Namu Amida Butsu" was a means of strengthening one's faith in Amida, not *merely* an expression of trust, and was considered by him an appropriate religious practice in a period of Dharma decline (called mappō in Japanese Buddhism). Unlike its later offshoot, Jōdo Shinshū, Hōnen's school continued the Buddhist monastic tradition. Hōnen's school was both threatening and alienating to the more formal and established Buddhist schools of the time, resulting in a five-year exile, terminated only one year prior to his death. (See also CHING-T'U; JŌDO SHINSHŪ; PURE LAND; SHINRAN; SUKHĀVATĪ.)

⌘ JUKAI ⌘

Japanese Buddhist term meaning "receiving the precepts." Jukai refers to the occasion where a would-be Buddhist disciple formally accepts the Buddhist precepts, thus becoming a member of the lay community. It usually takes places during a special week set aside especially for this ceremony. It generally includes an expression of faith in the "Three Jewels" of Buddhism (i.e., Buddha, Dharma, and Saṃgha) as well as an acceptance of ten main precepts. It often also includes the general vow of the bodhisattva to strive for attaining complete, perfect enlightenment (i.e, Buddhahood) for the sake of all sentient beings.

— K —

⌘ KAKUSHIN ⌘
(1207–1298)

Japanese monk who brought the Wu-mên-kuan (Japanese: Mumonkan) to Japan from China. Kakushin was ordained at Tōdai-ji in Nara, studied the Shingon school of Buddhism on Mount Kōya, and also studied Zen with a student of Eisai Zenji named Gyōyū. He traveled to China in 1249, becoming the disciple of China's most accomplished Ch'an master of the time, Wu-mên. Eventually, Kakushin received the seal of transmission known as inka-shōmei from Wu-mên, and was named his Dharma heir. When he returned to Japan in 1254, Kakushin was given a copy of his master's well-known text called the Wu-mên-kuan. Following his return to Japan, Kakushin became quite famous, building a monastery first known as Saihō-ji but later called Kōkoku-ji. As a result of his fame, he was repeatedly invited to the capital in Kyoto by the emperor. He was especially important in the Rinzai school of Zen for his work with kōans, and for bringing the Fuke school of Zen (Chinese: P'u-k'o), which he learned in China, to Japan. (See also WU-MÊN HUI-K'AI.)

⌘ KĀLACAKRA TANTRA ⌘

Text of the Atiyoga subdivision of the Anuttarayoga-tantra, literally meaning "Wheel of Time," and considered to be one of the most complex Tantric texts. It was probably introduced to Tibet from India in the eleventh century. It is comprised of three basic parts: (1) a section that considers the physical world and its aspects, including temporal factors, (2) a section that considers the psycho-physical world of the individual, and (3) a section focusing on visualization of the deities. It is still regularly practiced in the dGe-lugs-pa school of Tibetan Buddhism. (See also TANTRA.)

⌘ KALPA ⌘

Sanskrit technical term meaning "world cycle." Early Buddhism, consistent with the basic worldview of its Indian homeland, accepted the notion of a cycle of time that had neither an absolute beginning nor ending. This cycle of unending time is referred to as saṃsāra, and for the earliest tradition, helps to define Buddhist soteriology as a system promoting the cessation of suffering (duḥkha) in a continually enduring chain of rebirths in a never-ceasing time frame. Nonetheless, within the overarching picture of a ceaseless cycle of time, world cycles or kalpas are designated as a means of making the immense notion of temporal infinity more understandable in conventional human terms. Consequently, when one can fathom the vastness of time considered in terms of *even one kalpa*, then the notion of time's unending nature can be emphasized in a meaningful fashion.

⌘ KALYĀṆAMITRA ⌘

Sanskrit technical term literally meaning "good friend" or "noble friend," and most often applied to an individual's spiritual preceptor. It is the kalyāṇamitra who leads the adept through meditational training. Consequently, the choice of teacher is utterly critical. From the standpoint of appropriate training, a continuum is established, at least in the early tradition (as outlined in Buddhaghosa's Visuddhimagga), for precisely *who* makes the most suitable kalyāṇamitra, beginning with a Buddha, proceeding to an arhant, and eventually coming to, in the absence of all other possibilities, a conscientious person who has mastered self-control. Precisely because the practitioner's experience in meditation is focal to the attainment of salvation, the relationship with the kalyāṇamitra perhaps reflects the most important decision an individual can have in one's religious life.

⌘ KĀMA ⌘

Sanskrit term usually referring to sensual pleasure, but also applied to sexual desire, and occasionally, to longing in general. In elucidating craving (tṛṣṇā), the second of the four noble truths in Buddhism, three specific types of craving are noted of which *kama*-tṛṣṇā, craving for sensual pleasures, is the first. It is also listed as one of the āsravas or "impurities" in early Buddhism (i.e., the impurity of sensual desire) and one of the five hindrances in meditational training (i.e., *kāma*cchanda or "sensual desire"). It is also used as a cosmological term, linked with *loka* or *dhātu* to indicate the "world" or "realm" of desire, the lowest of the spheres of existence in Hīnayāna Buddhist cosmology.

⌘ KAMAKURA PERIOD ⌘

Period in Japanese history (1192–1338) during which power moved from the Heian court to a military group of samurai at Kamakura. The Kamakura Period witnessed much growth in Buddhism, as a number of new schools were introduced to Japan. Based largely on the writings of Genshin, Hōnen established the Pure Land School (Jōdo Shū). His work was extended by his disciple Shinran who founded the "True" Pure Land School (Jōdo Shinshū). Shortly thereafter, Nichiren became convinced that the truth of the Buddhist tradition could be found only in the Lotus-sūtra, and developed a Buddhist school, named after himself, that emphasized the efficacy of that scripture and a new religious practice based on chanting a phrase of homage to the text. Zen became important during this period, with Sōtō Zen being introduced by Dōgen Zenji and Rinzai Zen being introduced by Eisai Zenji. In addition to the significant developments for Buddhism during this period, Japanese culture also blossomed with the development of the Tea Ceremony, as well as Haiku poetry, and Nō Theater. The period can also be characterized by much discord between the military rulers, many of whom patronized Buddhist groups, and civil groups, eventually marshaling in a major new period of Japanese history.

⌘ KAMALAŚĪLA ⌘

Famous disciple of Śāntirakṣita who lived ca. 700–750 and wrote the Bhāvanākrama. Kamalaśīla and Śāntirakṣita were critical of Bhāvaviveka's position, known as the Svātantrika school, and extended it offering instead a Yogācāra-Mādhyamika (Svātantrika) position. Kamalaśīla also wrote commentaries on Śāntikrakṣita's Madhyamakālaṅkāra and Dharmakīrti's Nyāyabindu. Late in his life, he traveled to Tibet, and his text of the Bhāvanākrama was instrumental in defeating the Chinese monk Hvashang at the famous Council of Lhasa in Tibet in 792–794. (See also BHĀVANĀKRAMA; SĀNTIRAKṢITA.)

⌘ KANIṢKA ⌘

Third king of the Kuṣāṇa Dynasty reputed to have convened a major Buddhist council in Gandhāra. Upon gaining the throne sometime around 100 C.E., Kaniṣka tried to emulate the style of King Aśoka who reigned centuries earlier. Consistent with that estimate, Kaniṣka acceded to the suggestion of the monk Parśva to convene a council in Gandhāra. Vasumitra, a great scholar, became president of the council of 499 monks, assisted by the poet Aśvaghoṣa. The council was responsible for the production of a major Sarvāstivādin Abhidharma text known as the Mahāvibhāṣā. Despite his interest in Buddhism, and respect for King Aśoka, Kaniṣka remained somewhat greedy for conquest, and ruthless, throughout his reign, eventually extending his control far into the north. He was finally smothered in his blanket during an illness. Nonetheless, there was a significant flourishing of Buddhist culture under his reign.

⌘ KANJUR ⌘

See BKA'-GYUR

⌘ KAPILAVASTU ⌘

Home of Siddhārtha Gautama, the historical Buddha. Kapilavastu was the capital city of Siddhārtha's father, King Śuddhodana. It rested at the foothills of the Himalayas in what is now modern Nepal. As such, it was the stronghold of the Śākya clan. Lumbinī Garden, the actual birthplace of Siddhārtha is quite close to Kapilavastu. Consistent with a vow, made at the time of his "Great Renunciation," to return to his family and teach them the way to put an end to old age, sickness, and death, Buddha eventually returned to Kapilavastu, ordaining his son Rāhula as a monk and beginning an order of nuns, with his foster mother Mahāprajāpatī as the first member. It is regarded as one of Indian Buddhism's holy sites.

⌘ KAPLEAU, PHILIP ⌘

American Zen Rōshi and founder of the Zen Center of Rochester, New York, one of the major Buddhist centers in the United States. He was born in 1912, studied law, and became a court reporter. In this role, he worked at both the military tribunal in Nuremberg and the War Crimes Trials in Tokyo in 1946. At the beginning of the decade of the 1950s, Kapleau attended D.T. Suzuki's lectures in Buddhist philosophy at Columbia University, finally deciding in 1953 to travel to Japan in pursuit of genuine Buddhist training. He first practiced at Ryūtaku-ji Temple under Nakagawa Sōen Rōshi. Half a year later he began practice under Harada Rōshi at Hosshin-ji Temple, staying for several years. In 1956, Kapleau was taken to Yasutani Rōshi by Nakagawa Sōen Rōshi, and the former urged Kapleau to bring his Zen training to America. Two years later, Kapleau had a kenshō (or "enlightenment") experience. Prior to his return to America in 1966, Yasutani Rōshi authorized Kapleau as a teacher. In August 1966, the Zen Center was founded. In addition to publishing a number of important and influential books, such as *The Three Pillars of Zen* and *Zen: Dawn in the West*, Kapleau has been a leader in promoting Zen as an *American* religious practice, adapting Zen clothing, rituals, and the like for an American audience. (See also THE THREE PILLARS OF ZEN.)

⌘ KARMA ⌘

Sanskrit technical term, literally translated as "action," and referring to the Buddhist notion that any volitional activity accrues retribution appropriate to the nature of the deed. In the simplest sense, Buddhists believe that any act that is volitional (cetanā) in its basis creates a karmic "seed" that will eventually ripen (vipāka) and bear fruit (phala). Volitional acts may be judged to be "good" (kuśala) or "bad" (akuśala), while nonvolitional acts are generally designated as neutral. For an act to be negatively motivated, it must be motivated by one of the so-called three poisons on Buddhism: (1) lust (rāga), (2) hatred (dveṣa), or (3) delusion (moha). The opposite of each of these three motivating factors are then necessarily considered as the bases of positive karmic acts. Invariably, each individual is presumed to manifest free will in each experiential moment of his or her life, thus suggesting that one's station in life is intimately linked to the motivations behind one's actions. The law of karma consequently provides the underlying basis for a morality grounded in personal, individual responsibility. A small number of utterly heinous karmic acts, such as killing an arhant, are said to bear the fruit immediately, but otherwise, it is simply impossible to predict when a karmic seed will ripen and bear its fruit. As a result, most Buddhists are readily concerned with earning merit (puṇya) in hopes of gaining an auspicious rebirth. Precisely how karmic seeds are transferred from one life to the next was never effectively explained in any of the sects of Hīnayāna or Mahāyāna Buddhism, but led to a lively and continued debate.

⌘ KAR-MA BKA-RGYUD-PA (KARMA KAGYÜPA) ⌘

Subsect of the bKa-rgyud-pa school of Tibetan Buddhism, founded in the twelfth century by Dus-gSum mKhyen-pa (Düsum Khyen-pa, 1110–1193), known as the first Karmapa. The lineage of the tradition is established through the line of Karmapas that has remained unbroken from the time of the founder. The founder of the school built a number of monasteries, with many of his successors expanding their sphere of influence and importance of the subsect. They are known as the "Black Hat" sect because of the black hat, supposedly made of the hair of 10,000,000 dākinīs (or female demons) worn by the Karmapa on certain ritual occasions. The tradition has produced many famous lamas, including the nineteenth-century figure 'Jam-mgon Konsprul (Jamgön Kongtrül) and the most recent Karmapa Rigpe Dorje (1924–1982), who preserved the lineage during and after the Tibetan Holocaust, establishing a major center in Rumtek, Sikkim. (See also KARMAPA.)

⌘ KARMAPA ⌘

Title of the spiritual head and lineage holder of the Kar-ma bKa-rgyud-pa school of Tibetan Buddhism. The first Karmapa was Dus-gSum mKhyen-pa (Düsum Khyen-pa, 1110–1193). The Karmapa is presumably an embodiment of compassion, sometimes identified with the bodhisattva Avalokiteśvara. The lineage of the Karmapas is considered the oldest in Tibetan Vajrayāna. To date, sixteen Karmapas have been identified, the sixteenth being Rigpe Dorje (1924–1982). (See also KAR-MA BKA-RGYUD-PA.)

⌘ KARUṆĀ ⌘

Sanskrit technical term meaning "compassion," and important in all Buddhist traditions. Considered to be one of the chief attributes of a Buddha, it is among the prime motivating factors in Siddhārtha Gautama's pursuit of enlightenment. In the Hīnayāna sects it find its highest expression as a member of the fourfold Brahmā-vihāras or "divine abodes." In the Brahmā-vihāras it functions in consonance with love (maitrī), sympathetic joy (muditā), and equanimity (upekṣā) as an expression of the highest ethical standard of pursuit. In Mahāyāna it achieves its fullest development as one of the driving forces in the bodhisattva's religious practice. It is generally linked with wisdom (prajñā) in describing the two chief descriptive attributes of the bodhisattva. Karuṇā is said to be embodied in the bodhisattva Avalokiteśvara, who receives much attention in the Chinese and Japanese traditions (as Kuan-yin and Kwannon, respectively). Compassion is extremely important as the basis of the Pure Land tradition as well.

⌘ KASIṆA ⌘

Pāli technical term most often rendered as "entire" and employed as the title of a category of objects utilized in the Theravāda meditation tradition. They are ten in number and include: (1) earth, (2) water, (3) fire, (4) air, (5) blue, (6) yellow, (7) red, (8) white, (9) light, and (10) enclosed space. Irrespective of which kasiṇa is utilized as the focus of meditation, it is concentrated on in its "entirety," thus accounting for the name of the category of objects. It functions as a means of teaching the practitioner how to be concentrated and mentally steady. They are considered helpful in attaining the first jhāna or trance state.

⌘ KĀŚYAPA ⌘

Sometimes also referred to as Mahākāśyapa, a leading disciple of Buddha who became president of the first Buddhist council; Kāśyapa is also considered the first patriarch of Ch'an. A very senior and highly disciplined monk, Kāśyapa was selected to head the Buddhist council of Rājagṛha, held in the rainy season immediately following Buddha's death. He not only selected the 500 arhant monks who attended but personally questioned Upāli on the Vinaya and Ānanda on the Sūtras. He is also reputed to be the first patriarch of Ch'an Buddhism, resulting from a circumstance in which Buddha was surrounded by a number of disciples waiting to hear a discourse. To the dismay of the listeners, Buddha said nothing, but instead held up a flower, eliciting a smile from Kāśyapa. At that point, Buddha revealed that his Dharma was a sublime teaching, impossible to reach merely with words, and always transmitted directly from master to disciple. He proclaimed that he had just transmitted that Dharma to Kāśyapa, thus, in the minds of Chinese Buddhists, beginning the Ch'an lineage. The name Kāśyapa is also associated with a Buddha of a previous world cycle.

⌘ KATHĀVATTHU ⌘

Pāli Abhidhamma text, the title of which translates to "Points of Discussion." The "points" or "subjects" of discussion mentioned in the title of the text refer to issues apparently discussed in the third traditional Theravāda council, sanctioned by King Aśoka and held in his capital city of Pāṭaliputra. The Kathāvatthu is largely a polemical treatise defending the orthodox view of the time against rival viewpoints. As such it is important not only for the philosophical position it maintains but for its historical value in helping scholars sort out the essentials of early Indian Buddhist sectarianism.

⌘ KATSU ⌘

Shout used by Zen masters to help disciples break through rational thought patterns to achieve enlightenment. The practice is said to have originated with the Chinese Ch'an master Ma-tsu Tao-i (709–788), a third-generation leader in Hui-nêng's school. It was also utilized by Lin-chi I-hsüan (d. 866). Just as a blow with a stick, delivered at precisely the right moment, was thought to shake a student out of his attachment to empirical, conceptual patterns and enable him to experience reality directly, so also a shout was felt to produce the same effect. The shout was sometimes identified as "Kwatsu." (See also ZEN.)

⌘ KEGON ⌘

School of Japanese Buddhism derived from the Kegon-kyō or "Flower Ornament Sūtra" (Sanskrit: Avataṃsaka-sūtra; Chinese: Hua-yen Ching) and playing a role in the Nara period of Japanese history. Brought to Japan by the Chinese monk Shen-hsiang around 740, it was avidly promoted by Emperor Shōmu. The main monastery of the school was Tōdai-ji in Nara, where the emperor built a huge statue of the Buddha Vairocana. The emperor's keen interest in Kegon was political as much as religious, and the school was primarily attractive to the elite. With the coming of the Heian Period, the Kegon school lost most of its influence in Japanese Buddhist culture. (See also AVATAṂSAKA-SŪTRA; GAṆḌAVYŪHA-SŪTRA; HUA-YEN.).

⌘ KEIZAN JŌKIN ZENJI ⌘
(1268–1325)

One of the most important masters of Sōtō Zen. Keizan Jōkin Zenji founded Sōji-ji monastery in 1321 which, along with Eiheiji, represent the two most important monasteries in the Sōtō Zen tradition. He is considered the fourth patriarch of the school. Next to Dōgen Zenji, he is the most important figure in the Sōtō lineage. Dōgen Zenji is sometimes referred to as the father of Sōtō Zen, while Keizan Jōkin Zenji is cited as its mother. His best-known text is the frequently quoted Denkō-roku, but he also wrote the Sankon zazen setsu, Keizan shinki and Zazen yōjinki. Although his writings are more intuitive than Dōgen Zenji's, he did write most of the ceremonies utilized in Sōtō Zen. Under his leadership, Sōtō Zen was the largest Buddhist school of the time. (See also DŌGEN ZENJI.)

⌘ KENDŌ ⌘

Sword fighting in Japanese culture. In medieval Japan the art of sword fighting was extremely popular, and the tradition survives today. It was not unusual for trainees in the art of sword fighting to undertake Zen discipline as a corollary activity. Additionally, some Zen masters became quite adept in sword fighting. The activities were seen to be mutually influencing insofar as they both require a strong spontaneity and a genuine attitude of fearlessness. Today, there are a number of centers where *both* disciplines can be learned simultaneously.

⌘ KENSHŌ ⌘

One of several Japanese technical terms for enlightenment in Zen. Kenshō is sometimes translated as "realization," and is frequently used synonymously with another Zen technical term, satori. It is obviously a breakthrough experience available to any Zen practitioner at any time. Like all dramatic, visionary experiences, it is impossible to capture in descriptive, conceptual terms. It may arise suddenly, as the Rinzai school anticipates, or only after extended periods of sitting meditation, as Sōtō Zen suggests. Nonetheless, it should *not* be seen as the culmination of Zen practice, but simply an experience that can be continually deepened. (See also BODHI; ENLIGHTENMENT; SATORI; WU.)

⌘ KHMER ⌘

Alternative name for modern day Cambodians. While Cambodian history is traditionally said to begin in the first century C.E., the country was highly influenced by Indian culture for at least several centuries thereafter. By the late seventh century (exclusively) Khmer power was increasing, and around 800 a unified Khmer empire was established. Within 400 years, Theravāda Buddhism was introduced into the Khmer empire from Burma, and it is predominant today.

⌘ KHUDDAKA NIKĀYA ⌘

The fifth collection in the Sutta Piṭaka of the Pāli Canon, literally the "little" collection and containing fifteen selections of miscellaneous works. These include the: (1) Khuddaka-paṭhā ("Collection of Little Readings''), (2) Dhammapada (''Verses on Dhamma''), (3) Udāna (''Verses of Uplift''), (4) Itivuttaka (''Thus It Is Said''), (5) Sutta-nipāta (''Group of Suttas''), (6) Vimāna-vatthu (''Stories of Heavenly Mansions''), (7) Peta-vatthu (''Stories of the Departed''), (8) Theragāthā (''Verses of the Male Elders''), (9) Therīgāthā (''Verses of the Female Elders''), (10) Jātaka (''Birth Stories''), (11) Niddesa (''Exposition''), (12) Paṭisambhidā-magga (''Way of Analysis''), (13) Apadāna (''Stories''), (14) Buddhavaṃsa (''Lineage of the Buddhas''), and (15) Cariyā-piṭaka (''Basket of Conduct''). Some of the texts included in the Khuddaka Nikāya are among the oldest in the Theravāda tradition, while others rank among the most important. (See also ĀGAMA; TRIPIṬAKA.)

⌘ KINHIN ⌘

Zen walking. In the Zen tradition, great emphasis is placed on the practice of zazen, sitting meditation. Practitioners regularly practice zazen for several hours per day, and during intensive periods of training, for as many as fifteen or more hours per day. No matter how physically fit, human bodies require *some* movement in order not to become fatigued and a distraction to serious practice. As a result, the practice of alternating periods of zazen with walking meditation, called kinhin, was adopted. By allowing a short period for walking meditation every half-hour or so, the body remains refreshed, and thus meditation can proceed without additional distraction. (See also ZEN.)

⌘ KŌAN ⌘

Zen technical term literally meaning ''public case'' and used to facilitate the advancement of realization in Zen training. A kōan (Chinese: kung-an) was generally a story or phrase from the teaching that contained an enigmatic riddle that the disciple was asked by the master to solve. In most cases, the student would initially try to resolve the riddle by the use of rational, conceptual thinking and reasoning. However, since each kōan contained an utterly paradoxical circumstance, its solution depended *not* on logic, but on *insight*. The master utilized his private meeting with each disciple, known as dokusan, to measure the progress that was, or was not being made in the solution to each kōan. In these private meetings the Zen master could use his wisdom and compassion to encourage the disciple in making the intuitive leap into a genuine understanding of reality. There are nearly 2,000 kōans recorded, generally in collections such as the Mumonkan (Chinese: Wu-mên-kuan) and the Hekigan-roku (Chinese: Pi-yên-lu). For the most part, the kōan tradition is used extensively in the Rinzai but not the Sōtō tradition. (See also PI-YÊN-LU; WU-MÊN-KUAN; ZEN.)

⌘ KŌBŌ DAISHI ⌘

See KŪKAI

⌘ KO-I ⌘

Chinese term utilized to literally "stretch the meaning" of a Taoist phrase so as to convey a Buddhist meaning. During the earliest period of Buddhism's history in China, attempts were made to make Buddhist concepts and ideas understandable to its new Chinese audience by utilizing Chinese terms, most often from Taoism, to *approximate* Buddhist notions. In this way, terminology that was familiar to the Chinese was used, but in a *new* way. Because this "matching concepts" was so inexact, it was condemned by a number of early Chinese Buddhists like Tao-an (312–385) who insisted on developing a distinctly *Buddhist* terminology in Chinese.

⌘ KÖRÖSI, CSOMA SÁNDOR ⌘
(1784–1842)

Transylvanian sometimes regarded as the father of European Tibetology. Committed to a lifelong vow to find the origins of the Hungarian people, Körösi set out on foot, in 1820, to begin the search. Convinced by the English explorer William Moorcroft that the libraries in Lhasa had information about the origins of the Hungarians, Korösi studied Tibetan grammar, received a modest stipend from the British authorities to finance his research, and went to Tibet for several lengthy trips. He never did find the origins of the Hungarian people, but he did produce a Tibetan-English dictionary and grammar in 1834. He brought back much information that marked the beginning of modern, scholarly study of Tibetan Buddhism.

⌘ KORYO PERIOD ⌘

Period of Korean history (935–1392) during which Buddhism reached its peak of importance. Although Buddhism had been present in Korea for more than half a millenium, it was the Koryo period that witnessed the most extensive program of monastery construction, as well as a continued effort to sponsor art works. It was during this period that the Mongols, led by Genghis Khan invaded Korea.

⌘ KṢĀNTI ⌘

Sanskrit term literally meaning "patience," indicating one of the ten traditional perfections (pāramitās) of Mahāyāna Buddhism. The practice of kṣānti suggests that one must endure all sorts of suffering and inconvenience without becoming discouraged, and without being tempted to abandon the quest for complete perfect enlightenment. It is usually linked to the third stage (bhūmi) of the bodhisattva path, radiance (prabhākarī).

⌘ KṢITIGARBHA ⌘

See JIZŌ

⌘ KUAN-YIN ⌘

See AVALOKITEŚVARA

⌘ K'UEI-CHI ⌘

(632–682)

Famous student of Hsüan-tsang, considered as co-organizer of the Fa-hsiang school of Chinese Buddhism. As the chief disciple of Hsüan-tsang, he was a member of his teacher's translation group, and is said to have worked on the Ch'eng wei-shih lun, chief text of the Chinese Yogācāra school. He additionally systematized the work of his master, primarily in two texts known as the Fa-yüan i-lin-chang (Chapter on the Forest of Meanings in the Garden of Law) and the Ch'eng wei-shih lun shu-chi (Notes on the Treatise on the Completion of Ideation Only). Although K'uei-chi outlived his master by almost twenty years, following his death the Fa-hsiang school waned, severely damaged by the anti-Buddhist persecution of 845. (See also HSÜAN-TSANG.)

⌘ KUEI-SHAN LING-YU ⌘

(771–853)

Famous Ch'an master and Dharma heir of Pai-chang Huai-hai (720–814). He became a monk at age fifteen, training initially in the Vinaya school of Chinese Buddhism. Seven years later he became Pai-chang's student, remaining with him even *after* his enlightenment experience. For many years he served as a cook in his monastery, eventually being chosen by Pai-chang to head Ta-kuei monastery. He had an enormous monastic community and several dozen Dharma heirs, the two most famous being Yang-shan Hui-chi (807–883) and Hsiang-yen Chih-hsien (d. 898). With the former, he founded the Kuei-yang school of Ch'an (Japanese: Igyō), one of the traditional "five houses" of Ch'an. (See also PAI-CHANG HUAI-HAI.)

⌘ KŪKAI ⌘

(774–835)

Founder of the Shingon or esoteric school of Japanese Buddhism. Born into an aristocratic Nara family, Kūkai studied Confucianism and Taoism, in addition to Buddhism, in his teens. Ordained at twenty, he sailed to China in 804, where he studied Chên-yen (the Chinese Vajrayāna school of Buddhism) with Hui-kuo. Following Hui-kuo's death in 805, Kūkai returned to Japan the next year. He was appointed chief monk at Tōdai-ji monastery in 810, but eventually founded his own monastery on Mount Kōya in 816 that became the headquarters of his Shingon school. Kūkai placed great emphasis on the arts, as witnessed by his fame as a calligrapher, and promoted aesthetics in general. By the time of his death in 835, he was revered as a great teacher, attracting many brilliant disciples. He was buried on Mount Kōya, being given the posthumous title Kōbō Daishi, the "Great Teacher Kōbō," in 921. (See also SHINGON SCHOOL.)

⌘ KUMĀRAJĪVA ⌘

(344–413)

Kuchean monk who traveled to China, becoming one of the greatest translators in the history of Chinese Buddhism. Originally a Hīnayāna advocate, but eventually a proponent of Mahāyana, and especially the Mādhyamika treatises of Nāgārjuna, Kumārajīva arrived in Ch'ang-an in 401. In the capital of Ch'ang-an he headed an extensive translation bureau which rendered a large number of Buddhist Sanskrit texts into Chinese. Considered a member of the so-called Buddho-Taoist translation school because he utilized Taoist vocabulary to explain Buddhist doctrines, Kumārajīva's translations are regarded to be less accurate than those of Hsüan-tsang (596–664) but somewhat more readable. He is best known for his translations of Nāgārjuna's Mūlamadhyamaka-kārikās, Dvādaśa-dvāra-śāstra, and Mahāprajñāpāramita-upadeśa-śāstra, which serve as the basis of the San-lun school of Chinese Buddhism, as well as Āryadeva's Śata-śāstra, and a series of other well-known Mahāyāna texts such as the Amitābha-sūtra, Lotus-sūtra, and Vimalakīrti-nirdeśa-sūtra.

(See also BUDDHO-TAOISTS.)

⌘ KUNG-AN ⌘

See KŌAN

⌘ KUŚINAGARA ⌘

Capital of the Mallas in northern India where Siddhārtha Gautama, the historical Buddha, died. Following a meal of tainted food at the home of a blacksmith, Buddha arrived in Kuśinagara and made preparations for his death. Following several audiences with his followers, he died between two śāla trees. After a period of six days, the Malla rulers cremated the body on the seventh day, and erected a stūpa or memorial mound over the relics. As the place of Buddha's death, it was considered one of the holiest places in Buddhism.

⌘ KWANNON ⌘

See AVALOKITEŚVARA

⌘ KYOJONG ⌘

One of two major schools in Korean Buddhism. At the end of the fourteenth century, under the third king in the Yi Dynasty, Buddhism was suppressed, reducing the number of Buddhist sects to seven. The fourth king, Sejong, continued the suppression still further, reducing Buddhism to two schools, the Sonjong and the Kyojong. The Kyojong, or "Textual" school, was a union of the Hua-yen, Fa-hsiang, and San-lun traditions of Chinese Buddhism. The two major sects remained as the official divisions of Buddhism until 1935. (See also SONJONG.)

⌘ KYOSAKU ⌘

A rather long stick, often up to about three feet in length, that is used to "encourage" students engaged in zazen practice. During long and/or intensive periods of sitting meditation, students are apt to sometimes lose their focus and succumb to a wandering mind. This is often referred to as "monkey mind," in which the mind jumps around like a monkey in the forest. Additionally, students practicing zazen may also become stuporous or sleepy as well. In either case, the student benefits greatly by a quick blow on the upper back by a monitor carrying the kyosaku who walks back and forth, patrolling the meditation hall. It is neither a punishment for mental laziness nor an occasion of embarrassment amidst one's colleagues, but rather a simple call to wakefulness. It is an encouragement. Under precisely the right circumstances, it can bring about an experience of enlightenment, of kenshō or satori. (See also ZAZEN.)

⌘ KYŪDŌ ⌘

Japanese technical term meaning "way of the bow." Just as Kendō or sword fighting was popular in Japan not only as a traditional martial art but also as an activity that was mutually influencing with Zen training, so also Kyūdō or archery functions similarly. It promotes spontaneity, and serves as a means of integrating physical and spiritual training. A number of individuals have appeared who are *both* archery masters and serious students of Zen. Eugen Herrigel's wonderfully popular book *Zen in the Art of Archery*, first published in 1953, remains important reading in this area.

— L —

⌘ LALITAVISTARA ⌘

Buddhist Sanskrit text probably originating within the Sarvāstivādin school of Buddhism, but also having significant Mahāyāna influences, and translated as "Detailed Account of the Sport (of the Buddha)." The text is divided into twenty-seven chapters, and covers the period of Buddha's most recent previous lives, his decision to be reborn into our world, and his biography up to his preaching of his first sermon. It is preserved in Sanskrit, several Chinese versions, and in Tibetan. It is important for its use, in combination with other Buddhist texts of various schools, in outlining a reasonably accurate and complete account of Buddha's biography.

⌘ LAMA (BLA-MA) ⌘

Tibetan translation for guru, meant to indicate a master, teacher, or preceptor. The title is rather inclusive, and can apply to both (in Richard Robinson's terminology) "scholar-monks" such as Śāntirakṣita and "wonder-working yogins" such as Padmasambhava. While a lama's role as teacher and spiritual leader is significant in the Vajrayāna tradition, he is also a primary functionary in *performing* rituals. Thus, a lama has a major responsibility in the transmission of Buddhist teaching to his disciples, and for their development on the Buddhist path. If a lama is considered to be an incarnation of a particular individual, he is known as a tulku (sprul-sku). Some highly developed lamas are titled rinpoche, literally "precious one."

⌘ LAMOTTE, ÉTIENNE ⌘
(1903–1983)

Belgian Buddhologist, chief disciple of Louis de La Vallée Poussin, and renowned especially for his work on Indian Buddhism. For forty-five years (1932–1977), Lamotte was a professor at the Catholic University of Louvain. He was a member of the Académie Royale de Belgique and the Institut de France. He was also an Honorary Fellow of the International Association of Buddhist Studies. He will most likely be most remembered for his monumental volume *Histoire du Bouddhisme Indien, des origines à l'ère Śaka*, published in 1958 and translated into English by Sara Webb-Boin in 1988. Additionally, however, Lamotte was able to bring out editions and/or translations of a number of other extremely important Buddhist texts, including: the Saṃdhinirmocana-sūtra (1936), Vasubandhu's Karmasiddhiprakaraṇa (1936),

Asaṅga's Mahāyānasaṃgraha (1938–1939), the Vimalakīrti-nirdeśa-sūtra (1962), and the Chinese version of the introductory chapter of Nāgārjuna's Mahāprajñāpāramitā-śāstra (in five volumes, 1944–1980).

⌘ LAM-RIM ⌘

Tibetan term for "stages of the path," usually applied to a category of doctrinal manuals outlining the various stages of the Vajrayāna spiritual path. The oldest text of this variety is sGam-po-pa's (1079–1153) Jewel Ornament of Liberation, structured into six major sections. Utilizing this model, Tsong-kha-pa (1357–1419) wrote the Lam-rim chen-mo ("Graduated Path to Enlightenment"), perhaps the most important text of its type, especially useful for its elucidation of the meditational path.

⌘ LAṄKĀVATĀRA-SŪTRA ⌘

Mahāyāna text, probably written around 400, whose title translates to "Descent into Lanka," and whose doctrinal base focuses on the various themes of the Yogācāra school of Buddhism. The context of the sūtra is a discourse on Lanka in which Buddha responds to a series of questions posed to him by a bodhisattva named Mahāmati. The text is structured into nine chapters of mostly prose, concluding with an additional verse chapter. It discusses emptiness, the theory of eight-consciousness (vijñānas) central to Yogācāra doctrine, five "dharmas" culminating in the state of "suchness" or tathatā, a notion of three svabhāvas (i.e., self-natures) which is contrary to the Mādhyamika idea of two levels of truth, and two forms of Buddha (eternal and transforming). Perhaps the critical doctrine of the sūtra is its statement that the Tathāgata (i.e., Buddha) is present in all sentient beings, thus suggesting that all creatures dwell in the "Womb of the Tathāgata" (called Tathāgata-garbha), and presuming the obvious consequence: that Buddhahood is readily available to all. The text outlines the process of attainment whereby consciousness is essentially turned back on it base, reversed upon itself in a process called āśraya-parāvṛtti, in which all duality and distinctions cease. The sūtra had a strong influence on the Ch'an and Zen traditions.

⌘ LARGER SUKHĀVATĪVYŪHA-SŪTRA ⌘

Mahāyāna text important as one of the foundational bases of the Pure Land School of Buddhism. The text of the sūtra begins with Buddha on Vulture's Peak surrounded by a huge retinue of śrāvakas (i.e., hearers, disciples) and bodhisattvas. Using the premise of instructing Ānanda, Buddha rehearses the story of a monk Dharmākara who made a series of forty-eight vows under a prior Buddha known as Lokeśvararāja. Dharmākara begins pursuit of the bodhisattva path, focusing all his vows on one Buddha-Land. Eventually, Dharmākara is able to actualize his vows, becoming the Buddha Amitābha residing in the Pure Land of Sukhāvatī (the Western Paradise). Rebirth in Sukhāvatī is available to those who (1) make a vow to be reborn there, (2) employ their good merit to do so, and (3) meditate on Amitābha. The sūtra ends with a vision of Amitābha. (See also AMITĀBHA; AMITĀYURDHYĀNA-SŪTRA; SMALLER SUKHĀVATĪVYŪHA-SŪTRA.)

⌘ LAUGHING BUDDHA ⌘

Chinese way of depicting Maitreya, said to be the future Buddha. The figure is usually fat, most often sitting in a posture with the right leg somewhat elevated, and smiling. The figure is sometimes associated with Pu-tai, said to be an incarnation of Maitreya. (See also PU-TAI.)

⌘ LA VALLÉE POUSSIN, LOUIS DE ⌘
(1869–1939)

Belgian Buddhologist, known worldwide for his important translations, articles, and studies. La Valléee Poussin studied Oriental languages under Sylvain Lévi at the Sorbonne, but eventually went to Leyden to work with Hendrik Kern. While there, he learned Chinese and Tibetan. He became a professor at the University of Ghent in 1895, remaining there over thirty years. He founded the Société belge d'Étude orientales in 1921, and was one of the editors of the journal *Le Muséon*. He is best known for his multivolume French translation of Vasubandhu's Abhidharmakośa, published between 1923 and 1931. He also published a translation of Śāntideva's Bodhicaryāvatāra in 1907 and Hsüan-tsang's version of the Vijñaptimātratā-siddhi in 1930. Not only an editor and translator, he published important secondary works such as *Bouddhisme, opinions sur l'histoire de la dogmatique*, *Nirvāṇa*, and *The Way to Nirvāṇa*. Additionally, he contributed over two dozen articles to Hastings's *Encylcopedia of Religion and Ethics*. Largely through La Vallée Poussin's work, the so-called Franco-Belgian School of Buddhist Studies solidified, giving rise to an entire generation of Buddhist scholarship.

⌘ LESSER VEHICLE ⌘

See HĪNAYĀNA

⌘ LHASA ⌘

Capital city of Tibet. Lhasa, like most Tibetan towns, was small, probably never having more than (by Per Kvaerne's estimate) forty thousand residents. Nonetheless, it was the place where Atīśa (982–1054) spent most of his time. It was especially important to the dGe-lug-pa tradition which had several important monasteries, including Drepung, nearby. It remained of extreme importance to Buddhism until the time of the Communist Chinese takeover.

⌘ LIN-CHI I-HSÜAN ⌘
(d. 866)

Great Ch'an Buddhist master, disciple of Huang-po Hsi-yün (d. 850), and founder of one of the "five houses of Ch'an." Born sometime between 810 and 815, Lin-chi met Huang-po just prior to the anti-Buddhist persecution of 845, probably in the late 830s. After attaining enlightenment, an event that produces conflicting accounts, Lin-chi became head of a small monastery in the north called Lin-chi yüan. This little monastery soon became highly influential, as many esteemed masters came to visit Lin-chi. He had nearly two dozen Dharma heirs, but it was not until the seventh generation of disciples that Lin-chi's school came to the south. In Hunan it quickly became the most important of all Ch'an schools. Most of what we know of Lin-chi derives from the accounts of his students. He is known as Rinzai Gigen in Japan. (See also LIN-CHI SCHOOL.)

⌘ LIN-CHI SCHOOL ⌘

School of Ch'an founded by Lin-chi I-hsüan (d. 866) and regarded as the most important of the various Ch'an schools. One of the traditional "five houses of Ch'an," the Lin-chi school was highly influential in its homeland. It was developed fully by Lin-chi's successors, most notably Hsian-hua Ts'ung-chiang, Nan-yüan Hui-yung (d. 930), Feng-hsüeh Yen-chao (896–973), Shou-shan Sheng-nien (926–993), and Feng-yang Shan-chao (947–1024). Lin-chi brought an eclectic method of training to his school, encompassing most of the techniques in practice at the time. It was this tradition that Eisai (1141–1215) brought back to Japan, establishing the Rinzai Zen tradition. (See also LIN-CHI I-HSÜAN.)

⌘ LIU-TZŬ T'AN-CHING ⌘

Chinese Ch'an text the title of which translates to "The Platform Sūtra of the Sixth Patriarch." It was probably composed around 820 and considers the legend of Hui-nêng (638–713) who received Dharma transmission from Hung-jen that ultimately split Ch'an into Hui-nêng's "Southern School" and Shen-hsui's "Northern School." The text itself includes biographical material, as well as his sayings. It has been translated into English a number of times, most recently by Philip Yampolsky (1967).

⌘ LOHAN ⌘

Chinese technical term for early Buddhist notion of the arhant or "worthy one." Although the vast majority of the Buddhism that found its way into China, or developed in China, emphasized Mahāyāna, which generally deprecated the arhant as an individual whose attainment was self-motivated, lohans were seen as persons worthy of veneration. Especially in Ch'an, where self-effort was deemed not only commendable but necessary for enlightenment, were the lohans revered. Although the figure of the arhant was known as early as the seventh century in China, a virtual cult grew up around the lohans in the tenth century, beginning first with sixteen lohans, but eventually expanding to eighteen and even five hundred lohans. (See also ARHANT.)

⌘ LOKAKṢEMA ⌘

Indo-Scythian who arrived in China in the second century C.E., and was one of the first major Buddhist translators. Lokakṣema was the first known Mahāyāna missionary in China, working in Lo-yang from 168 to 188 C.E. Along with An Shih-kao, he built the basis of what later became the Chinese Buddhist canon. Among his most important works was a partial translation of the Aṣṭasāhasrikā-prajñāpāramitā-sūtra, the first Buddhist philosophical text translated into Chinese.

⌘ LOTUS-SŪTRA ⌘

Familiar, popular title of the Saddharmapuṇḍarīka-sūtra, more properly titled in full as "Sūtra on the Lotus of the Good Teaching." It is one of the most popular Mahāyāna discourses, and although it is extremely important in Indian Buddhism, it became even more highly valued in China and Japan, serving as the basis of the T'ien-t'ai school of Chinese Buddhism (Japanese: Tendai) and of the school founded by Nichiren. The context of the sūtra is a discourse delivered by Buddha from the famous location known as Vulture's Peak to a huge assembly of disciples of various categories. The main message of the text is that while there are a variety of paths available to disciples (usually identified as three: śrāvaka or "hearer," pratyekabuddha or "private-buddha," and bodhisattva or "enlightenment being"), there is *really only one true vehicle*. This "One Vehicle" Buddhism, or Ekayāna, includes *both* Hīnayāna and Mahāyāna. This central idea is demonstrated through a series of parables, the most important of which center around a burning house, a blind man, and a prodigal son. Emphasis is also placed on the nature of the Tathāgata, developing skill in means (upāya) or the ability to know how to properly utilize wisdom, and building proper character in the bodhisattva (stressing morality, understanding of emptiness, avoidance of doctrinal disputes, and compassion for all beings). (See also NICHIREN.)

⌘ LO-YANG ⌘

Beginning in 494, the capital of the Northern Wei Dynasty of Chinese Buddhism. Chosen by the emperor Hsiao-wen who abandoned the favorable military site of Ta-t'ung as no more campaigns were planned. It was near Lo-yang that Bodhidharma settled in the early sixth century, as Lo-yang was increasingly patronized by royal individuals. A temple for foreign monks, known as Yung-ming temple, was constructed in the city, and a nunnery was erected as well (called the Yao-kuang temple). The most majestic temple in Lo-yang, called Yung-ning temple, was erected by Empress Ling before her death in 528. By 550, Lo-yang was in ruins, the victim of a shrinking treasury and internal disorder.

⌘ LUMBINĪ ⌘

Garden site near Kapilavastu, capital of the Śākyas, where Siddhārtha Gautama was born. In the traditional legend, the future Buddha's mother Māyā was on her way to complete her pregnancy and delivery at the home of her own mother, when she paused in Lumbinī to enjoy the foliage of a lush garden. While there she began labor, delivering the child forthwith. Along with Bodhgayā (the site of enlightenment), Sārnāth (the site of the first sermon), and Kuśinagara (the site of Buddha's death), Lumbinī is one of the four holy places in Buddhism.

⌘ LUNG-MEN ⌘

Site of a huge series of caves constructed near Lo-yang in the early years of the Northern Wei Dynasty of Chinese Buddhism. The project was begun immediately after tranferring the capital from Ta-t'ung in 494, and continued into the Sung Dynasty. The most important of the caves were the Ku-yang-tung (showing influences of the Lotus-sūtra and Vimalakīrti-nirdeśa-sūtra) and Pin-yang-tung (based on the Sudāna-jātaka and Mahāsattva-jātaka). More than two thousand caves were built, housing nearly 150,000 Buddha figures. The leading figures include, in order of number, Amitābha (122), Avalokiteśvara (197), Śākyamuni (94), Maitreya (62), and Kṣitigarbha (33). The caves house inscriptions by the ruling class, monks, and religious societies. The caves clearly reveal that the form of Buddhism operative in the Northern Wei Dynasty was Mahāyāna.

⌘ LÜ SCHOOL ⌘

School of Buddhism emerging in the T'ang Dynasty of Chinese history that emphasized the Vinaya tradition as opposed to doctrinal, philosophical issues. Founded by Tao-hsüan (596–667), it relied on the Dharmaguptaka Vinaya, translated into Chinese by Buddhayaśas and Chu Fo-nien in 412 as the "Vinaya in Four Parts" (Ssu-fen-lü). This particular Vinaya contained 250 rules for monks and 348 rules for nuns, and seems to have been more important in Chinese Buddhism, both Hīnayāna and Mahāyāna than any of the numerous other complete Vinayas possessed by the various Indian Buddhist schools. Although most scholars tend to indicate that this strong emphasis on observance of Vinaya reflected Tao-hsüan's position requiring *both* monastic discipline *and* doctrinal teaching in the practice of Chinese Buddhism, they fail to suggest just why the *Dharmaguptaka Vinaya* became the version of choice in China. It might be conjectured that the Dharmaguptaka Vinaya is the *only* Hīnayāna Vinaya to include *rules governing the method of observance at stūpas*, a practice which by 600 was an important aspect of Chinese Buddhism. This school was also the basis for the Japanese Vinaya school, known as Ritsu, brought to Japan by Chien-chen in 754. (See also RITSU.)

⌘ LU-SHAN ⌘

Famous mountain which was a center of Buddhist activity in the late fourth century and thereafter. Mount Lu was the location where Hui-yüan (334–416) founded the White Lotus Society, and thus important for the Pure Land tradition in China. It also served as a refuge for the Sarvāstivādin monk Buddhabhadra (359–429) after he left Kumārajīva's translation center in Ch'ang-an. Tao-sheng (ca. 360–434), founder of the Nirvāṇa School of Chinese Buddhism, visited Mount Lu as well. The Ch'an master Tao-shin (580–651) is said to have resided on the mountain for ten years. As such, it demonstrates a rather long and important history for early Chinese Buddhism.

— M —

⌘ MĀDHYAMIKA ⌘

Indian Mahāyāna Buddhist school founded by Nāgārjuna, and emphasizing the emptiness (śūnyatā) of all components of experiential reality (dharmas) as its major doctrine. One of the most important schools of Buddhism across the face of the globe, it got its beginnings in the writings of Nāgārjuna, a second- or third-century C.E. philosopher, famous for his Prajñāpāramitā-inspired logical discourses. The title of the school essentially means "Middle Way," and uses as its primary text the Mūlamadhyamaka-kārikās of Nāgārjuna, a treatise that expounds in great detail about the genuine meaning of dependent-origination (pratītya-samutpāda) and emptiness (śūnyatā). Although ascribing to the merits of the bodhisattva path, and the efficacy of Mahāyāna ethical maxims, Nāgārjuna and the Mādhyamika school are far more concerned with emphasizing the nature of ultimate reality (paramārtha-satya) from Buddhist perspective. The Mādhyamika philosophy and the development of the school were continued by Nāgārjuna's most immediate successor Āryadeva. The negative dialectic of the school came to be one of its trademarks, and this emphasis was carried on by Buddhapālita (ca. 470–550) who headed a Mādhyamika subdivision known as the Prāsaṅgikas. Buddhapālita was rivaled by Bhavaviveka (ca. 490–570) who founded another Mādhyamika subdivision known as the Svātantrikas, a group which utilized a *positive* dialectic. Eventually the school became championed by such important Indian Buddhist figures as Candrakīrti, Śāntideva, Śāntirakṣita, Kamalaśīla, and others. In addition to its enormous influence on Indian Mahāyāna, it became the basis of a Chinese school (San-lun) and Japanese school (Sanron), as well as providing the philosophical core for much of Tibetan Buddhism. (See also ĀRYADEVA; BHAVAVIVEKA; NĀGĀRJUNA.)

⌘ MAGADHA ⌘

Famous region in northern India with much connection to early Buddhist history. One of Buddha's chief supporters was the royal patron Bimbisāra who ruled over Magadha from his capital city of Rājagṛha. Rājagṛha was site of the traditional first Buddhist council, held in the rainy season immediately following Buddha's demise. The capital was eventually moved to Pāṭaliputra, from which Aśoka ruled the Mauryan Dynasty. Not only was the third canonical council held during Aśoka's reign, but Buddhism began an extensive missionary movement, expanding greatly beyond Magadha.

⌘ MAHĀBODHI SOCIETY ⌘

Society founded by Anagārika Dharmapāla (1864–1933) in 1891, intended to focus on reviving Buddhism in India. At the time of its foundation, Bodhgayā, the site of Buddha's enlightenment, was under Hindu control. Thus, Dharmapāla's main goal was to regain control of the sacred location for Buddhists worldwide. He attended the World Parliament of Religions in Chicago in 1891, calling added attention to his work for the Mahābodhi Society. In 1925, a British branch of the society was formed. The society is still active today, with centers throughout the world. (See also DHARMAPĀLA, ANAGĀRIKA.)

⌘ MAHĀKĀŚYAPA ⌘

See KĀŚYAPA

⌘ MAHĀMAUDGALYĀYANA ⌘

Famous early disciple of Buddha. Originally from a Brahmin family, Mahāmaudgalyāyana heard a Dharma recitation from his close friend Śāriputra, and was thus inspired to join the Buddhist community. Upon entering the monkhood, he became enlightened rather quickly, becoming one of Buddha's dozen or so closest disciples. While his friend Śāriputra distinguished himself for knowledge of the Abhidharma or "Higher Dharma," Mahāmaudgalyāyana became known for his proficiency in miraculous powers. He was eventually murdered.

⌘ MAHĀMEGHAVANA ⌘

Site in Sri Lanka, housing the first Buddhist missionaries from India. Upon receiving Mahinda and other missionaries from King Aśoka's capital, King Devānaṃpiya Tissa offered them housing in a location known as Mahāmeghavana. When he learned that the visiting monks found the place agreeable, he donated it to the saṃgha, a sign of the king's willingness to accept the religion on the island. This may well have been the site of what later became known as Anurādhapura. A branch of the Bodhi Tree was imported and planted, and a monastery known as Tissārāma established, eventually developing into the famous monastery of

Mahāvihāra. As such, it is the first important Buddhist site on the island of Sri Lanka.

⌘ MAHĀMUDRĀ ⌘

Technical term in Vajrayāna Buddhism, literally translated as "Great Seal," and representing one of the highest teachings of the tradition. Known as phyag-rgya chen-po in Tibetan, the teaching was especially important in the bKa-rgyud-pa school of Tibetan Buddhism. As a meditational system, it first involves the cultivation of calming (śamatha), eventually developing insight (vipaśyanā), finally coming to the direct experience of emptiness and luminosity, embodied in the figure of Samantabhadra (considered the Dharma-kāya in this case). The lineage associated with the practice of Mahāmudrā presumably passes from Tilopa to Nāropa to Mar-pa, and to Mi-la ras-pa, thus becoming entrenched in the Tibetan Buddhist tradition.

⌘ MAHĀPARINIBBĀNA-SUTTA ⌘

Sixteenth discourse of the Dīgha Nikāya of the Pāli Canon titled "The Discourse of the Great Parinibbāna." This long sutta deals with the final portion of the Buddha's life. It considers his decision to die in his eightieth year, the circumstances of his passing, his cremation, and the distribution of his relics. It is important for its omissions as well as its inclusions. Most notable is Buddha's statement that the lesser and minor precepts of discipline can be abolished if the saṃgha wishes *without identifying precisely which precepts were to be considered lesser and minor*. As a result there was much uncertainty following Buddha's death. This text is important for both historical and doctrinal matters for Theravāda Buddhism. It should not be confused with the Sanskrit text known as the Mahāparinirvāṇa-sūtra, an essentially Mahāyāna discourse.

⌘ MAHĀPARINIRVĀṆA-SŪTRA ⌘

Sanskrit title of a Buddhist text which translates to "The Discourse of the Great Parinirvāṇa." Not to be confused with the Pāli text similarly titled, this is a Mahāyāna text, which, under the pretext of Buddha's final passing, expounds on Buddha-nature as equivalent to the Dharma-kāya and immanent in all sentient beings. Other traditional Mahāyāna ideas can be found in the text as well. It is an enormously lengthy text, far exceeding its Pāli counterpart.

⌘ MAHĀPRAJĀPATĪ ⌘

Buddha's foster mother who married his father Śuddhodana following the death of his natural mother, Queen Māyā. As is traditional with the mothers of future Buddhas, Siddhārtha Gautama's mother died seven days after his delivery. Not wanting his son to be raised without a mother, Śuddhodana married Māyā's sister Mahāprajāpatī (i.e. his sister-in-law). She raised Siddhārtha in Māyā's stead. Following his attainment of Buddhahood, and the death of her husband, Mahāprajāpatī petitioned Buddha to go forth into the homeless life as a female mendicant (bhikṣuṇī). Although he refused her initial entreaty, and several additional requests, Ānanda interceded on her behalf, convincing Buddha to relent and begin an order of nuns with Mahāprajāpatī as the first member.

⌘ MAHĀSĀṂGHIKA ⌘

Name of one of two Buddhist sects which splintered from the unified Buddhist community in the first sectarian division and whose name translates to "Great Group-ists" or "Great Community." Although early Buddhist scholarship in the West presumed that the initial schism in Buddhism occurred at the council of Vaiśālī, traditionally known as the "Second Council," later scholarship has proved this hypothesis incorrect. Apparently, shortly after the second Buddhist council, another *noncanonical* Buddhist council was held, the circumstances of which are still being debated in the scholarly literature. Nonetheless, it is clear that at this noncanonical council, the Buddhist community split into two groups: the Sthaviras or "Elders," and the Mahāsāṃghikas or "Great Group-ists." Their name indicates their presence as the majority party in the council proceedings. It appears that the council considered matters of Vinaya or doctrinal issues related to the nature of the arhant, or both. In any case, the Mahāsāṃghikas soon came to be identified as a liberal group with a progressive Buddhology suggesting the supramundane nature of Buddha. They seem also to possess a number of pre-Mahāyāna or proto-Mahāyāna notions, such as that of the bodhisattva. Eventually, the Mahāsāṃghikas divided internally into the Ekavyāvahārikas, Lokottaravādins, Gokulikas, Bahuśrutīyas, Prajñaptivādins, Caitikas, and perhaps one or two others.

⌘ MAHĀSENA ⌘

King who ruled Sri Lanka from 334–362, supporting the *Mahāyāna* tradition. Although Sri Lanka had been almost exclusively Theravādin prior to Mahāsena's rule, he supported a Mahāyāna monk known as Sanghamitta, and destroyed the Mahavihara, uprooting its monks and plowing over its land. In its place he built Jetavana, donated to the Mahāyāna monks. Mahāsena's son Sirimeghavaṇṇa overturned his father's policy, rebuilt the Mahāvihāra, and restored the Theravāda tradition.

⌘ MAHĀSIDDHA ⌘

Vajrayāna term meaning "Great Master," and applied to those individuals who have mastered the Tantras. The Mahāsiddha tradition arose around the eighth century and was typified by wandering saints who tended to be rather unconventional in their appearance and conduct. They were often long-haired lay members who hardly fit the traditional monastic archetype for Buddhist masters. They were notorious for possessing magical powers known as siddhis. The Vajrayāna traditions cites eighty-four Mahāsiddhas, of both genders and all social classes. As a group, they created a class of poetic spiritual songs known as dohas.

⌘ MAHĀVAṂSA ⌘

The "Great Chronicle," outlining Sri Lankan history up to the fourth century C.E. Traditionally ascribed to King Mahānāma (409–431), the text focuses on a period of history commencing with a supposed visit of the Buddha to Sri Lanka and extending up to the ninth century. It includes material on the Buddhist conversion of the island, the creation of the Mahāvihāra, the transplanting of a portion of the Bodhi Tree, historical conquests (particularly over the Tamils), and a wealth of other data. The text was updated periodically, up to the nineteenth century, through a supplement known as the Cūlavaṃsa. The Mahāvaṃsa and Dīpavaṃsa represent two of the great chronicles of Sri Lanka.

⌘ MAHĀVASTU ⌘

Sanskrit text of the Lokottaravādin subsect of the Mahāsāṃghika school, the title of which may be translated as the "Great Story." It belongs to the class of literature known as Avadāna, and is sometimes referred to by its full title: Mahāvastvavadāna. Its period of composition is difficult to date, but it may have been composed in various strata, dating as early as the second century B.C.E., and including material as late as the fourth century C.E. Its language is complex, generally categorized as belonging to "Buddhist" Sanskrit, but highly consistent with other texts of the Lokottaravādin subsect. The text itself contains stories related to Buddha's prior existences, biographical information about Buddha's career, stories about various disciples, and miscellaneous discourses. Although it is contained within the literature of a Buddhist school categorized as Hīnayāna, it presents many viewpoints that are clearly at least *proto*-Mahāyāna such as the bodhisattva path for practitioners. It is an extremely important work for understanding the transition from Hīnayāna to Mahāyāna.

⌘ MAHĀVIBHĀṢĀ ⌘

Short title for a famous Sarvāstivādin Abhidharma commentary, the full title of which is the Abhidharma-mahāvibhāṣā-śāstra. The Mahāvibhāṣā or "Great (Text of) Options," was composed at King Kaniṣka's Indian Buddhist council, intended as a commentary on the Jñānaprasthāna. The Sanskrit original is now lost, and, in the absence of a Tibetan version, our knowledge of the text comes from two Chinese translations, the primary one having been made by Hsüan-tsang. The methodology of the text involves presenting all opinions attributed to the masters on each point of philosophical contention and rendering an appropriate conclusion. The mere presence of the text suggests that vast differences of opinion that had developed among tha various Sarvāstivādin thinkers of the time. Additionally, the importance of the text cannot be overstated, as an entire school of thought, known as the Vaibhāṣikas and chiefly relying on the viewpoints of Vasumitra, developed as a result of the text. (See also VAIBHĀṢIKA.)

⌘ MAHĀVIHĀRA ⌘

A major ancient monastery in Sri Lanka, founded by King Devānaṃpiya Tissa (247–207 B.C.E.). The name Mahāvihāra or

"Great Monastery" reflects its role and importance in Theravāda Buddhism on the island. It developed from the Tissārama, given to visiting missionaries from King Aśoka's court, on the site of Mahāmeghavana in the capital city of Anurādhapura. Its residents became known as the Theriya school, in contrast to the monks of the rival monasteries of Abhayagiri (whose monks were referred to as the Dhammaruci school) and Jetavana (whose monks were of Mahāyāna inclination). Representing the orthodox tradition of Sri Lankan Buddhism, the Mahāvihāra residents reconciled with the Abhayagiri residents following a council in Anurādhapura held in 1165 under the reign of Parākramabāhu I (1153–1184). The city of Anurādhapura was abandoned around the thirteenth century, essentially terminating the history of the Mahāvihāra. (See also ABHAYAGIRI; ANURĀDHAPURA; JETAVANA.)

⌘ MAHĀYĀNA ⌘

Sanskrit term denoting a movement in Buddhism begun around 200 B.C.E. in India and identifying itself as the "Greater Vehicle." Primarily as a reaction against the highly ecclesiastic, somewhat pedantic, and self-motivated Buddhism of the time, this new movement emerged as a means of reemphasizing Buddhism as a liberating vehicle for the masses of Buddhist practitioners. In general, it offered a new literature, initially identified as the Prajñāpāramitā or "Perfection of Wisdom" literature, a new theory concerning the nature of Buddhahood, and a new path to a new goal. Drawing much of its philosophical content from the Mahāsāṃghika and Sarvāstivādin schools of early Buddhism, and its notions of community from an overarching emphasis on compassion (karuṇā) for all sentient beings, it stressed the emptiness (śūnyatā) of all phenomena, the transcendent nature of Buddha, and the attainment of Buddhahood for all beings by means of a course of practice known as the bodhisattva path. While it did not summarily reject early Buddhism, it perceived its overall approach to be inferior, thus the designation of all early Buddhist groups or nikāyas as Hīnayāna or "Lesser Vehicle." Like its precursor, once established, Mahāyāna began to splinter internally. Within several hundred years, Indian Mahāyāna included the Mādhyamika school founded by Nāgārjuna, the Yogācāra school founded by Asaṅga and Vasubandhu, and the Pure Land tradition. Additionally, Indian Buddhism was shortly joined by a third school, known as Vajrayāna, focusing on the esoteric tradition. As Buddhism spread to China, the overwhelming majority of individual schools that arose were based on Mahāyāna philosophy. It was equally the case as Buddhism moved through Korea and into Japan. As such, Mahāyāna-based Buddhism predominates in East Asia. (See also HĪNAYĀNA; VAJRAYĀNA.)

⌘ MAHĀYĀNASAṂGRAHA ⌘

Famous Yogācāra text written by Asaṅga and expounding the basic philosophical tenets of the school. The title translates to "Compendium of Mahāyāna," a clear expression of the text's contents. The Sanskrit version has now been lost, but a Tibetan version and several Chinese versions remain. The text is especially well known for its exposition of the three svabhāva (i.e., "self-nature") doctrine, including the: (1) parikalpita-svabhāva or imaginary realm, (2) paratantra-svabhāva or relative reality, and (3) pariniṣpanna-svabhāva or ulitmate reality. It also considers other basic Yogācāra doctrines, such as that of the eight consciousnesses, in a comprehensive survey of the school. (See also ASAṄGA.)

⌘ MAHĀYĀNA VINAYA ⌘

Generic term highlighting those texts which outline moral practice for those pursuing the bodhisattva path. Just as the Vinaya Piṭakas of the various Hīnayāna schools describe, in great detail, the regulations governing the proper and expected moral conduct of monks and nuns, as well as their method of application, so also practitioners on the Mahāyāna path are expected to maintain the highest ethical conduct. However, since Mahāyāna does not dictate an absolutely monastic way of life, a series of texts emerged that addressed ethical conduct more generally, without specific distinction between religious professional and lay disciple. These texts can collectively be referred to as Mahāyāna Vinaya. The most well known of these texts include the Bodhicaryāvatāra and Śikṣāsamuccaya of Śāntideva, the Brahmajāla-bodhisattva-śīla-sūtra, and the Bodhisattva-prātimokṣa-sūtra. Additionally, portions of a variety of other texts address issues applicable to Mahāyāna practice. Taken together, they describe an ethical life that is the embodiment of wisdom (prajñā), compassion (karuṇā), and skill in means (upāya). (See also BODHISATTVA-ŚĪLA.)

⌘ MAHINDA ⌘

Son of the Indian king Aśoka and leader of a Buddhist missionary enterprise to Sri Lanka. Some time around 250 B.C.E., Aśoka sought to expand Buddhism from the region around Magadha, expanding it into a "world" religion. As such, he sent his son Mahinda to Sri Lanka in hopes of establishing the Dharma in the island. Mahinda converted the king, Devānaṃpiya Tissa, and received a site on the island to support a monastic unit. This site eventually developed into the Mahāvihāra or "Great Monastery." A branch of the Bodhi Tree was brought from Bodhgayā and planted in Sri Lanka as well. In a short time, a valid ordination lineage for monks was established, and the religion began to grow on the island, remaining today as a stronghold of Theravāda Buddhism.

⌘ MAITREYA ⌘

Name of the future Buddha, literally translated as "Benevolent One." Although the notion is present in virtually all the Hīnayāna schools, where they view Maitreya as a bodhisattva progressing toward Buddhahood, the notion reaches its apex in Mahāyāna, where Maitreya is depicted as a virtual cult image. He is mentioned in a wide variety of Mahāyāna sūtras, and also comes to play a major role in Vajrayāna Buddhism where his heaven is said to represent a Pure Land. He is represented by a detailed and explicit iconography, and is identified as one of the five earthly Buddhas.

⌘ MAJJHIMA NIKĀYA ⌘

The second major portion of the Sutta Piṭaka of the Pāli Canon, literally the "middle length" collection and containing 152 discourses. It corresponds to the Madhyama Āgama of the Sanskrit Buddhist canon. In the Pāli version, it is organized into three sections, the first two of which contain fifty discourses each. Further, each section is subdivided into five groups of ten discourses with the penultimate section containing the extra two discourses. An extremely wide variety of subject matter is considered in the collection, ranging from a major discourse on the establishment of mindfulness (the Satipaṭṭhāna-sutta) to a sermon on the Āryan quest (Ariyapariyesana-sutta), from a discourse with Upāli, the master of disciplinary rules (Upali-sutta) to a sermon on the analysis of the elements (Dhātuvibhaṅga-sutta). In sum, it is a miscellany of doctrinal, social, practical, and ethical sayings of the Buddha. (See also ĀGAMA; TRIPIṬAKA.)

⌘ MAKIGUCHI, TSUNESABURŌ ⌘
(1871–1944)

Founder of the Value Creation Education Society or Sōka Kyoiko Gakki, from which the Japanese Buddhist school known as Sōkagakkai later emerged. A convert to the Nichiren Shōshū school of Buddhism in 1928, Makiguchi organized his society informally in 1930 along with his disciple Josei Toda. Sōka Kyoiko Gakki was formally founded in 1937, installing Makiguchi as its first president and Toda as chairman of the Board of Directors. The organization began publishing a magazine known as *Creation of Value*, but was ordered by the government to cease its publication in May 1942. In July of the following year, Makiguchi, Toda, and a number of their disciples were arrested for refusing to take part in a nationalistic Shintō worship ceremony. Makiguchi died in prison on November 18, 1944. When Toda was paroled the following year, he rebuilt the organization he and Makiguchi had founded. On May 3, 1951, Toda was installed as second president of the newly named Nichiren Shōshū Sōkagakkai or Value Creation Society. Since then, it has become one of the strongest of the "new religions." (See also NICHIREN SHŌSHŪ SŌKAGAKKAI.)

⌘ MAKYŌ ⌘

Unusual phenomena that may arise during zazen practice in Zen. Virtually all meditative traditions involve an intensely personal inner journey. As a result of confronting all aspects of oneself, forthrightly and directly, much energy, both positive and negative, is released. The release of this energy may take the form of various kinds of sensory experiences that are either pleasant, unpleasant, or both. Such experiences may involve sounds, body movement, imagined sights, and so forth. When these makyō appear, it is critical that the practitioner remain focused and undistracted, continuing to pursue the direct experience of one's own true (Buddha) nature. (See also ZAZEN.)

⌘ MANAS ⌘

Sanskrit technical term generally translated as "mind." In the early Buddhist tradition, manas was considered one of the twelve sense-fields (āyatanas) which included six pairs of base and object. In this schemata, the manas is the mind-organ (i.e., the base) and mental input such as memory functions as the object. Due to the importance of the mind in the meditative tradition, manas was a category of particular interest to the early Buddhist psychologists and philosophers engaged in Abhidharma analysis. With the development of Mahāyāna, and especially the Yogācāra school, manas took on a new focus as one of the eight consciousnesses. Here it was considered a subtle mental element, seventh of the eight consciousnesses, that functioned by receiving and disposing of data from the six prior consciousnesses. Along with the first six consciousnesses, it represented the surface of the mind, contrasted with the eighth consciousness, known as the "storehouse consciousness" (ālaya-vijñāna) which functioned as the basis of all other mind activity. (See also ĀLAYA-VIJÑĀNA.)

⌘ MAṆḌALA ⌘

A (sacred) circle that is a symbolic representation of the world, generally associated with a particular individual. Richard Robinson and Willard Johnson refer to the maṇḍala as "a divine cosmoplan and a theophany, able to manifest divinity itself when used by the meditator as a meditative object." Maṇḍalas are depicted in two or three dimensional form, representing the universe of a particular deity. A maṇḍala has a square base, with the central deity housed at the center of the diagram. Four entrances are present, in each of the cardinal directions. Each maṇḍala also contains a number of secondary deities and images, as well as other symbolic objects. Physically, maṇḍalas are most often painted on hanging cloth scrolls known as thangkas, but sometimes cast in metal or even constructed with colored sand. As a meditative device, the practitioner visualizes himself entering the maṇḍala, and in a complex series of ritual activities, gains initiation into the divinity portrayed in the diagram. This *empowerment* is of great significance in Vajrayāna Buddhism.

⌘ MAÑJUŚRĪ ⌘

A prominent bodhisattva whose name means "Sweet Glory," and who is especially important in a number of Mahāyāna sūtras. Although present in the Lotus-sūtra, he is a primary interlocutor in the Vimalakīrti-nirdeśa-sūtra where he, of all the bodhisattvas mentioned, comes closest to the brilliance and understanding manifested by Vimalakīrti. A tenth stage bodhisattva, he is often shown iconographically holding a lotus which supports a Prajñāpāramitā text and a sword, symbolizing the wisdom he manifests in aiding sentient beings. Mañjuśrī is said to appear to people in dreams, and those worshipping him are protected by his power. He is also sometimes referred to as Mañjughoṣa ("Sweet Voiced"). In Tibetan Buddhism a number of the most prominent figures are considered incarnations of Mañjuśrī.

⌘ MANTRA ⌘

A syllable, word, or phrase which utilizes the symbolic power of sound as a means to experience things as they really are. The term mantra was first used in the Hindu Vedas to designate a verse utilized to invite deities to witness a sacrificial act. The term derives from the Sanskrit verb root √man, literally meaning "to think." As such, mantras can be seen as "mental tools." In Buddhism, mantras function as a means of manifesting power, either through a Buddha's power or the marshaling of cosmic forces, in order to protect one from evil, attain favors, or assist in generating positive meditational states. Examples of mantras from a variety of somewhat divergent Buddhist sources might include: (1) Gate, gate, pāragate, pārasaṃgate, bodhi svāhā, an enigmatic passage from the Heart Sūtra, often translated as "Gone, gone, gone beyond, gone completely beyond, O what an awakening!" (2) Namu Amida Butsu, the so-called Nembutsu of the Pure Land tradition, translated as "Homage to Amida Buddha," and (3) Oṃ maṇi padme hūṃ, rendered "Om! O jewelled lotus lady." Mantras are neither necessarily logical nor grammatical. Their efficacy comes from the power they invoke and the mental state cultivated by incessant recitation. Due to their role in Vajrayāna Buddhism, this vehicle is sometimes called the Mantrayāna. (See also NAM MYŌHŌ RENGE KYŌ; NAMU AMIDA BUTSU; NEMBUTSU.)

⌘ MAPPŌ ⌘

Japanese term indicating the "Latter Day Dharma," a period of decline in the Dharma. It was adopted from the Chinese term mo-fa, utilized by Tao-ch'o (562–645), who predicted that Pure Land practice was most suitable for a period of decline of the Dharma. By the late Heian Period in Japanese history, with disarray and decadence prevalent in the Tendai and Shingon school, many Japanese Buddhists felt that a period of decline in the Dharma had begun. Beginning with the Kamakura Period (1192–1338), conditions were thus ripe for the introduction of new Buddhist schools designed to counteract, or at least be more applicable to, a period of mappō. Consequently, the Kamakura Period witnessed the arrival of the Pure Land and Ch'an (i.e., Zen) traditions from China, as well as the formation of the Nichiren school of Buddhism. In this latter school, Nichiren saw himself as the incarnation of the bodhisattva which the Lotus-sūtra predicted would preserve the Dharma during the mappō period.

⌘ MĀRA ⌘

Evil demon and lifelong adversary of Buddha who was quite literally the personification of "Death." Māra plays a role in both the beginning and end of Buddha's spiritual quest. Just prior to his attainment of enlightenment, Siddhārtha Gautama is assailed by Māra, first through an army of demons and then through the temptation of his daughters, but he fails to prevent the bodhisattva's attainment of enlightenment. Again near the end of Buddha's life, Māra attempts to convince Buddha to pass into final nirvāṇa (referred to as parinirvāṇa). He is continually depicted as the "Tempter" in various Buddhist traditions.

⌘ MĀRGA ⌘

See ĀRYA SATYAS; EIGHTFOLD PATH

⌘ MARKS OF EXISTENCE ⌘

See ANĀTMAN; ANITYA; DUḤKHA

⌘ MAR-PA (MARPA) ⌘

(1012–1097)

Important Tibetan Buddhist regarded as the founder of the bKa-rgyud-pa school of Tibetan Buddhism. As a married householder who was skilled in Sanskrit, Mar-pa went to India on three occasions in search of Dharma instruction. On his first visit he met a great master named Nāropa under whom he trained for many years at Nālandā. Following a second visit to India, he took Mi-las ras-pa as his disciple. On his third visit, late in life, Mar-pa met Nāropa a final time, and also met the famed teacher Atīśa (982–1054) who came to Tibet in 1042. Mar-pa is credited with bringing the Mahāmudra teaching to Tibet, as well as the "Six Dharmas of Nāropa." Sometimes called "The Translator," the bKa-rgyud-pa school of Tibetan Buddhism begins its lineage with Mar-pa. (See also BKA-RGYUD-PA; MI-LAS RAS-PA.)

⌘ MA-TSU TAO-I ⌘

(709–788)

Third generation leader of the Ch'an school of Hui-nêng. He was an immediate disciple of and only Dharma heir to Nan-yüeh Huai-jang (677–744). Along with Shih-t'ou Hsi-ch'ien (700–790), he is regarded as an originator of one of the two main lineages of the "Southern School" of Ch'an. Ma-tsu was regarded as the foremost master "west of the river" or in the provinces of Chiang-shi while Shih-t'ou was master "south of the lake" or around Hunan. He was the only Ch'an master in the period after Hui-nêng to be called a patriarch. He utilized a variety of methods to assist his disciples in realizing their own true natures and in attaining enlightenment. Sometimes this involved a shout, or gesture, or blow with a stick, but in each case it was designed to overcome ordinary, conceptual thinking. Although Ma-tsu had many Dharma heirs, his most famous was Pai-chang Huai-hai

(720–814), best known as the proponent of a series a rules used to regulate daily life and conduct in Chinese Buddhist monasteries. (See also SHIH-T'OU HSI-CH'IEN.)

⌘ MAURYAN DYNASTY ⌘

Period of Indian history from around 324–187 B.C.E. which highlighted great Buddhist growth and influence. Beginning with Candragupta, the Mauryan Dynasty commenced, with rule passing to his son Bindusāra, and then to King Aśoka. It was during this dynasty that Buddhism spread beyond its Indian borders, primarily through the missionary efforts of Aśoka. Of special importance was the conversion of Sri Lanka and its integral role in preserving the Theravāda tradition. Buddhism became thoroughly sectarian during this period, which also witnessed an increasing interest in philosophical matters and a careful development of the ecclesiastic order. A famous council was held at Pāṭaliputra during the reign of Aśoka, in an attempt to preserve Aśoka's version of the "orthodox" tradition. Despite the outcome of the council, it was only to be a short period before Buddhism experienced the development of a radical new movement that called itself Mahāyāna or "Greater Vehicle" Buddhism around the end of the Mauryan Dynasty. (See also AŚOKA.)

⌘ MĀYĀ ⌘

Queen of King Śuddhodana and birth mother to Siddhārtha Guatama, the historical Buddha. Queen Māyā is said to have conceived the child in a dream filled with mythological overtones, delivered the child from her right side while standing upright in Lumbinī Garden, and died seven days following delivery as is the tradition for mothers of Buddhas. Following her death, the king married her sister Mahāprajāpatī, thus providing a foster mother for Siddhārtha Gautama.

⌘ MEDITATION ⌘

See BHĀVANĀ

⌘ MEIJI RESTORATION ⌘

Movement begun in 1868 that marked the end of the military control of Japan by the samurai. The movement was spurred on by a Shintō nationalistic effort that essentially opposed Buddhism. It brought with it an initial Buddhist persecution that was rather quickly tempered. To some degree Buddhism became more secularized and modern, celibacy became the exception rather than the rule for monks, and lay organizations abounded. Additionally, it set the stage for what eventually became known as the "new religions" in Japan.

⌘ MENPEKI ⌘

Japanese Buddhist term literally meaning "wall facing." Menpeki describes the Zen practice of doing zazen while facing a blank wall. The classic prototype of the practice was Bodhidharma's purported nine years of wall facing, often illustrated in Ch'an art. In modern Zen, it is rather traditional for Sōtō practitioners to do zazen facing a wall while Rinzai adepts face the center of the meditation hall or zendō. (See also ZAZEN.)

⌘ MIDDLE WAY ⌘

A descriptive term applied to the teaching of Siddhārtha Gautama, the historical Buddha. Technically described as madhyamāpratipad, it means clearly different things to different schools of Buddhism. In the earliest tradition, it referred to Buddha's path through the extremes of life, a rejection of sensuous abundance and of serious austerity. It suggested that the fourth noble truth, that of the eightfold path, offered a middle course that would carry the serious practitioner to nirvāṇa. In the Mahāyāna tradition, the phrase is most often applied as a descriptive title of the school of thought begun by Nāgārjuna, that of Mādhyamika, the "Middle Path." The notion was also utilized by other Mahāyāna schools, particularly the Yogācāra. In modern times, the phrase has fallen prey to use as a rather sloppy generic term for all of Buddhism, irrespective of doctrinal position.

⌘ MI-LAS RAS-PA (MILAREPA) ⌘
(1040–1123)

Famous disciple of Mar-pa whose name means "Cotton-Clad Mila," and who is regarded as the greatest poet-saint in Tibetan Buddhism. While his early life is interesting, it is overshadowed by those events prior to and after he becomes Mar-pa's student.

He becomes Mar-pa's student in middle age, initially acting only as his servant. Mi-las ras-pa is subjected to a seemingly enormous number of tests and trials by the master for six years *prior* to receiving any significant Dharma instruction. He eventually receives teaching from Mar-pa, particularly concentrating on the "Six Dharmas of Nāropa," and becomes the second patriarch of the bKa-rgyud-pa lineage. Mi-las ras-pa spent many years living alone in the caves of the Himalayas, only gradually accepting disciples. During this period of solitude, he composed many songs reflecting teaching. These he shared with his closest disciple sGam-po-pa (1079–1153) who organized the bKa-rgyud-pa school and founded its first monasteries. (See also BKA-RGYUD-PA; MAR-PA; SGAM-PO-PA.)

⌘ MILINDAPAÑHA ⌘

Important noncanonical Theravāda text whose title translates to "The Questions of King Milinda," and which contains a running dialogue between the monk Nāgasena and the Bactrian King Menander. It is valuable not only because it documents one of the early encounters between Buddhist and Hellenistic cultures, but because it *also* focuses on a wide variety of issues that were critical for a thorough and accurate understanding of Theravāda Buddhism. A number of profoundly important dilemmas are considered in the dialogue, including how rebirth occurs in the absence of an ātman or soul, what truth is, why moral people encounter suffering while apparently evil people prosper, why suicide is not a valid antidote to earthly suffering, why philosophical discussion is not profitable, why textual materials appear to present contradictory contents, and a host of others. Often using extremely insightful similes, Nāgasena responds to all questions masterfully, resolving the king's concerns one by one. Legend has it that, following his encounter with Nāgasena, Menander abdicated his throne, leaving his son to rule, and joined the Buddhist saṃgha. (See also NĀGASENA.)

⌘ MISSIONS ⌘

Buddhist ventures into various regions, intended as an attempt to spread the Dharma beyond the current sphere of influence. As a religious tradition, Buddhism has a long and complicated his tory of missionary activity beginning with that undertaken by the Indian king Aśoka in the third century B.C.E. Other kings and rulers in various Buddhist cultures throughout Asia have followed this pattern in expanding the Dharma. Kaniṣka, for example, following Aśoka's example, expanded the Dharma in Central Asia. Equally, Mahāyāna Buddhism moved between East Asian countries repeatedly, as Theravāda missions moved freely in the countries of South Asia. It is important though to separate true *missions* from attempts at conquest or simple pilgrimages. Following a dearth of mid-millennium activity, Buddhism in the modern world has once again adopted a missionary framework, eagerly exporting itself to all corners of the globe. Consequently, it is now rather usual to find Tibetan Buddhist groups from all four major schools, Japanese Buddhist groups from a variety of Zen traditions, as well as Pure Land groups, eclectic Chinese Buddhist groups, and Theravāda communities from a variety of South Asian countries in the United States, Canada, Great Britain, South America, Australia, Africa, and the individual countries of continental Europe. The missions are so active that it is nearly impossible to track them accurately or establish any meaningful demographic data. Nonetheless, the above is a clear signal that Buddhists are maintaining an active missionary stance in the modern world. (See also AŚOKA.)

⌘ MONASTERY ⌘

See ĀRĀMA; ĀVĀSA; VIHĀRA

⌘ MONDŌ ⌘

Japanese term literally meaning "question and answer," describing the interchange that occurs in Zen between master and student or between masters. The questions usually concern some aspect of Buddhism and are designed to elicit responses reflecting the respondent's true or deepest understanding of the subject. It is by no means an intellectual discourse, but rather a spontaneous dialogue reflecting existential concerns.

⌘ MONK ⌘

See BHIKṢU; SAṂGHA

⌘ MOXA ⌘

Japanese Buddhist practice of burning small scars into the head of an ordinand. Adapted from a similar Chinese custom,

Japanese monks and nuns often had scars burned into their heads by placing a cone of incense on their scalp and igniting it at the end of their formal ordination ceremony. The particular number of scars varied, depending on the inclination of each monastic institution. Although the procedure is considered to be extremely painful, it is nonetheless widespread in practice.

⌘ MU ⌘

A negative syllable whose actual meaning is "no" or "nothing," but which is used in a positive sense as a Zen kōan. Its use apparently derives from an episode in Chinese Buddhism in which a Ch'an master asks Ma-tsu's disciple Chao-chou Ts'ung-shen (778–897) whether a *dog* has Buddha nature. Chao-chou's answer is "Wu!" the Chinese equivalent of the Japanese syllable Mu. It represents a spontaneous answer demonstrating Chao-chou's enlightenment. In Zen, the disciple who is charged with solving the Mu kōan must utilize his zazen practice to break conceptual thought patterns, transcend intellectual reasoning, and experience reality directly. Only then will he be able to understand Mu with the immediacy and totality required by his master's charge. (See also KŌAN.)

⌘ MUDRĀ ⌘

A "seal" or "sign" made with the hand(s) or body and intended to *symbolically* represent some aspect of Buddhist teaching. These symbolic representations became important in Mahāyāna Buddhism and critical in the esoteric Vajrayāna tradition. They traditionally involve liturgical recitation of mantras and relate to particular visualizations desired by the practitioner in developing advanced meditational states. There are numerous mudrās used in Buddhism, a number of which include the: (1) Dhyāni mudrā, in which the right palm rests on the left palm with both thumbs formed into a circle, lightly touching; often seen by practitioners in meditative posture, and generally associated with Amitābha; (2) Dharmacakra mudrā, in which the thumb and forefinger of each hand are joined, with the left palm facing inward to the body and the right palm facing outward, and with the circles formed by the thumb and forefinger of each hand touching each other; associated with a number of Buddhas, including Śākyamuni; and (3) Añjali mudrā, in which both palms are placed together and held at chest level; utilized as a gesture of respect or greeting. There are many others, each having a specific function and application.

⌘ MŪLAMADHYAMAKA-KĀRIKĀS ⌘

Sanskrit text attributed to Nāgārjuna and established as the basis for the Mādhyamika school of Indian Buddhism. Most scholars place Nāgārjuna in the time between 150 and 250 C.E., establishing his major text as relatively early in Mahāyāna history. The text title literally translates to "Root Verses on the Middle Way," and presumably reflects Nāgārjuna's personal description of his philosophical stance. The text itself is divided into twenty-seven very short chapters including a total of about 450 verses. It is a polemical treatise which refutes the views of other Buddhist (particularly Sarvāstivādin and Sautrāntika) and non-Buddhist schools. His method of refutation, the *reductio ad absurdum* argument, called prasaṅga in Sanskrit, became the hallmark of the text. Nāgārjuna used this method to defeat his opponents' arguments in terms of *their own* assumptions. The text insists on a strict application of the notion of emptiness (śūnyatā) as an epistemological tool designed to avoid the presumption that any *dharma* or "building block of reality" can have a fixed, permanent own-being (svabhāva). Chapter 13, verses 7–8, insist that even emptiness is empty, and that an individual who turns emptiness into a *viewpoint* is "incurable." Perhaps the highlight of the text, in which it establishes Mahāyāna's primary philosophical position, is Chapter 24, verse 18, in which Nāgārjuna maintains that, "It is dependent origination (pratītya-samutpāda) that we call emptiness." He goes on to say in the next verse that since no *dharma* exists independently, no *dharma exists which is not empty*. This latter point has enormous implications for Buddhist theory and practice. The importance of the text can, at least in part, be measured by the sizable number of commentaries it provoked, spanning several centuries. (See also NĀGĀRJUNA.)

⌘ MÜLLER, FRIEDRICH MAX ⌘
(1823–1900)

German Indologist who, as editor of the *Sacred Books of the East* series, was active in publishing translations of Buddhist texts, and who published some interesting if inexact research of his own on Buddhism. Following his doctorate from Leipzig in 1843, he studied Sanskrit and philosophy at Berlin, eventually leaving for Paris in 1845. There he met Eugène Burnouf who fueled Müller's interest in Indology. Müller also learned Pāli, and set about to conduct research on Theravāda Buddhism. Although renowned for his work in the history of religions, Müller was never able to move beyond two concerns which, unfortunately, inaccurately colored his overall view of Buddhism for the rest of his life: (1) his presumption that Buddhism was a nihilistic religion, and (2) his inability to understand the concept of nirvāṇa. There is little evidence to indicate that Müller read very many Buddhist canonical texts beyond the Dhammapada (which he translated from Pāli), and he is affectionately referred to in scholarly circles as an "armchair scholar" who never actually *visited* the Buddhist cultures he studied and wrote about. While the above seriously discredits the value of his judgments about Buddhism, it does not diminish his role as an important facilitator in bringing translations of many Buddhist texts to print for the first time.

⌘ MUMONKAN ⌘

See WU-MÊN-KUAN

— N —

⌘ NĀGĀRJUNA ⌘

Indian Buddhist scholar who lived sometime between 150 and 250 C.E., and who is the founder of the important Mahāyāna school known as Mādhyamika. As a philosopher, Nagarjuna is best known for the Buddhist texts attributed to him. His most famous text is the Mūlamadhyamaka-kārikās, a twenty-seven chapter text that includes approximately 450 verses and establishes the basis of Nāgārjuna's philosophy. He is also credited with writing the Dvādaśa-dvāra-śāstra, a text discussing the notion of emptiness (śūnyatā) in twelve headings, the Vigrahavyāvartanī, an attack on the logical school of Nyāya, the Mahāprajñāpāramitā-upadeśa-śāstra, a voluminous text extant only in Chinese (but perhaps *not* written by Nāgārjuna), the Suhṛllekha or

"Friendly Epistle" written to an Indian king, and a large variety of ancillary texts. The basic method utlized by Nāgārjuna is the *reductio ad absurdum* approach in which Nāgārjuna dismantles his opponents on the basis of *their own* arguments while offering his critics no opportunity to utilize the same approach on his work. The underlying theme of all Nāgārjuna's writings is that of emptiness, as established in the Prajñāpāramitā tradition. He is a thoroughgoing Mahāyānist in rejecting any notion of own-being (svabhāva), continually emphasizing what he calls the "middle way," and insisting that dependent origination, Buddha's theory of causality, is the clearest expression of the doctrine of emptiness. Although he was presumably a bodhisattva of high attainment, Nāgārjuna says little about this aspect of the Buddhist path, focusing instead on the indentity of nirvāṇa and saṃsāra, which he maintains to be two forms of the same reality. Nāgārjuna's writings, and the Mādhyamika school, had deep influence not only on later Indian Buddhism but also Buddhist schools in China, Japan, and Tibet. (See also MĀDHYAMIKA; MŪLAMADHYAMAKA-KĀRIKĀS.)

⌘ NĀGASENA ⌘

Theravāda monk who is the central figure in the famous Buddhist text known as the Milindapañha. Cast as the learned Buddhist authority in the Milindapañha or "The Questions of King Milinda," Nāgasena responds with brilliance to all the questions posed by the Bactrian king Menander, the major interlocutor of the text. Presumably from a Brahmin family, and having joined the saṃgha in his teens, Nāgasena is supposed to have lived around the first century C.E. He handles questions on philosophical dilemmas such as how rebirth occurs in the absence of a soul, on ethical concerns like why suicide is an unacceptable choice for the elimination of suffering, and a host of other matters in which similes are utilized in an extremely penetrating fashion to elucidate the fundamental Buddhist position. King Menander is reputed to have joined the saṃgha following his encounter with Nāgasena. (See also MILINDAPAÑHA.)

⌘ NAGATOMI, MASATOSHI ⌘

Buddhist studies professor at Harvard University's Yenching Institute who was considered to be among the foremost scholars of Buddhism in the United States. Having a career at Harvard spanning several decades, Professor Nagatomi had language facility and a breadth of knowledge matched by few scholars worldwide. Although he had been especially interested in Buddhist logic, he was equally at home working on the disciplinary texts of the monastic tradition as with the texts of Dharmakīrti. He worked closely with the Center for the Study of World Religions at Harvard in developing some of the finest young Buddhologists of the past two decades. In addition to his brilliant mind and extremely diligent pursuit of furthering the study of Buddhism, he was regarded as one of the most compassionate preceptors, willing to extend himself far beyond what is normally considered usual in academe for his students' progress and future. He also held a number of administrative positions in professional organizations, and was especially active in the American Academy of Religion.

⌘ NAKAGAWA SŌEN RŌSHI ⌘
(1908–1983)

Japanese Rinzai master, important for his influence on both Japanese *and* American Zen. Nakagawa Sōen Rōshi was the Dharma heir to Yamamoto Gempo (1865–1901), and was abbot of Ryūtaku-ji monastery for many years. Through the efforts of one of his good freinds, Nyogen Senzaki (1876–1958), Nakagawa Sōen Rōshi was persuaded to visit America many times, beginning in 1949. Sōen Rōshi in turn brought his Dharma heir Eido Tai Shimano Rōshi to America and, as a result, the Zen Studies Society was founded in New York in 1965 (now having a number of important affiliates).

⌘ NAKAMURA, HAJIME ⌘
(b. 1912)

Eminent Japanese Buddhologist who is among the world's leading authorities on Indian Buddhism. Although he has published many articles in both Japanese and Western language journals, he is especially well known for his 1980 volume *Indian Buddhism: A Survey with Bibliographical Notes*. It is really not so much a survey as it is an extremely comprehensive, annotated bibliography that brings together the best Asian and Western scholarship on the subject. His viewpoints on matters of textual scholarship are profoundly valuable and insightful for students and scholars alike.

⌘ NĀLANDĀ ⌘

Buddhist university in India, founded initially as a monastery by Śakrāditya, king of Magadha. It was a great center of Mahāyāna thought, noted for its extensive library and its congregation of Mādhyamika scholars. Not only was it a home for famous Buddhist teachers like Dignāga, but it was also a place of learning attractive to visiting pilgrims. As such, scholars like Hsüan-tsang and I-ching studied there before returning to China with texts and teaching. It eventually became something of a pipeline for importing Buddhist ideas and scholars to Tibet, an association which dramatically influenced Tibetan Buddhism for centuries. Nālandā was eventually destroyed by Muslim invaders.

⌘ NAM MYŌHŌ RENGE KYŌ ⌘

Japanese formula known as the daimoku which literally means "Homage to the Scripture of the Lotus of the Good Teaching." It was felt by the Japanese Buddhist innovator Nichiren (1222–1282) that the Lotus-sūtra was the most complete Buddhist text, the only one capable of leading Buddhists to salvation in the period of Dharma decline known as mappō. Consequently, Nichiren advised repeating the phrase Nam Myōhō Renge Kyō again and again both as an expression of faith in the Lotus-sūtra and as a vehicle in itself for facilitating enlightenment. It was adopted as part of the liturgy of the radically militant offshoot of Nichiren's school of Buddhism known as Sōkagakkai or the "Value Creation Society." As such it is employed as a mantra of empowerment thought to bring material rewards in the ordinary world as well as religious fruits. (See also DAIMOKU; NICHIREN; NICHIREN SHŌSHŪ SŌKAGAKKAI.)

⌘ NAMU AMIDA BUTSU ⌘

Japanese formula known as the nembutsu, literally meaning "Homage to Amida Buddha," and important in the Pure Land schools. As Pure Land Buddhism developed in India, China, and Japan, faith was placed in the saving grace of Amida (Sanskrit:

Amitābha; Chinese: A-mi-t'o) Buddha. As the abiding doctrinal tenet of the tradition, this faith was externally expressed in the mantric formula Namu Amida Butsu, repeated again and again by adherents of the belief. If properly recited, and with an appropriate mental perspective, it was felt that adepts could be reborn in the Western Paradise of Amida, from which salvation was more readily attainable. In China the practice was called nien-fo. It was felt that chanting of the nembutsu was the most effective Buddhist practice for individuals in a period of Dharma decline (mappō). (See also NEMBUTSU.)

⌘ NARA PERIOD ⌘

Period of Japanese history (710–784) when the capital was established at Nara, and during which Buddhism experienced much growth. Following almost two centuries of presence in Japan, during the Nara Period Buddhism included primarily the Jōjitsu, Kusha, Sanron, Hossō, Ritsu, and Kegon traditions. These groups were primarily academic in their approach to Buddhism. Under Emperor Shōmu, many Buddhist temples were erected, the most notable being Tōdai-ji, chief location of the Kegon school. Buddhist monks were influential at court during this period of Japanese history, with the resulting association between saṃgha and state provoking much internal political intrigue. The Taihō reforms of 702 sought to combat this uncertainty by including the saṃgha as a governmental department. By the conclusion of the Nara Period, Buddhism had expanded its initial influence significantly, gaining a foothold that was to be developed still further in successive periods of Japanese history.

⌘ NĀRO CHOS-DRUG (NĀRO CHÖDRUG) ⌘

The "Six Dharmas of Nāropa," a set of Vajrayāna doctrines taught to Nāropa by his guru Tilopa. These teachings were in turn transmitted to Mar-pa, Nāropa's student, who brought them to Tibet where they became an instrumental part of the bKa-rgyud-pa school of Buddhism. The six teachings include: (1) the product of inner heat, (2) experience of one's body as illusory, (3) the dream state, (4) clear light perception, (5) the in-between (rebirth) state, and (6) consciousness transference. When properly practiced, the "Six Dharmas of Nāropa" lead to the attainment of supernormal powers known as siddhi. (See also NĀROPA.)

⌘ NĀROPA ⌘

Vajrayāna practitioner and disciple of Tilopa who was instrumental in the development of Tibetan Buddhism through the teachings he imparted to his student Mar-pa. He was a scholar turned yogi, having abandoned his position at Nālandā university in order to pursue training under Tilopa. It was through Nāropa that Mar-pa received the Mahāmudrā teaching, as well as that set of teachings known as the "Six Dharmas of Nāropa." As a result of his association with Mar-pa, Nāropa is regarded as a critical figure in the bKa-rgyud-pa school of Tibetan Buddhism. (See also MAR-PA; TILOPA.)

⌘ NEMBUTSU ⌘

Japanese term for a mantra utilized in the Pure Land schools as an expression of faith in the saving grace of Amida Buddha (Sanskrit: Amitābha; Chinese A-mi-t'o). The nembutsu constitutes the primary religious practice in the Pure Land tradition for individuals hoping to be reborn in the Pure Land of Amida Buddha. Considered by its proponents to be the most effective religious practice in times of Dharma decline (mappō), it consists of a repetition of the formula Namu Amida Butsu or "Homage to Amida Buddha." It is an expression of tariki or "other-power," literally placing one's faith for salvation outside of one's *own* attainment, a practice which is sometimes contrasted with the notion of jiriki or "self-power" in Zen. Although cited in Japanese here, it has both a Sanskrit and Chinese counterpart (known as Nien-fo). (See also NAMU AMIDA BUTSU.)

⌘ NICHIREN ⌘
(1222–1282)

Founder of a Japanese Buddhist school named after him and professing the belief that salvation could be attained by reciting the name of the Lotus-sūtra. Born into a fisherman's family, Nichiren was ordained at age fifteen, and like many famous Buddhist figures before him, went to study at the Tendai monastic complex on Mt. Hiei. While he was critical of the other Buddhist schools of the time, he felt that the Tendai tradition came closest to the true Buddhist message. However, he felt that even this tradition had minimized emphasis on the Lotus-sūtra, which he felt was the most important scripture of the school, causing him to leave Mt. Hiei in favor of a monastery closer to his home. He set about to personally save Japan from the social and political ruin that he was certain would result from practicing the "wrong" religion espoused by the traditional Buddhist sects. He even predicted an invasion of Japan. As a result, he professed the notion that the Lotus-sūtra was the *only* Buddhist text suited to religious practice in a time of Dharma decline (mappō), and that recitation of its title was the means to liberation. The religious practice cultivated by Nichiren involved recitation of the phrase Nam Myōhō Renge Kyō or "Homage to the Scripture of the Lotus of the Good Teaching," while gazing at a diagram known as the gohonzon, a maṇḍala-like form with the above words inscribed on it. His revolutionary notions and approach resulted in his exile, and he was not allowed to return to Kamakura until 1274, following an attempted Mongol invasion that Nichiren felt vindicated him. A Buddhist school known as the Nichiren-shū grew up around the figure of Nichiren, emphasizing both his emphasis on the efficacy of the Lotus-sūtra and his extreme sense of Japanese nationalism. (See also DAIMOKU; GOHONZON; LOTUS-SŪTRA; NAM MYŌHŌ RENGE KYŌ; NICHIREN SHŌSHŪ SŌKAGAKKAI.)

⌘ NICHIREN SHŌSHŪ SŌKAGAKKAI ⌘

Radical, modern, militant offshoot of the Nichiren School of Japanese Buddhism. Founded by Tsunesaburō Makiguchi as the Value Creation Education Society, informally in 1930 with his disciple Josei Toda, and formally in 1937, this Japanese "new religion" later changed its name to the present Value Creation Society or Nichiren Shōshū Sōkagakkai in 1951. Politically aggressive, ostensibly campaigning for world peace, and promising material wealth to its constituents, the group emphasizes the practice of chanting the daimoku (i.e., Nam Myōhō Renge Kyō) while staring at the maṇḍala-like gohonzon. Under the leadership of its current president, Daisaku Ikeda, it has become a world religion, having made great missionary strides in Africa, Europe, and the Americas. (See also IKEDA, DAISAKU; MAKIGUCHI, TSUNESABURŌ; NICHIREN.)

⌘ NIEN-FO ⌘

See NEMBUTSU

⌘ NIKĀYA ⌘

Pāli and Sanskrit term generally rendered as "collection" or "group," and most often applied to collections of scriptures or individual Buddhist groups. In the composite of Theravāda scriptures known as the Pāli Canon, each of the individual "collections" of texts in the Sutta Piṭaka or "Basket of Discourses" is referred to as a Nikāya. Thus there is a Dīgha Nikāya, Majjhima Nikāya, Saṃyutta Nikāya, Aṅguttara Nikāya, and Khuddaka Nikāya. In its other major use as a descriptive label for individual Buddhist groups, nikāya is a specific term indicating a particular Buddhist sect. The Theravāda sect, for example, may be called the Theravāda nikāya. In modern scholarly literature, nikāya has served as a reasonable antidote to identifying a given sect as belonging to one of the so-called Hīnayāna, Mahāyāna, or Vajrayāna schools of Buddhism, as each of these generic titles can be viewed as pejorative by members of one of the other groups. In other words, members of the Sarvāstivādin school of Buddhism would hardly be fond of identifying themselves as Hīnayānist or *Lesser Vehicle* Buddhists as the Mahāyāna schools would choose to cite them. To utilize the designation *Sarvāstivādin nikāya* avoids the problem. It might be postulated that the terms Hīnayāna, Mahāyāna, and Vajrayāna could be employed as *historical* indicators rather than as *evaluative* designations, thus circumventing the problem, but this alternative has not been very effective, or readily implemented, in Buddhist literature.

⌘ NIRMĀṆA-KĀYA ⌘

"Apparition-Body," first of the three bodies of the Buddha in Mahāyāna, and used to represent the physical form of Śākyamuni Buddha. Developed most fully in the Laṇkāvatāra-sūtra, this idea of three forms of representing Buddha comes to maturity in the Yogācāra school. It suggests that the nirmāṇa-kāya or "apparitional body" is visible to ordinary individuals as an inspiration to begin the (Mahāyāna) Buddhist path. Once on the bodhisattva path, the nirmāṇa-kāya gives way to Buddha in another form: a quasi-physical preacher of Mahāyāna sūtras known as the saṃbhoga-kāya or "enjoyment body." Finally, when the path is completed, one attains the Dharma-kāya or "Dharma body," ultimate reality itself, the true nature of Buddhahood. In other words, each of the three bodies of Buddha speaks to an individual at a different level of spiritual development. Insofar as the student *begins* his training by personal inspiration in the rather concrete form of a physical teacher, the nirmāṇa-kāya is especially important. (See also TRIKĀYA.)

⌘ NIRVĀṆA ⌘

Sanskrit term for the goal of Buddhist religious practice. Etymologically, the word reflects a derivation from the Sanskrit prefix nir + $\sqrt{}$ vā, literally meaning "to be blown out" or "to be extinguished," "to be calmed" or "to be cooled." Depending on one's orientation, both from within Buddhism and from without, the term can be interpreted from a variety of perspectives. From the vantage point of early Buddhism, nirvāṇa (or its Pāli counterpart nibbāna) seems to have reflected a cessation of duḥkha or suffering and a simple termination of rebirth in saṃsāra. Within the various Hīnayāna nikāyas, there are differences of opinion about the specifics of nirvāṇa and just *who* achieves it. For the majority of early Buddhist schools which dutifully adhere to the anātman or "not-self" doctrine, the question of *precisely who or what experiences nirvāṇa* is a vital question, one that is presumably not answered by Buddha Śākyamuni, reflective of his concern for not speculating about philosophical issues. For the cluster of sects known by the collective term Pudgalavāda or "Personalists," they would offer a much different response, arguing that indeed it is the *individual* who experiences nirvāṇa. For Mahāyāna schools, emphasizing a bodhisattva path based on wisdom (prajñā) and compassion (karuṇā), nirvāṇa appears as a *selfish, individual* goal pursued by Hīnayānists, and should thus be *rejected* until all sentient beings can attain complete, perfect enlightenment. Further, a new meaning is attributed to the term, linking it to ultimate reality, and utilizing the concept of emptiness (śūnyatā) to suggest that nirvāṇa and saṃsāra are not ontologically different states, but rather differing ways of experiencing the same reality. Like their Hīnayāna counterparts, individual Mahāyāna sects also interpret the term differently. The problem is further complicated by external interpreters of the term, many of whom have neither the philological acumen or doctrinal perspective to understand the concept contextually in Buddhism. As such, nirvāṇa was often understood by early scholars as a simple *annihilation*, causing them to depict Buddhism as a profoundly *nihilistic* religious system. In light of the varied, colorful, inexact, and sometimes even malicious explications of the term, it makes Buddha's reported silence about the specifics of the term appear quite wise.

⌘ NŌ ⌘

Japanese form of drama, often reflecting Zen ideals. Originated by Zeami Motokiyo (1363–1444), this drama form combines dance, recitation, and song, making it a complete aesthetic experience that demonstrates those qualities of experience at the heart of Zen training. It is formal, slow, and precise, just the sort of encounter Zen trainees receive in their initial monastic exercises. (See also ZEN.)

⌘ NOBLE PERSONS ⌘

See ĀRYA-PUDGALA; ĀRYA-SAṂGHA

⌘ NON-INJURY ⌘

See AHIṂSĀ

⌘ NOT-SELF ⌘

See ANĀTMAN

⌘ NUN ⌘

See BHIKṢUṆĪ; SAṂGHA

⌘ NYĀNATILOKA ⌘
(1878–1957)

One of the best-known *Western* converts to Buddhism. Born Anton Walter Florus Gueth in Wiesbaden, Germany, he discovered Buddhism while studying music in Frankfurt following his college education. A talented violinist, he accepted an engagement which ultimately led him first to India and later to Sri Lanka. After a short stay in Sri Lanka, he traveled on to Burma where he became an ordained Buddhist monk in 1903. Returning to Sri Lanka, in 1911 he established a hermitage on the southwest coast of the island. Although he quickly became quite famous, ordaining many (especially European) monks, he contributed a number of important books to Buddhist literature, including a translation of Buddhaghosa's Visuddhimagga, *Guide through the Abhidhamma Piṭaka, The Word of the Buddha, Buddhist Dictionary,* and a number of others. He played an important role in planning the sixth Theravāda council, held in Rangoon in 1954, and was made a distinguished citizen by the Sri Lankan government in 1957.

— O —

⌘ ŌBAKU SCHOOL ⌘

One of the three major schools of Zen (along with Rinzai and Sōtō) in Japan. It was founded by the Chinese master Yin-yüan Lung-ch'i (d. 1673), known as Ingen Ryūki in Japanese, who visited Japan in 1654 when he was already more than sixty years old. He first stayed at Kōfuku-ji temple in Nagasaki, but quickly moved on to Kyoto. There he established the chief temple of his sect (Ōbakusan Mampuku-ji). Although a number of monks who had accompanied Yin-yüan returned to China, new monks arrived, among them Mu-an Hsing-t'ao (Japanese: Mokuan Shōtō), who founded Zuishō-ji temple near Tokyo. Although the school eventually developed a more Japanese character, it lost most of its influence, currently being the *least* influential of the Zen groups in Japan. (See also ZEN.)

⌘ OLCOTT, HENRY STEELE ⌘
(1832–1907)

Co-founder, with Madame H. P. Blavatsky, of the Theosophical Society, and longtime champion of Buddhist causes. Born in New Jersey, Colonel Olcott had a checkered career that included service in the U.S. Army, time spent as a successful criminal attorney, and work as a journalist. He met Madame Blavatsky in 1875, and within the year they founded the Theosophical Society. After establishing headquarters in India in 1879, he traveled to Sri Lanka in 1880, taking refuge in Buddhism on his arrival in Colombo. He worked diligently to promote Buddhist schools in Sri Lanka under the sponsorship of an organization he called the Colombo Buddhist Theosophical Society. At its height, the organization ran over 400 schools. He also formulated a Buddhist catechism of fourteen principles that was widely circulated in Buddhist countries.

⌘ OLDENBERG, HERMANN ⌘
(1854–1920)

Early German scholar of Buddhism regarded as one of the foremost authorities on Theravāda in continental Europe, and editor and translator of many important Buddhist texts. The son of a Protestant clergyman, Oldenberg studied Sanskrit and philology, earning his doctorate from Berlin in 1875. During his career, he held professorial appointments at Berlin, Kiel, and Göttingen. He eventually distinguished himself as a Pāli scholar, editing and translating the Dīpavaṃsa (1979) and editing the five volumes of the Vinaya Piṭaka (1879–1883). Perhaps his most significant contribution to the study of Buddhism is his classic volume *The Buddha, His Life, His Doctrine, His Community* (1881). Along with Thomas W. Rhys Davids, he was considered at the forefront of what has become known as the "Anglo-German School" of Buddhological scholarship. Toward the end of his life (1912) he visited India, long after his scholarly vision had been established.

⌘ ORDINATION ⌘

Act of establishing membership in the monastic component of the Buddhist saṃgha. The ritual act of ordination is open to members of both genders in Buddhism, but is an explicit, legal act of the saṃgha, and as such, requires certain formal, canonically dictated procedures. The actual ordination process is preceded not only by the stated *voluntary* intention of the ordinand but also by meeting certain established prerequisites regarding age, status, health, and so forth. In Hīnayāna Buddhism, two types of ordination are available: (1) Initiation as a *novice* (śrāmaṇera for males, śrāmaṇerī for females), at which time the ordinand repeats the threefold refuge formula (triratna), agrees to uphold ten specific rules of conduct (daśa śīla), is required to follow the monastic code embodied in a text called the Prātimokṣa, and is assigned two instructors known as the "teacher" (ācārya) and "preceptor" (upādhyāya). At that time the novice has his head shaved, receives his three robes, and is given a begging bowl. The first ordination is referred to as pravrajyā, literally "going forth." After age twenty, a member of the monastic community can ask for (2) higher ordination as a monk (bhikṣu) or nun (bhikṣuṇī). Higher ordination, carrying with it the full rights and responsibilities of an adult member of the monastic community, is referred to as upasaṃpadā. Each of the two ordinations described above *are not considered lifelong commitments.* At any time, a monk or nun may voluntarily elect to leave the monastic community and return to lay life. In Mahāyāna, a third type of ordination appears, that of the bodhisattva ordination, on which occasion the ordinand takes the formal vow of the bodhisattva: to gain complete, perfect enlightenment for the sake of all sentient beings.

⌘ ŌRYŌ SCHOOL ⌘

Rinzai Zen school originating from the Chinese Ch'an school of Huang-lung Hui-nan (1001–1069). The school disappeared in China before the end of the Sung Period. It was, however, brought to Japan by Eisai Zenji (1141–1215). It represents the first Zen school in Japan, and is counted among the Goke-Shichishū or the "five houses and seven schools" of Zen. It died out rather quickly in Japan. (See also ZEN.)

— P —

⌘ PADMASAMBHAVA ⌘

Tantric Mahāsiddha from Kaśmīr who came to Tibet in the late eighth century and was instrumental in the develpment of early Tibetan Buddhism. When King Khri-srong-lde-bstan (755–797) wanted to found a Buddhist monastery during his reign, Padmasambhava was invited to Tibet to exorcise the demons of the indigenous Bön religion from around the site. This being accomplished, the monastery of bSam-yas was established sometime around 787, on a site about thirty miles from Lhasa. It is difficult to estimate exactly how long Padmasambhava actually stayed in Tibet, but he had a profound impact on the Buddhist tradition there, generally being regarded as the founder of the rNying-ma-pa school of Tibetan Buddhism. He is still revered by this school under the name Guru Rinpoche. During his stay in Tibet, Padmasambhava hid a great many authoritative texts called Terma (gter-ma) of the rNying-ma-pa school which he expected to be discovered in the future to be expounded upon by appropriately qualified people known as Tertöns (gter-ston). Consequently, the school founded by Padmasambhava has the most extensive collection of gter-ma texts of any school of Tibetan Buddhism, including Padmasambhava's biography and The Tibetan Book of the Dead. (See also RNYING-MA-PA.)

⌘ PAGODA ⌘

Buddhist term, used almost exclusively in China, Korea, and Japan, for a relic container. The term, perhaps derived from the Sri Lankan equivalent (dägaba) of the Indian word stūpa, describes a sacred structure utilized as a shrine in East Asian Buddhism. Pagodas are frequently tall structures, generally more so than stūpas, already known in China by the fifth century C.E. Constructed from a variety of materials (usually some form of stone or wood), they are multistory buildings focused around a central axis that conveys an obvious cosmic symbolism. Ornamented with a variety of religious art forms, they provide an ideal structure for circumambulation in ritual observances. Precisely because of their role as relic containers of famous masters, they are considered especially sacred in Buddhist tradition. (See also STŪPA.)

⌘ PAI-CHANG HUAI-HAI ⌘
(712–784)

Famous Chinese Ch'an master, known not only for the importance of his meditational attainment but also for his rules regulating monastic behavior. Pai-chang was the Dharma heir of Ma-tsu Tao-i and the master of the well-known disciple Kuei-shan Ling-yu, founder of one of the "five houses" of Ch'an Buddhism. He is the author of the Pure Rule of Pai-chang (Pai-chang ch'ing-kuei), which established the first clearly formulated set of monastic rules for Ch'an monks. Prior to Pai-chang's rules, monks in China followed the Vinaya of the Dharmaguptakas, an Indian Buddhist sect. Pai-chang's system utilized the Vinaya emphasis of *both* Hīnayāna and Mahāyāna in structuring a framework uniquely adapted to Chinese monastic life. He is also known for his emphasis on monks establishing their own support through working in the fields. While he maintained the begging rounds as a form of meditational training, he advocated the notion that "a day without work is a day without food." His writings on the notion of "sudden enlightenment" in Ch'an have also been of primary importance to later generations of Buddhists in China and Japan.

⌘ PĀLI CANON ⌘

Title of the scripture collection of the Theravāda school of Buddhism. Pāli is an Indian dialect derived from, and quite similar to, Sanskrit. A variety of opinions exist as to precisely where Pāli was in use, but it is clear that it became the linguistic medium for the Theravāda nikāya. It also represents the only *complete* scripture collection for any Hinayāna sect. It is composed of a Vinaya Piṭaka or "Basket of Discipline," a Sutta Piṭaka or "Basket of Discourses," and an Abhidhamma Piṭaka or "Basket of Higher Teachings." Because of its threefold division, it is also referred to as the *Tipiṭaka* or "Three Baskets." Orthodox Theravādins are likely to maintain that the Pāli Canon represents all the "Buddhavacana" or teachings *actually* spoken by the Buddha during his forty-five year ministry. Modern scholarship, however, suggests that a careful linguistic and historical analysis reveals an alternative picture of the Pāli Canon involving a significant number of strata, styles, internal inconsistencies, and authors. In any case, the Pāli Canon is extremely well organized, comprehensive, and authoritative. A summary of its contents appears in the preliminary materials of this volume.

⌘ PĀLI TEXT SOCIETY ⌘

Society founded in England in 1881 by Thomas W. Rhys Davids intending to make texts of the Theravāda school of Buddhism available to a wide audience. As interest in Buddhism grew throughout Europe in the latter half of the eighteenth century, T. W. Rhys Davids wanted to make Romanized texts of the Pāli classics (including both scriptures and commentaries), along with translations, accessible to individuals, both as a scholarly endeavor and an attempt to preserve Buddha's teaching. Although funding for the projects was not always easy to obtain, within several decades it had published virtually the entire canon. The organization also began to publish the *Journal of the Pāli Text Society*, an important medium for the exchange of scholarly ideas. The organization continues today, with well over two hundred volumes to its credit.

⌘ PAÑCA-ŚĪLA ⌘

Five moral precepts, traditional to virtually all Buddhist schools. Members of the Buddhist laity, in addition to taking refuge in the "Three Jewels" of Buddha, Dharma, and Saṃgha, are required to adhere to five moral precepts of conduct, designed to aid in cultivating the "higher" life and assist in securing a more favorable rebirth, one that may be consistent with the attainment of salvation. The five precepts include: (1) not harming living beings, (2) not taking what is not given, (3) avoiding misconduct in sensual matters, (4) abstaining from false speech, and (5) avoiding substances that cloud the mind. The pañca-śīla are said to constitute the basic ethical framework of the laity. In modern application it appears that they are neither widely followed nor particularly comprehensive. A common practice among Buddhist lay disciples is to observe *one precept at a time* on the presumption that all five are simply too difficult. A number of Buddhist innovators in the modern world are addressing the problem revealed by the above in order to find new, contemporary, applications of the five precepts that make ethical life more genuinely accessible for Buddhists living in a vastly complicated, highly technological world.

⌘ PANCHEN LAMA ⌘

Title given to the abbot of Tashi Lhunpo Monastery by the fifth Dalai Lama. Just as the Dalai Lama in Tibetan Buddhism is thought to represent an incarnation of Avalokiteśvara, the Panchen Lama (pan-chen bla-ma) is felt to be an incarnation of Amitābha. Originally a religious title only, Panchen Lamas served as representative of the office of Dalai Lama following the death of each, until a new Dalai Lama could be identified. (See also DALAI LAMA.)

⌘ PARAMĀRTHA ⌘
(499–569)

Indian translator who arrived in China in 546 during the Liang Dynasty and is best known for his translating Asaṅga's Mahāyāna-saṃgraha into Chinese. He spent a number of years in southern China, eventually settling in Canton. He was important in the development of Chinese Buddhism insofar as his translations of Yogācāra texts were indispensable. In addition to the Mahāyāna-saṃgraha, he is reputed to have translated Vasubandhu's Viṃśatikā, the Madhyāntavibhāga-śāstra, and literally dozens of other texts. This work greatly facilitated the development of the Fa-hsiang school of Chinese Buddhism.

⌘ PĀRAMITĀ ⌘

Sanskrit technical term usually rendered as "perfection" and applied to a series of practices thought to be essential for spiritual progress. The term pāramitā is derived from the Sanskrit prefix pāram which generally denotes the other side of something, i.e., beyond, and the past participle of a verb meaning "to go." Thus, pāramitā means "going to the other side" or "having gone beyond," and by application "perfection." Although the term appears in the literature of various Hīnayāna sects, and is especially important to the Sarvāstivādins, it is in Mahāyāna that the notion of perfections becomes a critical component of Buddhist philosophy and practice. The concept appears early in the Prajñāpāramitā literature, emphasizing *six* pāramitās: (1) dāna (giving), (2) śīla (morality), (3) kṣānti (patience), (4) vīrya (vigor), (5) dhyāna (meditation), and (6) prajñā (wisdom). And of course the intended ideal emerges: wisdom can be *perfected* by all beings if certain religious principles are understood and rigorous religious practices are observed. The practices involve traversing the bodhisattva path as opposed to the way of the arhant in earlier Buddhism. Eventually, four additional perfections were added: (7) upāya (skill-in-means), (8) praṇidhāna (vow), (9) bala (power), and (10) jñāna (knowledge). These ten pāramitās are correlated with the ten stages of the bodhisattva path, each perfection corresponding to a particular stage (bhūmi). As a result, a highly ambitious path is outlined which is a guideline for a distinctly Mahāyāna Buddhist practice.

⌘ PARINIRVĀṆĀ ⌘

Technical term for the final nirvāṇa, i.e., death, of the historical Buddha. In the early Buddhist tradition, Buddha maintained that he was simply a man who had discovered a way to put an end to suffering, and with it, eliminated his future rebirth in the world of saṃsāra. This experience, described in his biography as the attainment of enlightenment or nirvāṇa, marks the beginning of his status as a *Buddha*. In consistence with his repeated proclamation of *human* status, his biological death could be anticipated. When it occurred, it was stated that he had passed into final nirvāṇa, parinirvāṇa, not to be reborn. (See also NIRVĀṆA.)

⌘ PĀṬALIPUTRA ⌘

Famous city in early Buddhism, associated with Magadha, and corresponding to modern Patna. Pātaliputra was the capital of the Mauryan Dynasty, and was the site of the traditional third council held during the reign of King Aśoka. It was also, however, important to Buddhism at a much earlier time in Indian history, as the possible site of a noncanonical council which may have occurred 137 years following Buddha's death, and which marked the beginning of the Buddhist sectarian movement. As such, it was an extremely vital location for Buddhism during a notable period of its early history.

⌘ PI-YÊN-LU ⌘

One of the great collections of "public case" records known as kung-an in Chinese (Japanese: kōan), of critical importance in Ch'an Buddhism. Literally meaning "Blue Cliff Records," it represents a collection of 100 riddle-like dilemmas composed by Hsüeh-tou Ch'ung-hsien (980–1052). His achievement is considered a poetic masterpiece, complex in its structure and brilliant for its insight. About a century later, it was collected into its present form by Yüan-wu K'o-ch'in (1063–1135), an important figure in the Sung Dynasty Ch'an tradition. Called the "Zen Master of

Full Enlightenment" by the emperor, Yüan-wu added an introduction to the text, as well as explanations and commentaries. Although the work received great acclaim early in its history, it fell into disuse for nearly two hundred years, largely due to the opposition of Yüan-wu's successor, Ta-hui Tsung-kao. Along with the Wu-mên-kuan, it represents one of the great masterpieces of Ch'an literature. It became extremely important in the Zen tradition of Japan, known as the Hekigan Roku. It is now accessible in the West as well in a variety of English translations. (See also KŌAN.)

⌘ POṢADHA ⌘

Buddhist Sanskrit form of the Pāli term Uposatha, representing the monthly fast and observance days in Buddhism. These days are marked by the full-moon, new-moon, and two half-moon days. For members of the lay community, particularly in the Theravāda tradition today, the laity congregates at their local monastery, spending the day in serious *fasting* and *observance* of the precepts, as well as in reflection. It is often the occasion for Dharma instruction. For members of the monastic community, the new-moon and full-moon days are marked by the recitation of the Prātimokṣa-sūtra, the text representing the monastic disciplinary code of the saṃgha. Attendance at this recitation is required for all monks and nuns except in the case of illness, and the recitation is not completed until all monastic offenses are confessed and appropriate disciplinary action taken. It is also the occasion for transacting necessary monastic business according to the requirements of the Vinaya.

⌘ PRAJÑĀ ⌘

Sanskrit technical term, literally translated as "wisdom," and representing one of the primary goals of all Buddhist schools. The term appears repeatedly in virtually all schools of early Buddhism as a means of indicating that wisdom, especially intuitive wisdom, is an expected consequence of serious Dharma study and rigorous meditational practice. It is necessarily the resultant of insight. In Mahāyāna the meaning and use of the term is expanded enormously. As one of the pāramitās, it appears at the sixth stage of the bodhisattva path, thus indicating its value as a significant achievement. Moreover, in the Prajñāpāramitā literature, it is the perfection of *wisdom* that is sought after, and which arises only when a true understanding of emptiness (śūnyatā) is developed. Along with compassion (karuṇā), it is considered one of the primary attributes of the bodhisattva, a virtue necessary for the attainment of Buddhahood.

⌘ PRAJÑĀPĀRAMITĀ LITERATURE ⌘

Generic term for a series of Mahāyāna texts known as the "Perfection of Wisdom" discourses. These texts, the earliest of which date from around 100 B.C.E., represent the first Mahāyāna literature, and are aptly named, due to their special interest in understanding the nature of wisdom or prajñā. The foremost scholar of Prajñāpāramitā literature, Edward Conze, notes the period of composition of this class of literature to extend for about 1,000 years, divided into four phases: (1) establishment of a basic text representing the initial "impulse" of the movement, (2) expansion of the basic text, (3) restatement of the basic doctrines into shorter texts and verse summaries, and (4) a period of influence by the Tantric tradition. The oldest text in this category is the "Perfection of Wisdom Discourse in 8,000 Lines" (Aṣṭasāhasrikā-prajñāpāramitā-sūtra). This text was later expanded into versions of 18,00, 25,000, and, eventually, 100,000 verses. It was then shortened into much shorter versions, the two most famous of which are the "Diamond Sūtra" (Vajracchedikā-prajñāpāramitā-sūtra) and the Heart Sūtra (Hṛdaya-prajñāpāramitā-sūtra). Finally, a series of Tantric texts emerges, one of which is called the "Perfection of Wisdom in One Letter." A large number of commentaries on this class of literature appeared, and both the texts and commentaries alike have been translated into Chinese and Tibetan. The style of the Prajñāpāramitā literature is interesting in that it presents an ongoing dialogue between Buddha and a series of disciples at varying stages of personal development. For the most part, those disciples usually associated with the early, Hīnayāna tradition (such as Śāriputra) are generally afforded the lowest position of expression, while those figures identified as bodhisattvas (such as Subhūti) are most highly regarded. In other words, the new Mahāyāna path is emphasized at the expense of the older framework. Such is also the case regarding doctrinal issues, with the Prajñāpāramitā texts launching an endless diatribe about the inadequacy of the Abhidharma approach and the efficacy of the doctrine of emptiness (śūnyatā). Moving out of India rapidly, the Prajñāpāramitā literature appears in China as early as 179 with Lokakṣema's translation of the 8,000 Line version. (See also AṢṬASAHASRIKA-PRAJNAPARAMITA-SUTRA; DIAMOND-SŪTRA; HEART-SŪTRA.)

⌘ PRAMĀṆAVĀDA ⌘

One of a variety of Sanskrit technical terms used to identify the general area of Buddhist logic. The founder of this school is usually cited to be Dignāga (ca. 400–485 or 480–540 are possible dates), rejecting the old logic of the so-called Nyāya school and founding the New Buddhist Logic. He is best known for two texts: the Pramāṇasamuccaya and the Nyāyamukha. He was in residence at Nālandā University for many years, having Dharmakīrti as his chief disciple. Dharmakīrti (ca. 650) elaborated Dignāga's logic, earning a reputation as the representative Buddhist philosopher. His most famous treatise is the Pramāṇavārttika. Dharmakīrti was followed by a number of later logicians, the most famous of whom were Śāntikrakṣita and Kamalaśīla (both eighth century). (See also DHARMAKĪRTI; DIGNĀGA; KAMALAŚĪLA; ŚĀNTIRAKṢITA.)

⌘ PRĀSAṄGIKA ⌘

Division of the Mādhyamika school founded by Buddhapālita (ca. 470–540). Following the basic establishment of the Mādhyamika school by Nāgārjuna, there was some disagreement as to the efficacy of Nāgārjuna's use of a negative dialectic and *reductio ad absurdum* argument as the basic approach of the school. While Bhāvaviveka (ca. 490–570) opposed Nāgārjuna and utilized a *positive* dialectic, founding the Svātantrika division of Mādhyamika, Buddhapālita upheld the orthodox approach, establishing the Prāsaṅgika division. By the seventh century, Candrakīrti advanced the Prāsaṅgika school dramatically. (See also BUDDHAPĀLITA; CANDRAKĪRTI; MĀDHYAMIKA.)

⌘ PRĀTIMOKṢA-SŪTRA ⌘

Monastic disciplinary text included in the Vinaya, and preserved in separate versions for monks and for nuns. The Prātimokṣa-sūtra is an inventory of offenses organized into categories classified according to the gravity of the offense. It is recited twice monthly, at the Poṣadha observance on the new-moon and full-moon days, and is employed as a device for insuring proper monastic discipline. As a ritual liturgy, it includes in addition to the categories of offenses, a series of verses that introduce and conclude the text, an introduction (nidāna) used to call the saṃgha together and instrument the confessional procedure, and an interrogatory formula, recited after each category of offenses, aimed at discovering who was pure and who was not. In the monks' version the categories of offenses include the: (1) Pārājika dharmas, offenses requiring explusion from the community, (2) Saṃghāvaśeṣa dharmas, offenses involving temporary exclusion from the saṃgha while undergoing a probationary period, (3) Aniyata dharmas, undetermined cases involving sexual matters, (4) Naiḥsargika-Pāyantika dharmas, offenses requiring expiation and forfeiture, (5) Pāyantika dharmas, offenses requiring simple expiation, (6) Pratideśanīya dharmas, miscellaneous matters which should be confessed, (7) Śaikṣa dharmas, rules concerning matters of etiquette, and (8) Adhikaraṇa-Śamatha dharmas, legalistic procedures utilized in settling disputes. The nuns' version contains seven categories, the third listed above being excluded. Nearly all of the schools of Hīnayāna Buddhism had their own versions of the Prātimokṣa-sūtra, with the rules varying in number in each case. The monks' version ranged from 218 to 263 rules while the nuns' version ranged from 279 to 380 rules. The Poṣadha observance was not considered concluded until all offenses listed in the Prātimokṣa-sūtra had been confessed and appropriate punishment meted out, thus guaranteeing on a fortnightly basis that all members of the saṃgha were pure in their behavior and worthy of community respect. (See also VINAYA PIṬAKA.)

⌘ PRATĪTYA-SAMUTPĀDA ⌘

Buddha's theory of causality, generally referred to as "dependent origination." This theory apparently became known to Buddha shortly after his attainment of enlightenment, and he is reputed to have meditated on it forward and backward. It establishes that nothing in the world happens by accident, as it were, but rather that all occurrences are causally conditioned.

Buddha presents a rather simple statement of this notion in asserting that "Because of this, that becomes; because of that, something else becomes," and so forth. To illustrate, the doctrine is further explained with respect to a causal sequence involving twelve specific links called nidānas, and including: (1) ignorance (avidyā), (2) mental constituents (saṃskāras), (3) consciousness (vijñāna), (4) name and form (nāmarūpa), (5) six sense organs (ṣaḍāyatana), (6) contact (sparśa), (7) feeling (vedanā), (8) craving (tṛṣṇā), (9) grasping (upādāna), (10) becoming (bhava), (11) birth (jāti), and (12) old age and death (jarāmaraṇa). The doctrine not only undermines the potential substantial nature of any compounded entity, but also suggests which three links in the chain might most readily be broken, thus ending the causal process, resulting in the attainment of nirvāṇa: ignorance, craving, and grasping. Although propounded by Buddha, and utilized as part of the doctrinal basis of each *early* Buddhist school, Mahayana also emphasizes the doctrine, suggesting that it underscores precisely what it means by the notion of emptiness (śūnyatā), that no composite entity can have any ontological status of its own, that all entities lack own-being (svabhāva).

⌘ PRATYEKABUDDHA ⌘

Literally a "private" or "solitary" Buddha, meant to describe an individual who has attained enlightenment, but who neither teaches nor becomes part of an active community. Some sources indicate that the pratyekabuddha differs from a Buddha in that he lacks certain attainments, such as omniscience. Along with the Śrāvaka-yāna or "Vehicle of the Śrāvaka" (literally "hearers") and Bodhisattva-yāna or "Vehicle of the Bodhisattva," it is one of three paths to enlightenment.

⌘ PRETA ⌘

A "hungry ghost," one of six traditional destinies (gatis) in Buddhism. It is included as one of the lower three destinies, represented in art as a being with an enormous stomach but tiny mouth, rendering the preta incapable of ever ingesting enough food. As a result, they are continually tormented by hunger. Although this condition seems to have been preceded by worldly greed in a previous life, like all destinies, it is only a transitory period in the cycle of saṃsāra.

⌘ PUDGALAVĀDA ⌘

General term for a cluster of early Indian Buddhist schools collectively called "Personalists" because of their insistence on a so-called pudgala that seems to transmigrate from life to life. The group appears to be a main trunk of the Sthavira group. The main sect is referred to as the Vātsiputrīyas, subdivided into the Saṃmatīyas, Dharmottarīyas, Bhadrāyanīyas, and Ṣaṇṇagarikas. They may well have emerged prior to the council held by King Aśoka around 250 B.C.E., but certainly no later than shortly thereafter. They argued that the pudgala was neither the same as nor different from the five aggregates (skandhas). And while the pudgala, as bearer of karmic retribution, maintainer of continuity from life to life in the cycle of saṃsāra, and experiencer of nirvāṇa provided a makeshift answer to issues of philosophical and practical consequence for early Buddhists, it *also appeared to be a surrogate ātman*. As such, all Pudgalavāda schools were thoroughly criticized by other Buddhist schools and branded as heretical. Despite this critique, the Chinese pilgrims Hsüan-tsang and I-ching reported an extremely large presence of Pudgalavādin monks in the monasteries they visited, indicating a rather long, and perhaps persuasive history for the schools.

⌘ PŪJA ⌘

"Ceremony," usually involving a respectful offering. The meaning of the term has been extended considerably in Buddhist usage to include worship, reverential salutation, religious services, ritual formularies, and even meditative practices. Pūja ceremonies are generally case specific to the culture and sectarian affiliation of the group involved, and thus may vary considerably from country to country. It is not unusual for flowers, incense, food, bowing, and other offerings to be involved. Singing and chanting may also be part of the pūja, as are various meditations, visualizations, and mudrās.

⌘ PUṆYA ⌘

Sanskrit technical term meaning "merit," and applied to the result of skilful action(s). It is linked to the doctrine of karma, in which positive volitional acts are said to produce merit and thus have a resultant kuśala or "good" karma. Theravadin cultures also presume that merit can be earned by such actions as donating gifts to the community, from virtually any act of genuine giving, from performing pūjas, or even reciting Buddhist texts. To some degree, one even finds the suggestion that the merit earned by one individual can be "shared" with others, increasing the spiritual welfare of all. This idea of the "transference of merit" became a key notion in the development of Mahāyāna, in which a major thrust of the bodhisattva ideal and path is to transfer one's merit to other sentient beings for their welfare. Since the boshisattva vows to gain complete, perfect enlightenment for the sake of all sentient beings, he can advance *all* beings in the spiritual path by his own meritorious pursuits.

⌘ PURE LAND ⌘

Mahāyāna Buddhist notion identifying a Buddha-kṣetra or "Buddha-Land" where a Celestial Buddha resides. In Mahāyāna cosmology, there are virtually countless Buddhas, and so also there are countless "Pure Lands" where these Buddhas dwell. By their very nature, these Pure Lands are paradises, resplendent with manifold benefits and beauties, and as such, ideal places for rebirth. Nonetheless, existence even in a Pure Land cannot be considered *permanent*, and must be viewed as only a more favorable location from which to pursue one's ongoing path to salvation. It is, however, an especially important oasis in times of Dharma decline when earthly conditions seem *not* to favor spiritual development and advancement. A number of Pure Lands became quite important in the development of Mahāyāna. Of particular note is the Pure Land of Amitābha Buddha, known as Sukhāvatī, and praised in a variety of Mahāyāna texts. Pursuit of rebirth in Amitābha's Pure Land developed into a formal Buddhist school which gained a wide following in East Asian Buddhism. It must be noted, though, that other Pure Lands, such as that of the "Healing Buddha" Bhaiṣajyaguru-Buddha, are mentioned throughout the literature. (See also AMITĀBHA; AMITĀYURDHYĀNA-SŪTRA; CHING-T'U TSUNG; JŌDO SHINSHŪ;JŌDOSHŪ;LARGERANDSMALLERSUKHĀVATĪVYŪHA SŪTRAS.)

⌘ PU-TAI ⌘

The so-called laughing Buddha often seen in Chinese art. Pu-tai was presumably a tenth-century Chinese monk who wandered about with a sack on his back to carry his belongings. In Ch'an he is considered an incarnation of the future Buddha Maitreya. (*See also* LAUGHING BUDDHA.)

— Q —

⌘ QUESTIONS OF KING MILINDA ⌘

See MILINDAPAÑHA

— R —

⌘ RĀHULA ⌘

Siddhārtha Gautama's only child, a son, born just prior to his decision to renounce the world. Siddhārtha's age at the time of his great renunciation is reputed to have been twenty-nine, thus Rāhula, whose name translates to "the fetter," was born to Siddhārtha and his wife Yaśosdharā just six years prior to the attainment of Buddhahood. Rāhula eventually joins the saṃgha at an early age, under the direction of Śāriputra, angering Yaśodharā to have her only child leave the family at such a tender age. In deference to her anger, Buddha decrees that it is unacceptable for novices (śrāmaṇera) to join the saṃgha *without* parental permission. Rāhula predeceased his father.

⌘ RĀJAGṚHA ⌘

Important city for early Indian Buddhism, located about 50 miles from modern Patna. During Buddha's lifetime, it was the capital of Magadha, the kingdom ruled by Buddha's friend and royal patron Bimbisāra. Although Buddha spent his last twenty-five rainy seasons at Śrāvastī, he is reported to have spent a number of earlier rain retreats at Rājagṛha. Rājagṛha was also the site of many monastic dwellings, including the very first gift of such a structure, known as Veṇuvana ārāma, to the saṃgha by Bimbisāra. Following Buddha's death, Rājagṛha was the site of the first Buddhist council.

⌘ RATNAKŪṬA-SŪTRA ⌘

Mahāyāna title that is actually a collection of forty-nine individual sūtras. The texts which were collected into the Ratnakūṭa-sūtra were apparently quite early, and were said to have influenced Mahāyāna thought even from the time of Nāgārjuna. There must have been a Sanskrit original, for Hsüan-tsang is reputed to have taken it to China, and it is cited in other Sanskrit texts, but the series now exists only in Chinese and Tibetan translations. Topically, it includes a wide variety of materials, loosely organized.

⌘ RATNASAMBHAVA ⌘

One of the five Celestial Buddhas. His name translates to "Jewel Born," and he is usually identified with the Pure Land of the south. He is linked to the bodhisattva Ratnapāṇi. In Tantric literature he is associated with the color yellow, and is illustrated in art making a mudrā with the right hand downward, palm outward. (See also AKṢOBHYA; AMITĀBHA; AMOGHASIDDHI; VAIROCANA.)

⌘ RDO-RJE (DORJE) ⌘

Symbol of the thunderbolt or diamond in Tibetan Buddhism, equivalent to the Sanskrit word vajra. It is compounded with the word "Vehicle" to indicate the third major school of Buddhism, that of the "Diamond Vehicle" (Vajrayāna). Historically, last of the Buddhist schools to develop in India, its name suggests that, like the diamond, it cuts through everything in coming to the experience of ultimacy. Like the diamond, which is the most perfect naturally occurring substance due to its low entropy or disorder, the rdo-rje is clear and perfect. It represents the masculine in Buddhism, identified by upāya or skilful means. As a ritual object, the rdo-rje is used in a vast variety of Tibetan rites and empowerment ceremonies, often in consort with the bell, a feminine symbol of wisdom (prajñā). Philosophically, such activity demonstrates the fashion in which wisdom and skillful means, or male and female duality, are mutually influencing.

⌘ RDZOGS-CHEN (DZOGCHEN) ⌘

Ati-yoga tradition of meditation brought to Tibet by Padmasambhava and Vimalamitra, and forming the essential practice of the rNying-ma-pa school of Buddhism. It was systematized by kLong-chen-pa in the fourteenth century. In this system, ultimate reality, referred to as Dharma-kāya, is personified as the Buddha Samantabhadra. In the simplest sense, rDzogs-chen aims at the pure awareness of this ultimate reality.

⌘ RHYS DAVIDS, CAROLINE AUGUSTA FOLEY ⌘ *(1858–1942)*

Pāli scholar, editor, translator, and wife of Thomas William Rhys Davids. C.A.F. Rhys Davids held a D.Litt. degree, and for many years was a reader in Pāli at the School of Oriental and African Studies at the University of London. Her editions and translations of Pāli texts are far too numerous to list, and in addition to these landmark works, she also published a number of important secondary studies such as *Gotama the Man* and *Sakya or Buddhist Origins*. She worked diligently with her husband in the Pāli Text Society, being especially interested in Abhidhamma texts. She also investigated stratification within the Pāli Canon, and argued, among other issues, that the Pāli Canon presented Buddhism as a monk-based institution which *was contrary to Buddha's original message*. She also maintained a long friendship with the brilliant Pāli scholar I. B. Horner, who also was active in the Pāli Text Society. An extremely fascinating portrait of both C.A.F. and T. W. Rhys Davids is offered in Guy Richard Welbon's book *The Buddhist Nirvāṇa and Its Western Interpreters*. (See also RHYS DAVIDS, THOMAS W.)

⌘ RHYS DAVIDS, THOMAS WILLIAM ⌘ *(1843–1922)*

Pāli scholar, editor, translator, and husband of Caroline Augusta Foley Rhys Davids. The son of a Congregational minister, he rejected his early training as a solicitor, entering the University of Breslau (Germany) to study Sanskrit. After receiving his Ph.D. in 1864, he entered the Ceylon Civil Service. Puzzled over a legal case concerning a Buddhist temple, and unable to read the language involved (Pāli), he set about to get an education suited to his task. He eventually resigned from the Civil Service in 1872, returned to England, and began a legal practice. He was nonetheless more interested in Buddhism, thus beginning a series of translations from the Pāli language he learned in Ceylon. As early as 1877, he published his first book *The Ancient Coins and Measures of Ceylon*. In 1878 his still famous *Manual of Buddhism* appeared. Following his series of Hibbert Lectures in 1881, he founded the Pāli Text Society and embarked on a career of editing and translating that is still virtually unrivaled in Buddhology. In 1882 he assumed the position of professor of Pāli at University College, London. He also worked tirelessly for the Royal Asiatic Society. In 1894 he married Caroline Augusta Foley, and while the couple continued their prodigious work, they also raised three children (one of whom was killed in 1917 during the First World War). Also in 1894, both Thomas W. and Caroline A.F. Rhys Davids visited Cornell University, presenting a lecture series that eventually became *Buddhism: Its History and Literature*. He also was appointed to the position of professor of Comparative Religion at Victoria University, Manchester, in 1904. He finally retired to Chipstead, Surrey, where he worked until his death. (See also RHYS DAVIDS, CAROLINE AUGUSTA FOLEY.)

⌘ RINZAI ZEN ⌘

School of Buddhism brought to Japan by Eisai Zenji (1141–1215) and continuing the Lin-chi Ch'an tradition from China by combining meditative practice with the use of kōans. Eisai traveled to China first in 1168 and again in 1187, receiving the seal of enlightenment in the Huang-lung lineage of the Lin-chi Ch'an tradition, known in Japan as the Ōryō school. Although this was the first Zen school in Japan, it died out rather quickly, being supplanted by the Rinzai Yōgi school of Zen. The Rinzai Yōgi school has produced a long line of famous masters dating back to the thirteenth century. They paved the way for more recent individuals like Hakuin Zenji (1685–1768). The Rinzai school of Zen, along with Sōtō, is one of two active schools today. It continues to rely on kōan practice and strict discipline, and for this reason has become very popular outside Japan. (See also EISAI ZENJI; ZEN.)

⌘ RISSHŌ-KOSEIKAI ⌘

Modern Japanese Buddhist group, based on the teachings of Nichiren, and founded by Niwano Nikkyō (b. 1906) and Naganuma Myōkō (1889–1957) in 1938. While emphasizing the efficacy of the Lotus-sūtra, this "new religion" of Japan also makes Śākyamuni Buddha a figure to be worshipped. The ethical aspects of the eightfold path and boshisattva path are encouraged, as well as honoring one's ancestors. The organization offers an extensive counseling program based on the teaching of the four noble truths and the Lotus-sūtra, is secularized, and has a rigorous publication program. Like many of the new religions of Japan, it is exceedingly popular.

⌘ RITSU SCHOOL ⌘

Japanese Vinaya school of Buddhism. It was brought to Japan from China by Chien-chen, a monk of the Lü school, in 754. He built an ordination platform at Tōdai-ji temple, as well as several other branches. This school adhered to the Dharmaguptaka Vinaya, known in Chinese as the "Vinaya in Four Parts" (Ssu-fen-lü). It contained 250 rules for monks and 348 rules for nuns. In the Heian Period (794–1185) the school declined, especially because the Tendai master Saichō eliminated the formal Vinaya as too rigorous, retaining only a modified version. It experienced a modest revival during the Kamakura Period (1192–1338), and continues today as a small school. (See also LÜ SCHOOL.)

⌘ RNYING-MA-PA ⌘

Earliest of four major schools of Tibetan Buddhists, literally titled "Ancient Ones." The school of Buddhism traces its origin back to the foundation of Buddhism in Tibet in the seventh and eighth centuries. It seems to possess authentic Indian Buddhist teachings brought to Tibet primarily by Padmasambhava. It is perhaps the least political of the Tibetan Buddhist schools. Early in its history, Tibetan Buddhism was persecuted by King gLang-dar-ma (836–842). In response to the threat, many of the sacred texts were hidden by Padmasambhava and others for protection and designated gter-ma or "treasures" to be resurrected at a safer time. Thus, the rNying-ma-pa school has the largest corpus of gter-ma literature of any of the four schools. Its religious practice revolves around the rDzogs-chen (or Ati-yoga) technique. Within about a century there was to be something of a renaissance in western and central Tibet, focusing on figures such as Atīśa, Marpa, and others, and radically changing the nature of Tibetan Buddhism, resulting in three new major schools of Buddhism.

⌘ ROBINSON, RICHARD HUGH ⌘
(1926–1970)

Buddhologist and Mādhyamika specialist, educated at the University of London, and founder of the Buddhist studies program at the University of Wisconsin. The University of Wisconsin was the first American institution to establish an educational program leading to graduate degrees in Buddhist studies, and it was developed almost exclusively by Richard Robinson. Fluent in all the Buddhist canonical languages, Robinson was primarily interested in the work of Nāgārjuna and the other Mādhyamika writers, and especially in China, but he also possessed an extensive background and intense curiosity that produced fruitful results across the face of Buddhist Studies. Like Louis de La Vallée Poussin and other major scholarly figures of the twentieth century, Robinson trained a large number of scholars before his untimely death in a 1970 home accident. A number of his former students are still at work editing his last projects in hopeful anticipation of eventually making several volumes of his translations available posthumously.

⌘ RŌSHI ⌘

Quite literally "elder teacher," a Zen master who has received the seal of enlightenment from his master. This title is generally withheld until one has attained the maturity and balance that augments and enhances Dharma realization. There is really no distinction at all as to *who* may be a Rōshi; it can be a member of the monastic tradition, a member of the laity, or an individual of either gender. The key factors are realization (kenshō, satori) and maturity. In the Rinzai tradition, where kōan study is utilized, faithful completion of such study *is not* a guarantee of being confirmed as a Rōshi. In modern times, the term is sometimes used in deference to an individual's standing, but such usage is inconsistent with the authentic meaning of the term.

— S —

⌘ SADDHARMAPUṆḌARĪKA-SŪTRA ⌘

See LOTUS-SŪTRA

⌘ SAICHŌ ⌘

(767–822)

Founder of the Tendai school of Japanese Buddhism. Just prior to the capital being moved to Heian, Saichō built a small monastery on Mt. Hiei. With the support of the emperor, he was sent to study in China, focusing primarily on T'ien-t'ai, but also considering Ch'an, esoteric Buddhism, and the Vinaya tradition. Upon his return, he consolidated his learning into a single tradition known as Tendai which, by its scope, was clearly more expansive than its Chinese (T'ien-t'ai) counterpart. Recognizing the importance of a moral life, Saichō established a twelve-year training period for his monks, undertaken in solitude in the monastery on Mt. Hiei. He tried to stress the independence of Tendai from the Buddhist schools of the Nara Period. He even tried to establish this location as a Mahāyāna ordination center, but his plans were opposed, and the center did not develop until after his death. Nonethless, the monastic complex housed as many as 30,000 monks. Like T'ien-t'ai, Saichō's Tendai school stressed the efficacy and universality of the Lotus-sūtra, and the potential of all beings to become Buddhas. After his death, he was posthumously titled Dengyō Daishi, "Master Who Transmitted the Teaching." (See also TENDAI.)

⌘ ŚĀKYA ⌘

Indian clan to which the family of Siddhārtha Gautama, the historical Buddha, belonged. Nestled in the foothills of the Himalayas, in what would be modern-day Nepal, their capital was in Kapilavastu. The clan, belonging to the warrior class (i.e., kṣatriya) was ruled by King Śuddhodana. (See also ŚĀKYAMUNI.)

⌘ ŚĀKYAMUNI ⌘

Epithet of the historical Buddha, literally meaning "sage of the Śākya clan." Upon the attainment of enlightenment, a number of epithets were used to describe, identify, or indicate the Buddha. Śākyamuni simply identifies him with reference to his clan, and in this way, is distinguished from other Buddhas, previous or Celestial. (See also ŚĀKYA.)

⌘ SAMĀDHI ⌘

Buddhist technical term, often translated as "concentration," but also rendered in a variety of other ways. It is used to collectively describe three stages of the eightfold path that are usually grouped together: right effort, right mindfulness, and right concentration (itself). Although it is described to arise at varying times, and under varying circumstances, in the numerous Buddhist meditational systems, they all agree that it refers to the product of mental cultivation; that it results from some kind of mental training, and describes a desired state of mental development that is *nonordinary*. It is clearly a precursor to the highest meditational experiences in Buddhism, variously described in the individual Buddhist traditions.

⌘ SAMANTABHADRA ⌘

One of the great bodhisattvas in Mahāyāna, usually associated with Vairocana Buddha. His name translates to "Universal Sage," and in the Lotus-sūtra he protects preachers of that text. He is often depicted on a six-tusked white elephant, and with Mañjuśrī, identified as a helper of Śākyamuni Buddha. He is said to represent the embodiment of wisdom (prajñā). Samantabhadra is especially important in Chinese Buddhism, where he is highly venerated. In the Vajrayāna tradition, Samantabhadra is associated with the primordial Buddha (or Ādi-Buddha), and thus represents the Dharma-kāya. He is represented as blue in color, and the iconography sometimes exhibits him in union with his consort.

⌘ ŚAMATHA ⌘

Meditational term denoting "calming" of the mind, generally indicated as a preliminary to the cultivation of insight (vipaś yanā). The goal of Buddhist meditation necessarily is the attainment of enlightenment. To be sure, each Buddhist school that emphasizes meditation, describes a series of practices designed to facilitate that attainment. Irrespective of whether the highest states of meditation are described to be trances (jhānas), as in the Theravāda tradition, states described by Kamalaśīla in his Bhāvanākrama or "Stages of Meditation," experiences cited by Chih-i in his Mo-ho chih-kuan or "Text on Great Calm and Insight," or esoteric typologies in the Vajrayāna schools (such as Tsong-kha-pa's Lam-rim chen-mo), they are all predicated on the attainment of calm, of śamatha. The underlying basis for and logic behind this requirement is that insight can only occur when the psychological and physiological distractions that inhibit spiritual attention are removed. There is no better method for the accomplishment of that requirement than śamatha practice, invariably involving (at first) a simple breathing technique designed to lower the body's physiological function while teaching the mind to become focused and attentive. (See also VIPAŚYANĀ.)

⌘ SAṂBHOGA-KĀYA ⌘

"Enjoyment-Body," second of the three bodies of the Buddha in Mahāyāna, and used to represent the quasi-physical form of Buddha as preacher in the Mahāyāna sūtras. Developed most fully in the Laṅkāvatāra-sūtra, this idea of three forms of representing Buddha comes to maturity in the Yogācāra school. It suggests that the "apparitional body" or nirmāṇa-kāya is visible to ordinary individuals as an inspiration to begin the (Mahāyāna) Buddhist path. Once on the bodhisattva path, the nirmāṇa-kāya gives way to the saṃbhoga-kāya. Finally, when the path is completed, one attains the Dharma-kāya or "Dharma body," ultimate reality itself, the true nature of Buddhahood. Thus, each of the three bodies of Buddha speaks to an individual at a different level of spiritual development. (See also TRIKĀYA.)

⌘ SAṂGHA ⌘

Sanskrit word for "group," generally accepted in the Buddhist context as the designation for the Buddhist community. In the broadest sense, it includes four basic groups of individuals: (1) monks or "bhikṣus," those males who have renounced worldly life for the homeless career of the mendicant, (2) nuns or "bhiṣuṇīs," those females who have renounced worldly life for the homeless career of the mendicant, (3) male lay disciples or "upāsakas," who follow a lesser series of regulations and remain in worldly life, and (4) female lay disciples or "upāsikās," who follow a lesser series of regulations and remain in worldly life. What all four of these groups share is a common commitment to the "three jewels," of Buddhism: Buddha, Dharma, and Saṃgha. That means that they affirm belief that Siddhārtha Buddha, the historical Buddha, accomplished the enlightenment he claimed; they affirm his doctrine as an efficacious statement of both the theoretical and practical application of his enlightenment experience; and they affirm faith in the community of like-minded individuals who are committed to actualizing his teaching. While the laity agrees to adhere to a fivefold ethical code known as the pañca-śīla, the monastic members take on five additional precepts, a rigid monastic code, and a more rigorous lifestyle in the wanderers' community. As Buddhism became sectarian, with individual saṃghas growing up at first in India and later in other countries, the saṃgha retains its meaning as an umbrella-like "cover term" for all those *at least* professing faith in the "three jewels" and accepting the pañca-śīla. (See also BHIKṢU; BHIKṢUṆĪ; UPĀSAKA; UPĀSIKĀ.)

⌘ SAṂSĀRA ⌘

The cycle of perpetual existence in Hinduism and Buddhism. It is a description of the universe that has enormous implications for religious life, for it is founded on the assumption that the universe has existed eternally, that it had no ultimate "creation" and knows no final "destruction." Coupled with the Buddhist notion of rebirth, conditioned by the quality of one's volitional or "karmic" behavior, an individual presumably experiences rebirth after rebirth in an endless chain. According to Buddha, it is of little value to speculate about the *nature* of this circumstance, for the more important task requires developing an *antidote* to perpetual rebirth, to find a way out of this world characterized as filled with suffering or "duḥkha." Of course each Buddhist school propounds its own path, based on the initial teaching of Buddha. Nonetheless, the overarching premise is that saṃsāra is a generic term for the expected state of affairs: a perpetual, continued cycle of time.

⌘ SAṂSKṚTA ⌘

Technical term indicating that which is "conditioned" or produced by causes. In the Abhidharma traditions of the early Buddhist schools, the elemental building blocks of experiential reality were referred to as *dharmas*, in this usage not to be confused with the generic term for Buddha's teachings. Dharmas were said to be of two kinds: (1) *conditioned (saṃskṛta)*, or those items which, by their various combinations, produce the compounded world of our ordinary experience, and which adhere to the laws of causality as espoused by traditional Buddhist doctrine, and (2) unconditioned (asaṃskṛta), or those items which are beyond conditioned reality, outside ordinary causality, and therefore, not subject to the law of impermanence. The various schools each propounded a certain number of saṃskṛta dharmas, case specific to their school and reflective of their doctrine. There was significant debate about their nature and number in the various schools. (See also DHARMA.).

⌘ SAMYAK SAMBUDDHA ⌘

Sanskrit epithet of Buddha, literally meaning, "complete, perfect enlightenment." In the historical development of Buddhism, it was deemed pertinent to describe just how the enlightenment of Buddha differed from the enlightenment of other arhants, if at all. It would not be unreasonable to assume that such a delineation may have been as *politically* motivated as doctrinally. Nonetheless, it was argued that a Buddha's enlightenment was not only self-discovered, but that it carried with it the attainment of omniscience (sarvajñatā) and ten powers (daśabala). The arhant's attainment of enlightenment contained *neither* of the above elements, and thus a Buddha is described as having attained complete, perfect enlightenment while an arhant has not.

⌘ SAṂYUTTA NIKĀYA ⌘

The third major portion of the Sutta Piṭaka of the Pāli Canon, literally the "connected discourse" collection and containing 56 groups of suttas, grouped according to subject matter. It corresponds to the Saṃyukta Āgama of the Sanskrit Buddhist canon. In the Pāli version, the individual suttas are generally short, covering an expansive series of topics reflective of Buddha's long teaching career.

⌘ SAN-LUN ⌘

The "Three Treatise School," a classical school of Buddhism in China. It was founded by Kumārajīva (344–413) based on Nāgārjuna's Mūlamadhyamaka-kārikās and Dvādaśa-dvāra-śāstra as well as Āryadeva's Śata-śāstra, hence the name "Three Treatise School." It corresponds to the Indian Madhyamika school of Buddhism. Kumārajīva passed the teaching on to his disciples, especially Tao-shêng (360–434), Seng-chao (374–414), and Seng-lang (d. 615). Following Kumarajiva's death, a period of decline in San-lun was experienced, with interest reawakened by Chi-tsang (549–623), considered to be the greatest master of the San-lun school. After Chi-tsang, the school lost importance in China, but was eventually exported to Japan via a Korean student of Chi-tsang. (See also CHI-TSANG; KUMĀRAJĪVA; SANRON; SENG-CHAO; TAO-SHÊNG.)

⌘ SANRON ⌘

One of six academic traditions of Japanese Buddhism during the Nara Period, imported without substantial modification, from China. It corresponds to the Indian Mādhyamika and Chinese San-lun schools of Buddhism. The school was brought to Japan in 625 (along with the Jōjitsu school) by the Korean monk Ekwan, a disciple of Chi-tsang's who lived at Genkō-ji temple. The Sanron school never had the impact on Japan that its counterpart did on China. (See also SAN-LUN.)

⌘ ŚĀNTIDEVA ⌘

Indian Mahāyāna monk associated with the Mādhyamika school of Buddhism and author of at least two major texts. Śāntideva probably lived ca. 650–750, and was an influential monk at Nālandā University. He is best known for his two texts known as the Bodhicaryāvatāra and the Śikṣāsamuccaya. The former, intended for the spiritual development of the Mahāyāna bodhisattva, is a text of ten chapters (containing over 900 stanzas) focusing on a variety of subjects ranging from the cultivation of the "thought of enlightenment" (bodhicitta) to the practice of the "perfections" (pāramitās). The latter is a collection of items arranged around 27 kārikās or verses which functions as a handbook or practical guide to Mahāyāna practice and thought. He is also credited as the author of a third, lesser known text, known as the Sūtrasamuccaya. (See also BODHICARYĀVATĀRA; ŚIKṢĀSAMUCCAYA.)

⌘ ŚĀNTIRAKṢITA ⌘

Famous Indian scholar who lived ca. 680–740 and is best remembered for his texts known as the Tattvasaṃgraha and Madhyamakālaṅkāra. Along with his student Kamalaśīla (ca. 700–750), he was critical of the position of the Svātantrika of Bhāvaviveka, and extended it, offering a Yogācāra-Mādhyamika (Svātantrika) position. He is reputed to have traveled to Tibet, had a role in the founding of Tibet's first monastery at bSam-yas, and (along with Padmasambhava) was important in early Tibetan Buddhism. (See also KAMALAŚĪLA.)

⌘ SANZEN ⌘

Rinzai Zen equivalent of the general term in Zen practice known as dokusan, representing a private meeting with the Zen master. During this meeting, the student's development is considered, as well as any problems encountered. It provides the master an opportunity to deal with *each* student individually. Today it has become virtually synonymous with dokusan. (See also DOKUSAN.)

⌘ ŚĀRIPUTRA ⌘

Famous early disciple of Buddha. Originally from a Brahmin family, Śāriputra joined the saṃgha after hearing a Dharma discourse by the monk Aśvajit. Along with his friend Mahāmaudgalyāyana, he became enlightened quickly and established a reputation as a master of the Abhidharma. Legends indicate that he predeceased Buddha by a short period, perhaps several months.

⌘ SĀRNĀTH ⌘

City near Benares where, in a Deer Park, Buddha preached his famous first sermon known as the Dharmacakrapravartana-sūtra.

Because the site marks the beginning of his formal Dharma exposition, it is considered as one of the holy locations in Buddhism. The spot was marked by the erection of a stūpa, and is the location of an Aśokan edict.

⌘ SARVASTIVADA ⌘

Indian Buddhist sect which splintered from the main Sthaviravāda trunk during the mid-third century B.C.E. It takes its name from the affirmation of the doctrine of "sarvam asti," literally "holders of the doctrine that all is." Doctrinally, the sect affirms ontological realism, arguing that the world is composed of 75 dharmas (72 of which are compounded or "saṃskṛta" and 3 of which are uncompounded or "asaṃskṛta") which exist throughout the three periods of time (i.e., past, present, and future). In other words, while the basic building blocks of reality change, continuity is maintained. Although it was the Sarvāstivādins who were presumably expelled from the kingdom at Aśoka's third council at Pāṭaliputra, the school became perhaps the most forceful of all the Hīnayāna sects, establishing a stronghold in Kaśmīr and Gandhāra that endured as long as Indian Buddhism itself. The sect possessed a complete canon in Sanskrit, much of which is preserved today in Sanskrit fragments, as well as Chinese and Tibetan translations. Its Abhidharma tradition is both famous and erudite, best known for Vasubandhu's Abhidharmakośa and the Mahāvibhāṣā, composed at Kaniṣka's council under the supervision of Vasumitra. Within 100 years of their appearance, the Sautrāntika school develops from the Sarvāstivādins. A number of Sarvāstivādin doctrines are considered as precursors of Mahāyāna ideas.

⌘ SA-SKYA-PA ⌘

School of Tibetan Buddhism founded by 'Brog-mi (Drok-mi), taking its name from the monastery he founded in 1073. 'Brog-mi was a contemporary of Atīśa, and studied at Vikramaśīla monastery in India for eight years. In his teaching he emphasized the "new" Tantras of Atīśa and Rin-chen bzang-po. The abbots of the monastery founded by 'Brog-mi (and coming from the Khon family) had enormous power during the twelfth and thirteenth centuries, were highly respected for their extensive learning, and were permitted to marry. 'Brog-mi passed on the Sa-skya-pa lineage to his son, and thereafter it was usual to pass the lineage from uncle to nephew. The school was also especially interested in matters of Buddhist logic. Sa-skya Paṇḍita established a relationship with Mongolia, and his nephew Chos-rGyal 'Phags-pa (1235–1280) was prelate to Kublai Khan. The school also strongly influenced Tsong-kha-pa and the dGe-lugs-pa sect. The school is still prominent in the modern world, both in Asia and the West. (See also 'BROG-MI.)

⌘ SATIPAṬṬHĀNA-SUTTA ⌘

Pāli name of a meditational discourse, the title of which means "the setting up of mindfulness." The text appears in two versions in the Pāli Canon: (1) a long account known as the Mahāsatipaṭṭhāna-sutta as the twenty-second discourse of the Dīgha Nikāya, and (2) an only slightly shorter text simply called the Satipaṭṭhāna-sutta and located as the tenth discourse of the Majjhima Nikāya. The two texts outline an extremely important form of Theravāda meditation, focusing on the development of mindfulness of (1) body, (2) feeling, (3) mind, and (4) mental objects. Like other systems of Buddhist meditation, it operates on the principle that calm (samatha) is initially developed which finally leads to insight (vipassanā). Properly practiced, the technique developed in the Satipaṭṭhāna-sutta is said to lead to the realization of nibbāna through the attainment of trance states (jhānas). Its Sanskrit counterpart, known as the Smṛtyupasthāna-sūtra, is also widely known. The general practice of the setting up of mindfulness has been prevalent throughout Buddhism's history, and is taught extensively today in all Theravāda countries, as well as in the West.

⌘ SATORI ⌘

Zen term for enlightenment. It expresses the ideal of Buddhist "realization," and is sometimes used synonymously with another Zen technical term, kenshō. Precisely because it involves a visionary experience, it is impossible to describe in conceptual terms. It may arise suddenly, as the Rinzai school suggests, or gradually, following long periods of sitting meditation, as the Sōtō Zen school argues. It is by no means the culmination of Zen practice, but rather an experience that can be deepened. (See also BODHI; ENLIGHTENMENT; KENSHŌ; WU.)

⌘ SAUTRĀNTIKA ⌘

Hīnayāna school developing from the Sarvāstivadin lineage probably in the middle of the second century B.C.E. The sect rejects the Abhidharma Piṭaka, utilizing the Sūtra Piṭaka as its doctrinal authority. While it rejects the Sarvāstivādin notion that "everything exists" (sarvam asti), it affirms that the subtlest form of the "aggregates" or skandhas (referred to as mūlāntika) transmigrates from life to life. In this sense the school is closer to the Pudgalavādin schools than the Sthavira schools. In order to avoid a critique similar to that heaped on the so-called Personalist schools, the Sautrāntikas carried the interpretation of the doctrine of momentariness to an extreme, so that time appears to be *almost* a mere succession of moments with no *duration*, a simple stream. This notion was later to be instrumental to the Yogācāra school in developing its theory of karmic seeds (or bījas) that seem to pass from life to life. The school also argues that with the attainment of nirvāṇa, the skandhas cease, thus providing the attainment of nirvāṇa with a distinctly negative interpretation.

⌘ SENG-CHAO ⌘
(374–414)

Disciple of Kumārajīva and one of the Buddho-Taoists, perhaps one of the last major figures in the San-lun school of Chinese Buddhism. He became a monk following a reading of the Vimalakīrti-sūtra, studied with Kumārajīva, and accompanied his master to Ch'ang-an. Seng-chao's importance lies in the fact that he was perhaps the first Chinese Buddhist to capture San-lun philosophy in a genuinely Chinese fashion. This was demonstrated by his best known writings: "Prajñā has no Knowing," "Things do not Shift," "Emptiness of the Non-Absolute," and "Nirvāṇa has no Name." He is well known to the Chinese Ch'an masters, and is quoted often. One Chinese emperor (cited in Walter Liebenthal's monograph *Chao Lun*) even referred to him as a "patriarch of the school of meditation." (See also BUDDHO-TAOISTS.)

⌘ SESSHIN ⌘

Zen technical term, literally meaning "to collect the mind," and indicating an extended period of intensive zazen (or sitting meditation) practice. Ordinary life in a Zen monastery usually involves a variety of practices such as physical work, ceremonials, recitations, and zazen. During periods of sesshin, zazen is the major practice, with all other activities, including sleep, minimized. Between periods of zazen, interviews with the master (dokusan) and demonstrations of realization (known as teishō) are interspersed. The sesshins are designed to provide periods of rigorous and intensive training to assist the practitioner in the pursuit of realization. The length and intensity of the sesshin varies from temple to temple. (See also ZAZEN.)

⌘ SGAM-PO-PA ⌘
(1079–1153)

Disciple of Mi-la ras-pa, a major figure in the bKa-rgyud-pa lineage of Tibetan Buddhism, credited with beginning the monastic tradition in that lineage. Sometimes called the "Doctor of Dvag-po," sGam-po-pa became a monk in the bKa-gdams-pa lineage at age twenty-six, following the death of his wife. Six years later, he undertook a period of training with Mi-las ras-pa, acquiring his major teaching (and Dharma transmission) in just over a year. These teachings included the "Six Dharmas of Nāropa" and Mahāmudrā. He is famous for his text known as The Jewel Ornament of Liberation. Following sGam-po-pa, the bKa-rgyud-pa tradition split into four major groups. (See also BKA-RGYUD-PA; MI-LAS RAS-PA.)

⌘ SHAMBHALA ⌘

A mythical kingdom, of uncertain location, which will produce the Buddhist figure ushering in the new age following a period of adversity and despair. It is presumably the place of origin of the Kālacakra Tantra. Speculation abounds as to just where Shambhala might be, but the myth itself is often associated with the coming of the future Buddha Maitreya.

⌘ SHAN-TAO ⌘
(613–681)

Disciple of Tao-cho (562–645), and considered to be the third patriarch of the Chinese Ching-t'u school of Buddhism. He wrote a Chinese commentary on the Amitāyurdhyāna-sūtra, helped give the school its classical style, and outlined a series of practices leading to rebirth in the Pure Land. These practices included: (1) uttering Buddha's name, (2) chanting sūtras, (3) meditating on Buddha, (4) worshipping Buddha images, and (5) singing praises of Buddha. Of these, nien-fo, or uttering Buddha's name was primary while the others were secondary. (See also T'AN-LUAN; TAO-CHO.)

⌘ SHAO-LIN MONASTERY ⌘

Chinese Buddhist monastery built in 477 during the Northern Wei Dynasty. It is perhaps most famous as the monastery to which Bodhidharma came in southern China and in which he is reported to have sat facing the wall for nine years. It was at Shao-lin monastery that Hui-k'o, Bodhidharma's eventual disciple, gained the confidence of the master and was admitted to his service. A popular American television series touted Shao-lin monastery as the birthplace of kung-fu, a martial art developed by the Buddhist monks there.

⌘ SHEN-HSUI ⌘
(606–706)

One of the main students of Hung-jen, the fifth Ch'an patriarch in China, and founder of the "Northern School" of Ch'an. Shen-hsui is reputed to have lost a genuine chance to become Hung-jen's Dharma heir when a verse by Hui-nêng was judged by the master to be superior to his. Although Hui-nêng was recognized to be the true Dharma successor, Shen-hsui nevertheless claimed to be Hung-jen's heir. Because he propagated his teaching in Ch'ang-an and Lo-yang, he was said to be the master of the "Northern School" of Ch'an. Some texts mention Shen-hsui as an advocate of the Lankāvatāra-sūtra, although it is not specifically mentioned in his writings. Although the "Northern School" was initially quite successful, it was eventually overshadowed by the "Southern School," which enjoyed a longer and more successful history. (See also HUI-NÊNG.)

⌘ SHIH-T'OU HSI-CH'IEN ⌘
(700–790)

Disciple of Ch'ing-yüan Hsing-ssu (660–740) and teacher of Yueh-shan Wei-yen, important Ch'an teacher in the lineage of

Hui-nêng. Upon attaining enlightenment, he set up residence in Hunan Province. Because he lived in a hut on a large flat rock, he gained the epithet "Stone-head," which he carried throughout his life. In the "Southern School" of Ch'an, he was regarded as the foremost master "south of the lake" while Ma-tsu Tao-i (709–788) was regarded as foremost master "west of the river" (i.e., in the provinces of Chiang-shi). A spirited interplay developed between their students, adding vitality to the "Southern School." Three of the traditional "five houses of Ch'an" emerged from Shih-tou's lineage. (See also MA-TSU TAO-I.)

⌘ SHIKANTAZA ⌘

Sōtō Zen practice of "just sitting," and corresponding to the Ts'ao-tung Ch'an practice known as Chih-kuan-ta-tso. It is stressed by Dōgen Zenji (1200–1253), the founder of Sōtō Zen. It is characterized by no "trying" and no distraction from just sitting, recognizing that *sitting in meditation itself* is the actualization of the Buddha nature inherent in all sentient beings. (See also CHIH-KUAN-TA-TSO.)

⌘ SHIN ARAHAN ⌘

Young Theravāda monk who taught and impressed King Anawrahtā (1040–1077) of Pagān. He fled Thatōn because of excessive Hindu influences, eventually arriving in Pagān and converting the king. Shin Arahan was placed in charge of the saṃgha in unified Burma. Although the Theravāda school of Buddhism became standard at the time, the saṃgha later splintered, with three other distinct saṃghas emerging.

⌘ SHINGON SCHOOL ⌘

Esoteric school of Buddhism in Japan, founded by Kūkai (774–835). Ordained at twenty, Kūkai traveled to China in 804, studying the Chên-yen or "True Word" school extensively. Upon his return to Japan in 805, he became head monk at Tōdai-ji, but left to found his own monastery on Mt. Kōya in 816. This monastery became the main center of the Shingon school. Like all schools of Buddhist Tantra, the Shingon school emphasizes ritual practices involving mantras, maṇḍalas, and mudrās, as well as various meditational practices. It identifies with Vairocana Buddha, and engages in a variety of initiation (abhiṣeka) and empowerment rites. (See also CHÊN-YEN; KŪKAI; TANTRA; VAJRAYĀNA.)

⌘ SHINKŌ SHŪKYŌ ⌘

Literally, the "New Religions," a term used in Japan to denote those forms of contemporary, popular Buddhism which grew out of older, established forms but which diverge, in some respects, from the doctrine, practice, and goal of the parent group. Examples of such groups would include Sōkagakkai and Risshō Koseikai.

⌘ SHINRAN ⌘

(1173–1262)

Student of Hōnen (1133–1212) who broke away from his teacher's school of Jōdo-shū or "Pure Land" Buddhism to found the Jōdo Shinshū or "*True* Pure Land" school. Although Shinran shared Hōnen's emphasis on the importance of Amida Buddha, he underscored the eighteenth of Amida's vows, virtually guaranteeing rebirth in the Pure Land to anyone reciting Amida's name. In so doing, he changed Japanese Pure Land practice from an affirmation and strengthening of faith, to an acknowledgement of trust and expectation. It is the highest expression of tariki or "other power." Additionally, Shinran moved away from the monastic ideal, taking a wife (for which he was expelled from the monastic community), and structuring a community composed of lay members. In this community, in which abbots' positions are maintained by *heredity*, the only religious practice utilized is the recitation of the nembutsu or recitation of the mantra Namu Amida Butsu, "Homage to Amida Buddha." The teachings of Shinran were preserved by one of his students under the title Tannishō. The school founded by Shinran remains the largest Buddhist school in Japan today. (See also JŌDO SHINSHŪ.)

⌘ SHŌBŌGENZŌ ⌘

Principal text of the Sōto Zen school of Buddhism, written by Dōgen Zenji, and literally meaning "Treasury of Knowledge Regarding the True Dharma." Dōgen did not produce the first chapter until 1231, eventually completing the text over the last two decades of his life. It includes such topics as how junior monks must behave in the presence of senior monks, rules for the meditation hall, mealtime rules, aspects of zazen, what is meant by enlightenment, and so forth. It serves as a compendium of Sōtō teaching that is deemed essential for all practitioners in that lineage. (See also DŌGEN ZENJI; SŌTŌ ZEN.)

⌘ SIDDHĀRTHA GAUTAMA ⌘

Son of the Śākyan King Śuddhodana and his queen, Māyā, later to attain enlightenment and become the historical Buddha in the present world cycle. Born into a noble family, the child was originally conceived in a mythically fraught dream in which a six-tusked white elephant entered the side of Queen Māyā. Born from his mother's right side, he took a number of steps, declared the present life to be his last birth, and proclaimed that he would be ruler over all. Following a sheltered youth of luxurious indulgence, he married, fathered a child, and in his twenty-ninth year, renounced the world to search for an end to suffering produced by old age, sickness, and death. After six years of training under various teachers, he made a solitary breakthrough, eliminated his final impurities, and attained Buddhahood, a state of becoming awakened to the world as it really is. Between the ages of thirty-five and eighty, he wandered throughout the countryside, preaching his Dharma or "Doctrine," and established a significant community, known as the saṃgha. In his eightieth year, he died, being cremated the following week, with his relics distributed to various groups to serve as stūpas or reliquary mounds. The biography of his life is preserved in fragments of texts in the various Buddhist traditions, and in a series of reasonably complete biographies such as the Mahāvastu or "Great Story," the Lalitavistara or "Detailed Account of the Sport (of the Buddha)," the Buddhacarita or "Acts of the Buddha," and a number of others. (See also BUDDHA.)

⌘ SIGĀLOVĀDA-SUTTA ⌘

Important Theravāda ethical text contained in the Dīgha Nikāya of the Sutta Piṭaka. It describes not only the four motives which are inappropriate as bases for action: (1) impulse (chanda), (2) hatred (dosa), (3) fear (bhaya), and (4) delusion (moha), but more importantly, it outlines and comments upon proper conduct in six specific types of social relationships: (1) children and parents, (2) teacher and pupil, (3) husband and wife, (4) friends, (5) servants and workpeople, and (6) monastic and laypersons.

⌘ ŚIKṢĀSAMUCCAYA ⌘

Buddhist Sanskrit text by Śāntideva, literally meaning "Compendium of Training," and addressing the issue of ethical conduct for bodhisattvas. It is arranged in three parts: (1) a series of 27 kārikās or verses, forming a framework for the text, (2) a commentary of the verses, providing substance to their teaching, and (3) a voluminous series of quotations, usually from older texts, and providing context to the issues discussed. It is clearly a Mahāyāna text as evidenced by the strong emphasis on emptiness (śūnyatā) pervading the body. Combined with Śāntideva's other major ethical text known as the Bodhicaryāvatāra, it provides a comprehensive picture of the moral life required by those pursuing the bodhisattva path. (See also BODHICARYĀVATĀRA; ŚĀNTIDEVA.)

⌘ ŚĪLA ⌘

Technical term, often translated as "conduct" or "virtue" and usually used to designate rules of ethical training for Buddhists. Unlike the formal and externally enforced code embodied in the Vinaya Piṭaka, śīla appears to be a noncodified, internally enforced ethical guideline designed to assist in the development of proper human conduct. The majority of the guidelines that can be identified as śīla appear to come from *outside* the Vinaya Piṭaka. They can be found in such Pāli texts as the Maṅgala-sutta of the Khuddaka Nikāya, the Metta-sutta of the Suttanipāta, and the Sigālovāda-sutta of the Dīgha Nikāya. In the simplest sense in early Buddhism, śīla is listed as a fivefold practice for the laity, insisting on (1) respect for life, (2) nontheft, (3) proper conduct in sexual matters, (4) abstention from false speech, and (5) abstention from substance abuse. For monks and nuns, five additional precepts were added, including: (6) abstention from solid food after noon, (7) avoiding music, dance, and dramatic presentations, (8) abstention from scents, unguents, and other bodily adornments, (9) avoidance of high beds, and (10) avoidance of handling gold and silver. With the rise of Mahāyāna, new texts appeared which defined śīla for bodhisattvas, emphasizing wisdom (prajñā), compassion (karuṇā), the ideals embodied in the perfections (pāramitās), and the skillful means (upāya) of proper application of these ideals to everyday life. (See also BODHISATTVA-ŚĪLA; ETHICS; MAHĀYĀNA VINAYA; VINAYA PIṬAKA.)

⌘ SKANDHA ⌘

Technical term literally meaning "heap" or "bundle," but usually translated as "aggregate," and applied to the five constituents of an individual that comprise one's personality-being. Since Buddha appears to have rejected the notion of a permanent abiding ātman or "self," he described the individual as a collection of five aggregates, including: (1) physical form (rūpa), (2) feeling (vedanā), (3) perception (saṃjñā), (4) mental constituents (saṃskāras), and (5) consciousness (vijñāna). All the aggregates are characterized by impermanence, not-self, and suffering, the traditional "three marks of existence" in Buddhism. They are sometimes called the aggregates of grasping (upādāna-skandha) because individuals make them objects of desire. Mahāyāna additionally argues that not only are the skandhas characterized by impermanence, not-self, and suffering, but they are also empty (śūnyatā). In the strictest sense, then, individuals are simply a combination of mere physical and mental phenomena, devoid of any ātman or abiding essence.

⌘ SMALLER SUKHĀVATĪVYŪHA-SŪTRA ⌘

Mahāyāna text important as one of the foundational bases of the Pure Land School of Buddhism. As opposed to the larger version of the text, with Buddha on Vulture's Peak, here the Buddha Amitābha presides over the Pure Land of Sukhāvatī. Birth in the Pure Land *is not* a result of good works, as in the larger version, and is not even mentioned. The key issue in the smaller text focuses on the metaphor of sound. The sounds present in the Pure Land are to remind one of the Buddha, Dharma, and Saṃgha. Additionally, these sounds, and that of Amitābha's name, are prerequisites to meditation. Consequently, they must be repeated if salvation is to be attained. (See also AMITĀBHA; AMITĀYURDHYĀNA-SŪTRA; LARGER SUKHĀVATĪVYŪHA-SŪTRA.)

⌘ SOJI-JI ⌘

Along with Eihei-ji, one of two main monasteries of the Sōtō Zen school of Japanese Buddhism. It was originally a monastery associated with the Hossō school, but became a Zen monastery in 1321 when Keizan Jōkin became abbot. Just prior to the turn of the twentieth century, it was destroyed, eventually to be rebuilt not on its original site, but in Yokohama.

⌘ SŌKAGAKKAI ⌘

See NICHIREN SHŌSHŪ SŌKAGAKKAI

⌘ SONJONG ⌘

One of two major schools in Korean Buddhism. At the end of the fourteenth century, under the third king in the Yi Dynasty, Buddhism was suppressed, reducing the number of Buddhist sects to seven. The fourth king, Sejong, continued the suppression still further, reducing Buddhism to two schools, the Sonjong and the Kyojong. The Sonjong, or "Meditation" school, was a union of the Vinaya, T'ien-t'ai, and Ch'an traditions of Chinese Buddhism. The two major sects remained as the official divisions of Buddhism until 1935. (See also KYOJONG.).

⌘ SŌTŌ ZEN ⌘

School of Buddhism brought to Japan by Dōgen Zenji (1200–1253) and continuing the Ts'ao-tung Ch'an tradition of China. Originally a student of Eisai (1141–1215), Dōgen went to China in 1223. He experienced enlightenment under the Ch'an master T'ien-t'ung Ju-ching (1163–1228), and received Dharma transmission from him. Returning to Japan, he eventually became abbot of Kōshō-ji monastery, and about a decade later founded Daibutsu-ji monastery, later referred to as Eihei-ji, one of the two main monasteries of Sōtō Zen. Although the goal of Sōtō Zen, gaining enlightenment, remains identical to that of Rinzai Zen, the methods of the two main schools of Zen are quite different. Sōtō utilizes a practice known as shikantaza or "just sitting." It presumes that *sitting in meditation itself* (i.e., zazen) is an expression of Buddha nature. Rinzai combines sitting meditation with the use of kōans, enigmatic, riddle-like "public cases" designed to dramatically push the mind beyond conceptual thought patterns, fostering sudden illumination. Sōtō Zen continues to play a prominent role in modern Japanese Buddhism, and is one of the popular Zen forms exported outside Japan. (See also DŌGEN ZENJI.)

⌘ SPRUL-SKU (TULKU) ⌘

Technical term for a reincarnated lama in Tibetan Buddhism. Beginning in the thirteenth century, Tibetan Buddhists maintained that some individuals reincarnated themselves following their death in keeping with the Trikāya notion of the "Three Bodies of the Buddha." By identifying the *specific* individuals who were the beneficiaries of these incarnations, a doctrinal and monastic perpetuity could be maintained within each tradition. As such *lineages* were established they became quite important in the ongoing history of Tibetan Buddhism and Tibetan Buddhist schools. Of course the most obvious, and important, of these incarnations is the Dalai Lama, head of the dGe-lugs-pa school. The head of each of the major schools, however, *also* incarnates himself, as well as other lineages *within* each school.

⌘ SPYAN-RAS-GZIGS (CHENREZI) ⌘

In Tibetan Buddhism, the bodhisattva of infinite compassion, Avalokiteśvara. Identified as the "Lord Who Looks Down," he was one of the most important Celestial Bodhisattvas in Mahāyāna Buddhism. In Tibet, he was considered as patron of the land, and sometimes associated with King Srong-btsan-sgam-po (616–650). In the iconography, he is shown in a variety of ways, often with eleven heads and one thousand arms or with four arms and sitting on a lotus flower. (See also AVALOKITEŚVARA.)

⌘ ŚRĀMAṆERA ⌘

Term for a male novice in the Buddhist saṃgha. These are individuals, often young in age, who take the initial ordination requiring a recitation of the threefold refuge formula and adherence to the daśa-śīla or "ten vows." The training of novices is usually entrusted to older, highly disciplined monks, including both a "teacher" (ācārya) and "preceptor" (upādhyāya), who provide both doctrinal and disciplinary instruction. The ordinand has his head shaved, receives his three robes, and is given a begging bowl. This initial ordination is known as the pravrajyā, literally "going forth." After attaining the proper age (20) or, upon completing the appropriate probationary period if already of proper age, the novice can receive the full ordination known as upasaṃpadā. (See also ŚRĀMAṆERĪ.)

⌘ ŚRĀMAṆERĪ ⌘

Term for a female novice in the Buddhist saṃgha. She follows the same regulations as the male novice regarding ordination and training. (See also ŚRĀMAṆERA.)

⌘ ŚRĀVAKA-YĀNA ⌘

The "vehicle of the śrāvaka." The Śrāvaka-yāna is another way of identifying the immediate disciples of the Buddha, the "hearers" and their spiritual descendants who responded to the oral teachings of the Buddha. Their goal in the early Buddhist tradition was the attainment of nirvāṇa. Along with the Pratyekabuddha-yāna, the path taken by the "private" or "solitary" buddhas who attained enlightenment on their own, never to embark on a teaching career, the Śrāvaka-yāna represents part of Hīnayāna Buddhism. In Mahāyāna, the path taken was that of the Bodhisattva-yāna, the selfless individual who accepted rebirth into saṃsāra again and again in hopes of bringing all sentient beings to complete, perfect enlightenment.

⌘ STCHERBATSKY, FEDOR IPPOLITOVICH (THEODORE) ⌘ *(1866–1942)*

Russian Buddhologist, primarily known through his interest in Buddhist logic, but widely published in a variety of areas. From a wealthy family, and linguistically gifted, Stcherbatsky had a long and varied career in the study of Buddhism. His major publications include *Soul Theory of the Buddhists* (1919), *The Central Conception of Buddhism and the Meaning of the Word "Dharma"* (1923), *The Conception of Buddhist Nirvāṇa* (1927), and *Buddhist Logic* (1930). He had an especially spirited, and long lasting, debate with Louis de La Vallée Poussin about the nature of nirvāṇa in the Buddhist tradition.

⌘ STHAVIRA ⌘

Sanskrit technical term meaning "elder." It was the name taken by one of the two initial sectarian groups in Indian Buddhism. Although there is still much conjecture about precisely where and when Indian Buddhism became sectarian, it is clear that the two original groups formed identified themselves as Mahāsāṃghikas or "Great Group-ists," and Sthaviras or "Elders." The Mahāsāṃghikas seem to be so named because their members were in the vast *majority* of Buddhists at the council that established sectarianism as an inevitable result of internal Buddhist conflict. The Staviras, rather than assuming a minority position, argued that they represented the elder, *orthodox* disciplinary and doctrinal tradition of the Buddha. Etymologically, the Pāli equivalent of Sthavira is Thera. Consequently, the Theravādin nikāya has argued that *it is one of the first, authentic Buddhists groups,* and since the Mahāsāmghikas no longer exist, that the Theravādin nikāya is the *oldest* remaining Buddhist school. *Historically, this claim is neither accurate nor verifiable.* It is quite clear that the Theravādin nikāya is a later development in Indian Buddhism, originating about 200 years after the beginning of Buddhist sectarianism. (See also MAHĀSĀṂGHIKA.)

⌘ STOREHOUSE CONSCIOUSNESS ⌘

See ĀLAYA-VIJÑĀNA

⌘ STŪPA ⌘

Buddhist memorial monument usually containing the remains of a famous historical figure. They are present in one form or another in most Buddhist cultures. In Theravāda countries, they are referred to in Pāli as thūpas. In some East Asian cultures they are called pagodas. In Tibet, the traditional phrase identifying them is mch'od-rten (chörten). Nonetheless, in *all* Buddhist cultures, they are objects of veneration, utilized to facilitate recollection and respect for a famous individual. In Buddha's case, stūpas were erected in recognition of the major events of his life: birth at Lumbinī Garden, enlightenment at Bodhgayā, the first sermon at Sārnāth, and death at Kuśinagara. Sometimes sacred texts were housed in stūpas in place of the actual physical remains of an individual. Stūpa architecture has gone through a variety of developmental phases, beginning with a simple hemispheric structure erected over a circular base and with a pillar-like or post-like top, but eventually evolving to the complex maṇḍala-like structure of the famous Javanese stūpa known as Borobuḍur. Many stūpas are pilgrimage sites for Buddhists, and are always locations for pūja or other forms of worship. (See also BOROBUḌUR; PAGODA.)

⌘ SUBHŪTI ⌘

Disciple of Buddha identified as being foremost of those dwelling in peace. Although he is mentioned very little in the early tradition, he becomes the principal interlocutor in the early Mahāyāna Prajnāpāramitā literature. There he is often utilized to represent the figure of the bodhisattva, skilled in knowledge about emptiness (śunyata), and superior to the figure of the śravaka.

⌘ ŚUDDHODANA ⌘

Father of Siddhārtha Gautama and ruler of the Śākya clan. He was head of a small kingdom in the foothills of the Himalayas (in what would be modern-day Nepal) with its capital at Kapilavastu. His clan was part of the warrior (kṣatriya) class, thus positioning him in an advantageous social position. His queen bore him a son who was named Siddhartha (literally "he who will accomplish his goal") on the basis of a prophecy offered by the sage Asita. After the death of Siddhārtha's biological mother, Queen Māyā, the king married her sister Mahāprajāpatī. Although Śuddhodana resisted Siddhārtha's great renunciation from the world, he considered Siddhārtha's attainment of Buddhahood a critically important achievement, converting to the tradition just prior to his own death.

⌘ SUFFERING ⌘

See DUḤKHA

⌘ SUKHĀVATĪ ⌘

"Land of Happiness," or "Pure Land," a special cosmological paradise over which Amitābha Buddha presides, located in the western region. It is described in detail in a variety of texts, including the Larger and Smaller Sukhāvatīvyūha-sūtras and the Amitāyurdhyāna-sūtra. Rebirth in Sukhāvatī is obtained by placing one's faith in Amitābha and reciting his name. (See also AMITĀYURDHYĀNA-SŪTRA; CHING-T'U; JŌDO SHINSHŪ; JŌDO SHŪ; LARGER AND SMALLER SUKHĀVATĪVYŪHA-SŪTRAS; PURE LAND.)

⌘ ŚŪNYATĀ ⌘

Doctrine of "emptiness" or "voidness," stressed in many Mahāyāna scriptures, beginning with the Prajñāpāramitā-sūtras. It goes beyond the early Buddhist position of anātman (not-self), stating that even dharmas, the momentary building blocks of experiential reality, have no ontological existence in their own right. The doctrine of emptiness thus emphasizes the relational aspect of existence, a presumably proper understanding of the early Buddhist doctrine of dependent origination (pratītya-samutpāda). In this way, emptiness becomes an epistemological tool used to "unfreeze" the fixed notions of our minds. It is important to understand that śūnyatā, utilized in this fashion, *is not* an ontological state, and that *even emptiness* is empty. However, it would be incorrect to surmise that the negative terminology associated with the concept is indicative of a subtle nihilism in Mahāyāna. To argue that all dharmas are empty does *not* mean that they do not exist, but rather identifies them as *appearances* which should not be perceived as objects of grasping. Because the doctrine of emptiness is critical to *all* Mahāyāna schools of Buddhism, it becomes of paramount importance, not only to the Mādhyamika and Yogācāra schools of Buddhism in India (including all of their respective subdivisions), but to all the Mahāyāna schools across the geographic landscape, ancient and modern. Śūnyatā also plays a critical role in all the Vajrayāna schools as well. Consequently, it is probably not unreasonable to cite this doctrine as *the single most important Mahāyāna innovation.*

⌘ SUPERNORMAL POWERS ⌘

See ABHIJÑĀ

⌘ SŪTRA PIṬAKA ⌘

Literally the "Basket of Discourses," a collection of Buddha's sermons identified as "canonical" at the first Buddhist council of

Rājagṛha. In the Sanskrit collection, four Āgamas are counted as part of the Sūtra Piṭaka: (1) the Dirgha Āgama, a series of long discourses, (2) the Madhyama Āgama, a series of middle length discourses, (3) the Saṃyukta Āgama, a series of "linked" discourses, and (4) the Ekottarika Āgama, a series of "increased-by-one" discourses. Each of these Āgamas corresponds to a counterpart (called a Nikāya) in the Sutta Piṭaka of the Pāli Canon, *the only complete textual collection of discourse material identified with one Buddhist school.* The Pāli texts include the (1) Dīgha Nikāya, (2) Majjhima Nikāya, (3) Saṃyutta Nikāya, and (4) Aṅguttara Nikāya. The Pāli Canon also has a fifth Nikāya, known as the Khuddaka Nikāya, but it does *not* correspond to the Sanskrit Kṣudraka Āgama. In the Sūtra Piṭaka one can find all of Buddha's basic doctrinal positions, as well as a miscellany of ethical and meditational teachings. (See also TRIPIṬAKA.)

⌘ SUZUKI, DAISETZ TEITARO ⌘
(1870–1966)

Japanese Buddhist scholar who wrote extensively on Mahāyāna Buddhism in general, and was one of the first interpreters of Zen to a Western audience. Suzuki's father, a physician, died when his son was only six years of age. Following his mother's death, and with a self-taught knowledge of English, he studied informally at the Imperial University in Tokyo. Since his family had a Rinzai Zen affiliation, he undertook some Zen training, eventually coming to serve as translator for Sōyen Shaku, the Dharma heir of his first teacher. After Sōyen Shaku's participation in the World Parliament of Religions in Chicago in 1893, he arranged for D. T. Suzuki to work with Paul Carus, an author and editor at Open Court Publishing Company in LaSalle, Illinois. Suzuki stayed with Carus from 1897 to 1909, at which point he returned to Japan. He married Beatrice Lane in 1911, returned to America in 1936, and then spent the war years in Japan. Suzuki returned to America again for a long stay between 1950 and 1958, giving frequent lectures at American universities. In his long career, he published a variety of books and articles. While at Open Court, he published *Outlines of Mahayana Buddhism.* He went on to publish *Studies in the Laṅkāvatāra Sūtra,* followed shortly by a translation of the same text: *The Laṅkāvatāra Sūtra.* Additionally, he wrote *Manual of Zen Buddhism, The Training of the Zen Buddhist Monk, Essays in Zen Buddhism* (published in three series), *Introduction to Zen Buddhism, Zen and Japanese Culture, Shin Buddhism,* and *On Indian Mahayana Buddhism.* He also was a frequent contributor to the well-known journal *The Eastern Buddhist.* Although he was often maligned by the scholarly community, he had during his life, and continues to have, a faithful and devoted audience of readers.

⌘ SUZUKI, SHUNRYU ⌘
(1904–1971)

Son of a Sōtō Zen priest and Rōshi, he was born in Tsuchisawa, Kanagawa Prefecture. At thirteen, he became the disciple of one of his father's students. At nineteen, he attended the high school associated with Komazawa University, completing the curriculum, as well as an undergraduate degree. He moved on to Eiheiji monastery, becoming a monk, and also spent time at Sōji-ji. In sequence, he married and also became a lifetime student of Kishizawa Rōshi. His wife died in 1951, leaving him a widower with four children. In 1958 he remarried and accepted a three-year position as priest of a temple in San Francisco. Emerging from this assignment was the creation of the San Francisco Zen Center in 1961. In the three decades of its existence, it has been one of the most important, and stable, Buddhist organizations in America. Suzuki Rōshi was one of the first Zen masters to install a Western student as Dharma heir, passing on his lineage to Richard Baker Rōshi. Following a prolonged illness, Suzuki Rōshi died on December 4, 1971. His book *Zen Mind, Beginner's Mind* is one of the most useful and popular books for Zen students today.

⌘ SVABHĀVA ⌘

Sanskrit term literally meaning "own-being" or "own-nature," said to be *lacking* in experiential reality as defined by Mahāyāna Buddhism. As an extension of the Buddhist understanding of anātman, Mahāyāna argues that if an entity indeed possessed a svabhāva, an ontological "own-being," it would exist in and of itself, thus contradicting the law of dependent origination (pratītya-samutpāda). As a result, Mahāyāna reasons that all building blocks of experiential reality, known as dharmas, are empty (śūnyatā) of svabhāva. This is a critical teaching of all Mahayana texts, but especially emphasized in the Prajñāpāramitā-sūtras.

⌘ SVĀTANTRIKA ⌘

Division of the Mādhyamika school founded by Bhāvaviveka (ca. 490–570). Following the basic establishment of the Mādhyamika school by Nāgārjuna, there was some disagreement as to the efficacy of Nāgārjuna's use of a negative dialectic and *reductio ad absurdum* argument as the basic approach of the school. Bhāvaviveka opposed Nāgārjuna and utilized a *positive* dialectic, founding the Svātantrika division of Mādhyamika. Bhāvaviveka, in turn, was opposed by Buddhapālita (ca. 470–540), who upheld the orthodox approach, establishing the Prāsaṅgika division of Mādhyamika. (See also BHĀVAVIVEKA; MĀDHYAMIKA.)

— T —

⌘ T'AI-HSÜ ⌘
(1889 1947)

Modern Chinese Buddhist reformist active in the Chinese Buddhist revival of the early twentieth century. A monk since his mid-teens, T'ai-hsü had a thorough grounding in the T'ien-t'ai and Hua-yen schools of Buddhism, but eventually specialized in the Fa-hsiang school. In 1911 he became abbot of a monastery in Canton. Within a decade he had begun to publish a periodical known as the Hai-chao-yin or Sound of the Tide (1918) and founded the Wu-ch'ang Buddhist Institute (1922). In a bold move to further reform the Chinese Buddhist community, T'ai-hsü organized the Chinese Buddhist Society in 1929. By 1947, the organization claimed nearly five million members. T'ai-hsü also supervised an extensive publication effort during the first decades of the twentieth century. His main doctrinal theme focused on promoting a synthesis of various Chinese Buddhist schools in a harmonious fashion. The reform movement that flourished as a result of the work of T'ai-hsü (and others) was cut short by the occupation of the mainland by the Chinese Communists in 1949.

⌘ TAISHŌ SHINSHŪ DAIZŌKYŌ ⌘

The Chinese Buddhist Canon is called the *Ta-ts'ang-ching* or "Great Scripture Store." Although the first complete printing was completed as early as 983 C.E., the now standard modern edition of this work is known as the *Taishō Shinshū Daizōkyō*, published in Tokyo between 1924 and 1929. It contain 55 volumes containing 2,184 texts, along with a supplement of 45 additional volumes. A summary of its contents appears in the section on The Buddhist Scriptures of this volume.

⌘ T'ANG DYNASTY ⌘

Period of Chinese history from 618–906, during which time Buddhism in China reached its peak of importance. By the time of the T'ang Dynasty, nearly all of the Buddhist schools were represented on Chinese soil: Chü-shê, San-lun, Fa-hsiang, T'ien-t'ai, Hua-yen, Ch'an, and Ching-t'u. During the T'ang Dynasty, however, they took on a *fully* Chinese character. Buddhism was aggressively supported by a number of T'ang rulers, resulting in an upscale development of monasteries, cave temple projects, and the like. Unfortunately, in 845, Buddhism was also severely persecuted by the Emperor Wu-tsung. Despite the emperor's death the following year, an enormous number of monks and nuns were laicized, monastic property was seized, images were melted down, and the economic base of the Chinese Buddhist saṃgha was thoroughly disrupted. Those Buddhist schools that were either textual, intellectual, or totally monastery-based essentially perished from the landscape, while the traditions that were based on personal, individual practice, especially including the Ch'an and the Pure Land traditions, survived.

⌘ T'AN-LUAN ⌘
(476–542)

Next to Hui-yüan, the most important figure in the Chinese Pure Land movement. While searching for immortality through Taoist methods, T'an-luan met an Indian missionary named Bodhiruci who had arrived in Lo-yang in 508. Sometime around 530 Bodhiruci converted T'an-luan to the Pure Land doctrine, and T'an-luan eventually became known as the first patriarch of the

Ching-t'u school in China. His commentaries on the traditional Pure Land texts form the theoretical basis for the school. His career was marked by a continual effort to spread the Pure land doctrine and practice throughout Chinese society. (See also BODHIRUCI; SHAN-TAO; TAO-CHO.)

⌘ TANTRA ⌘

Technical term, literally meaning "continuity" or "thread," and generally applied to the esoteric school of Buddhism that developed in India, but which quickly spread (especially) to Tibet, China, and Japan. The school espoused a doctrinal system that emerged from Mahāyāna philosophy and emphasized techniques of spontaneity centered around the use of mantras, maṇḍalas, and provocative psychological techniques. It attempted to move beyond all dualities, symbolized especially by the masculine and feminine principles, by their very union. In this system, the masculine principle is identified with skilfull means (upāya) and the feminine principle with wisdom (prajñā). The term is also applied to a class of literature composed of four types: (1) Kriyā-tantra (2) Caryā-Tantra (3) Yoga-tantra, and (4) Anuttarayoga-tantra. The latter two classes are generally regarded as "higher" than the previous two, this determination being made by the spiritual development of the practitioner for whom each was intended. In Tibet, the oldest Buddhist school known as rNying-ma-pa further divides Anuttarayoga tantra into three additional categories: (1) Mahāyoga, (2) Anuyoga, and (3) Atiyoga. This later practice is known as rDzogs-chen (dzogchen). (See also ANUTTARAYOGA-TANTRA; CHÊN-YEN; GUHYASAMĀJA-TANTRA; HEVAJRA-TANTRA; KĀLACAKRA-TANTRA; SHINGON; VAJRAYĀNA.)

⌘ TAO-AN ⌘

(312–385)

Early Chinese Buddhist scholar important for popularizing the Prajñāpāramitā literature, cataloguing the Buddhist scriptures, fostering the Vinaya tradition, and emphasizing devotion to Maitreya. He was a student of a Kuchean Buddhist monk named Fo-t'u-teng. It was from Fo-t'u-teng that Tao-an learned the prajñā texts. His search for scriptures led him to the production of the Tsung-li chung-ching mu-lu (Comprehensive Catalogue of Sūtras) a collection of Buddhist translations made from the Han Dynasty up to 374. This collection was sometimes called simply "An's Catalogue." Tao-an also encouraged Vinaya translations, recognizing that Chinese Buddhism *at that time* lacked a *complete* disciplinary text. He also created *his own* rules, aimed at addressing *Chinese* Buddhism. He also was instrumental in organizing a cult devoted to the worship of Maitreya, the future Buddha. He spent the last years of his life in Ch'ang-an encouraging the translation of Indian Sarvāstivādin literature. Tao-an also can be considered one of the so-called Buddho-Taoists who utilized Taoist terminology to express Buddhist ideas to the early Chinese Buddhist community. (See also BUDDHO-TAOISTS.)

⌘ TAO-CHO ⌘
(562–645)

Important Pure Land master in China, following the tradition of T'an-luan. His main text was the An-lo-chi (Collection of Essays on the Pure Land). The main issue confronted by Tao-cho involved the proper religious practice for individuals during a period of Dharma decline (mo-fa), resulting in his firm emphasis on recitation of the nien-fo, proclamation of homage to A-mi-t'o (Sanskrit: Amitābha) Buddha. He even recommended using beans to count the number of times a disciple repeated the recitation. (See also SHAN-TAO; T'AN-LUAN.)

⌘ TAO-SHÊNG ⌘
(360–434)

Disciple of Kumārajīva who was important in the development and transmission of the San-lun school of Chinese Buddhism. Sometime around 397, he arrived at the Buddhist center of Lushan, where he met and studied with Hui-yüan and Sanghadeva. Around 405, he moved on to Ch'ang-an, becoming a close disciple of Kumārajīva. He had a compelling interest in a text known as the Mahāparinirvāṇa-sūtra, a Mahāyāna text not to be confused with a text of similar name in the Pāli Canon. He worked toward synthesizing this text with the philosophy espoused in the Prajñāpāramitā texts. He also argued in favor of the theory of "sudden enlightenment," that realization occurs in a flash of insight, thus instigating a conflict with those who argued that enlightenment results from a *gradual* progression through the bodhisattva path, gaining a partial realization at stage seven, but not complete enlightenment until the culmination of stage ten.

⌘ TARA ⌘

Female Bodhisattva whose name means "Savioress," and who is said to be born from two tears shed by Avalokiteśvara. Since Avalokiteśvara is associated with compassion, Tārā becomes its feminine manifestation. As such, she became exceedingly important in Tibetan Buddhism, where a cult grew up around her worship. She is reputed to have twenty-one forms, varied by color, posture, and the like. She is most often represented as green or white. She was the subject of an immense doctoral dissertation by Stephan Beyer at the University of Wisconsin, the result being published as *The Cult of Tārā*.

⌘ TĀRANĀTHA ⌘

Eminent Tibetan Buddhist historian of the minor Jo-nang-pa lineage, born in 1575. He is primarily known for his *History of Buddhism in India*, apparently written in 1608. It is regarded as an important source for information on early Indian Buddhism.

⌘ TARIKI ⌘

Japanese technical term, most often translated as "other-power," indicating a religious attainment achieved through such activities as placing one's faith in the saving grace of a Buddha or other religious figure. Tariki (Chinese: t'o-li) is almost always played off against jiriki or "own-power," a term readily utilized in the Zen tradition to indicate a religious attainment, such as satori, achieved through one's one striving through a particular means such as zazen. Tariki is most often associated with the Pure Land tradition, in which rebirth in the Pure Land is facilitated by chanting the nembutsu or expression of faith in the saving grace of Amida Buddha. Tariki is also called the "easy path," again contrasted with jiriki, the "difficult path." (See also JIRIKI.)

⌘ TATHĀGATA ⌘

Sanskrit term literally meaning "Thus-Come," and used as an epithet of Buddha. Subsequent to his attainment of enlightenment and his establishment as a Buddha, Siddhārtha Gautama was identified by a number of epithets in various Buddhist literary texts. Most frequent among these honorific titles were Śākyamuni or "Sage of the Śākya Clan," Jina or "Conqueror," and Tathāgata. He is also referred to as an Arhant (worthy one) and as Samyak Sambuddha (Completely and Perfectly Enlightened One).

⌘ TATHĀGATA-GARBHA ⌘

Sanskrit technical term literally meaning "Womb of the Tathāgata," and utilized in Mahāyāna thought to suggest that all sentient beings possess the potential for Buddhahood. The term is especially important in Yogācāra texts, where it is used almost as an equivalent to the phrase "Buddha-nature," employed to indicate the inherent potential for Buddhahood in everyone. It also has an additional meaning in Yogācāra, especially in the Laṅkāvatāra-sūtra, where it is equated to the ālaya-vijñāna or "storehouse-consciousness."

⌘ TATHATĀ ⌘

Mahāyāna Buddhist term most often rendered as "suchness" or "thusness," indicating a formless, immutable absolute state. It is regularly used in conjunction with a variety of other nondescriptive terms as a synonym for enlightenment. It has sometimes been suggested that "suchness" and "thusness" have been offered as translation equivalents for tathatā so as to avoid presenting the idea that enlightenment can be described in objective terms, as a state having "this" or "that" set of characteristics. Tathatā captures the nonstatic, unreified state of ultimacy consistent with Mahāyāna thought.

⌘ TENDAI ⌘

Japanese Buddhist school equivalent to the Chinese T'ien-t'ai, brought to Japan by Saichō (767–822) in the eighth century. After building a small monastery on Mt. Hiei, Saichō was sent to China to study, focusing essentially on T'ien-t'ai, but also including other schools. Upon returning, he consolidated his teaching into the Tendai school. Doctrinally, there is little difference between the Chinese and Japanese versions of the school, including great emphasis on the Lotus-sūtra as the primary scripture of the school. A twelve-year training period for Tendai monks was instituted, indicative of the great emphasis the school placed on the moral life. There is also an esoteric aspect to the Tendai school. (See also SAICHO; T'IEN-T'AI.)

⌘ TENJUR ⌘

See BSTAN-'GYUR

⌘ THANGKA ⌘

Tibetan scroll paintings capturing various iconographical themes in the Tibetan Buddhist tradition. Quite often thangkas emphasize either the famous bhavacakra or "wheel of life" or previous existences of the Buddha as reflected in the Jātaka stories. They may also be used, however, as representations of key lineages or individuals, in a *particular* Tibetan Buddhist school. The painting of thangka's is an extremely difficult enterprise, perhaps to be viewed as a meditative exercise in itself, with the tradition passed on from master to disciple. Many of the oldest thangkas that were carried from Tibet during the holocaust are extremely valuable today. Additionally, the practice of painting thangkas continues in both Asia and the West.

⌘ THERAGĀTHĀ ⌘

The eighth of fifteen collections of texts included in the Khuddaka Nikāya of the Pāli Canon. The Theragāthā or "Verses of the Male Elders," contains a series of 264 poems attributed to 259 male disciples of the Buddha. They are arranged in twenty-one books, ranging from poems of one verse only up to a final poem of seventy-one verses. The text celebrates the fruits of attainment, including such benefits as freedom from mundane woes and the benefits of the meditative life. (See also THERĪGĀTHĀ.)

⌘ THERAVĀDA ⌘

Sole surviving sect of Hīnayāna Buddhism, prevalent in South and Southeast Asia today. The title of the group literally means "Those Who Hold the Doctrine of the Elders." It emerged out of Mahinda's mission to Sri Lanka during the reign of King Aśoka, apparently very closely related to the Vibhayjavādin group Aśoka regarded as orthodox. The group also bears striking affinities to the Mahīśāsaka and Kāśyapīya sects, which also appear to have grown from the Vibjayavādin lineage. From Sri Lanka, where the Theravāda sect has had an almost continuous lineage of over two millennia, the Theravāda tradition has come to dominate South Asia. It is the most important Buddhist group in Burma, Laos, Thailand, and Cambodia, and has in recent decades become highly active in Europe and North America. It is thoroughly conservative in all aspects of its doctrinal and monastic tradition. Additionally, it is the holder of the first complete set of Buddhist scriptures preserved intact in *one* canonical language: the Pāli Canon. It currently maintains a strong and socially active monastic tradition, but almost exlcusively composed of monks.

⌘ THERĪGĀTHĀ ⌘

The ninth of fifteen collections of texts included in the Khuddaka Nikāya of the Pāli Canon. The Therīgāthā or "Verses of the Female Elders," contains a series of 73 poems composed by 71 authors. Like the Theragāthā, poems in this collection are arranged according to length, in sixteen books. In general, the poems of the female elders are shorter than those of the male elders. Thematically, the text is quite similar to the Theragāthā. However, it is also clear that the females' poems are more personal, filled with episodes drawn from their personal lives. They reflect the writings of a vibrant group of personally and spiritually free women, quite the exception to the society in which they lived. (See also THERAGĀTHĀ.)

⌘ THREE JEWELS ⌘

See TRIRATNA

⌘ THE THREE PILLARS OF ZEN ⌘

Title of a contemporary volume compiled and edited by Philip Kapleau Rōshi, completed in Japan and first published in the United States in 1967. Intended for a Western audience, and for one of the very first times, portraying Zen through the eyes of a *Western* master, *The Three Pillars of Zen* focuses on the teaching, practice, and enlightenment of Zen. In the section on training and practice, in addition to including Yasutani Rōshi's introductory lectures on Zen training, it also includes ten private interviews between Yasutani Rōshi and Western students. Moreover, Bassui Zenji's (1327–1387) sermon on one-mind is presented, along with letters to his disciples. In the section on enlightenment, eight contemporary enlightenment experiences of Japanese and Western students are included, as well as Yaeko Iwasaki's enlightenment letters to Harada Rōshi in 1935 and his comments on them. A third and final section of the book includes (1) Dōgen Zenji's notions on "Being-Time," (2) ten "ox herding" pictures along with commentary, (3) zazen postures illustrated, and (4) a miscellany of Zen and Buddhist vocabulary terms. Now, a quarter-century after its appearance, it remains one of the most important and influential books for Western students and practitioners of Zen.

⌘ THREE REFUGES ⌘

See TRIŚARAṆA

⌘ TIBETAN BOOK OF THE DEAD ⌘

See BARDO THÖDOL (BAR-DO THOS-GROL)

⌘ T'IEN-T'AI ⌘

School of Chinese Buddhism founded by Hui-ssŭ (515–576), organized by Chih-i (538–597), and largely based on the teaching of the Lotus-sūtra. The name of the school is taken from the name of the mountain on which Chih-i exercised: T'ien-t'ai Shan. Although Chih-i actually *wrote* very little, his teachings were collected and preserved by one of his disciples, Kuan-ting (561–632). These teachings focused primarily on the Lotus-sūtra and included three great works: (1) Miao-fa lien-hia ching hsüan-i (Profound Meaning of the Lotus Sūtra), (2) Miao-fa lien-hua ching wen-chü (Commentary on the Lotus Sūtra), and (3) Mo-ho chih-kuan (Great Concentration and Insight). The T'ien-t'ai system is explained in five chronological periods. The first, or Avataṃsaka-sūtra period, is said to have lasted only three weeks, and dated from Buddha's attainment of enlightenment. Because his disciples did not understand his teaching, he began the second period, known as the Āgama period, lasting twelve years, and during which time Buddha preached his basic *but not final or complete* teaching. The third, or Vaipulya period, lasted eight years and presented the basic Mahāyāna teachings. In the fourth period, known as the Mahāprajñāpāramitā period and lasting twenty-two years, he emphasized the doctrine of śūnyatā, as taught in the Perfection of Wisdom literature. The fifth and final period, called the Lotus-sūtra Period, corresponds to the last eight years of Buddha's life, and here Buddha taught the doctrine of Eka-yāna, that there is really only one vehicle, and that the Śrāvaka-yāna, Pratyekabuddha-yāna, and Bodhisattva-yāna are only *apparent* contrasts. Additionally, T'ien-t'ai classifies Buddha's doctrine into two quartets of teachings with the first including (1) sudden doctrine, (2) gradual doctrine, (3) secret doctrine, and (4) indeterminate doctrine. Sudden doctrine was taught in the Avataṃsaka period. Gradual doctrine was taught over the second, third, and fourth chronological stages. Secret doctrine and indeterminate doctrine were used when Buddha taught disciples of differing capacities at the same time. The second quartet of teachings includes (1) Piṭaka doctrine, (2) common doctrine, (3) special doctrine, and (4) round or perfect doctrine. In the Avataṃsaka period special and round doctrines were taught. The Āgama period utilized only the Piṭaka doctrine. The Vaipulya period utilized all four of these doctrines, and the Mahāprajñāpāramitā period employs mostly the round doctrine, but also the common and special doctrines. Only the Lotus-sūtra period can be considered totally round and complete. (See also CHIH-I; LOTUS-SŪTRA.)

⌘ TILOPA ⌘

(989–1069)

Great Mahāsiddha and teacher of Nāropa. His name literally means "crusher of sesame," presumably a reflection of his long-time occupation in Bengal, following a long period of collecting esoteric teachings and practices throughout India. Although Tilopa is often described as being quite erratic, appearing only partially clothed, and acting "crazy," he transmitted the Tantric practices he unified to Nāropa. Under the name of the "Six Dharmas of Nāropa," these teachings were taken to Tibet where they were instrumental in the bKa-rgyud-pa school of Tibetan Buddhism. (See also NĀROPA.)

⌘ TI-LUN ⌘

Chinese Buddhist school based on Vasubandhu's commentary on the Daśabhūmika-sūtra. The Chinese text, translated by Bodhiruci and Ratnamati in 508, was called the Shih-ti ching-lun or Ti lun for short, hence the name of the school. Buddhabhadra's translation of the Avataṃsaka-sūtra (Chinese: Hua-yen Ching) into Chinese had been completed as early as 418–420, but gained little interest until the Ti-lun school appeared, as many Ti-lun masters were expert on the Avataṃsaka-sūtra. Consequently, the Ti-lun school may have foreshadowed the rise of the Hua-yen school, then being absorbed into it.

⌘ TI-TS'ANG ⌘

See JIZO

⌘ TRIKĀYA ⌘

Mahāyāna Buddhist concept, literally referring to "three bodies of Buddha." The doctrine, predominantly developed in texts associated with the Yogācāra school of Buddhism (such as the Laṅkāvatāra-sūtra), is a reflection of a sophisticated Mahāyāna Buddhology. It argues that Buddha is revealed in a variety of ways to a variety of individuals, each reflective of the individual's particular level of spiritual development. At the lowest level, one encounters the nirmāṇa-kāya or "apparitional body." This body is depicted as the historical Buddha, visible to ordinary, common worldlings as an inspiration to begin the Mahāyāna Buddhist path. It exists only insofar as it is an apparitional manifestation of ultimate reality. Once on the path, the practitioner, now known as a bodhisattva, encounters Buddha in another form: as saṃbhoga-kāya or "enjoyment body," a subtle-bodied, quasi-material preacher of Mahāyāna scriptures, neither fully human nor fully absolute. At the completion of the path, one attains Dharma-kāya or "Dharma body," the true nature of Buddhahood, ultimate reality itself, an abstract resolution of all dualities, beyond any conceptualization or designation. Thus, the mature notion of the trikāya offers three ways of relating to the essential notion of Buddhahood, each reflective of the psychological development of the practitioner, culminating in the proper experience of Buddhahood as ultimate reality itself, empty of any dualities whatsoever. (See also DHARMA-KĀYA; NIRMĀṆA-KĀYA; SAṂBHOGA-KĀYA.)

⌘ TRIPIṬAKA ⌘

Sanskrit technical term meaning "Three Baskets," and used as the title for the scripture collection of early Buddhism. The three individual "baskets" of Buddhist scripture include the: (1) Vinaya Piṭaka or "Basket of Discipline," (2) Sūtra Piṭaka or "Basket of Discourses," and (3) Abhidharma Piṭaka or "Basket of Higher Philosophy." The scripture collection of only one early Buddhist school is preserved intact, that of the Theravāda school, handed down in Pāli as the Tipiṭaka. The Tripiṭakas of other Hīnayāna schools are preserved in an incomplete number of Sanskrit texts that have appeared in various manuscript collections, supplemented by translations of the missing portions in Chinese or Tibetan. The other scripture collections, as preserved in Chinese and Tibetan, are described in the section titled The Buddhist Scriptures of this volume. (See also ABHIDHARMA PIṬAKA; AṄGA; SŪTRA PIṬAKA; VINAYA PIṬAKA.)

⌘ TRIRATNA ⌘

Sanskrit technical term meaning "Three Jewels," and referring to three major features of Buddhism: Buddha, Dharma, and Saṃgha. The first jewel identifies Buddha as the enlightened one, an individual who put an end to entrapment in the cycle of perpetual rebirth in saṃsāra. In consistence with the meaning of the title "Buddha," derived from the Sanskrit verb root √ budh, the first jewel identifies one who has become awakened. The second jewel identifies Dharma as the basic teaching of the Buddha. Generically, it includes the various doctrines maintained by all the Buddhist schools. The Saṃgha or community is the third jewel. Although most Buddhists think of this jewel as inclusive of all those groups in the lay and monastic community, in the strictest sense, this jewel includes *only those individuals who are included in the Ārya-saṃgha,* persons who have attained status as "noble persons" (or ārya-pudgalas). (See also TRIŚARAṆA.)

⌘ TRIŚARAṆA ⌘

Sanskrit technical term meaning "Three Refuges." It refers to a formula utilized in the ceremony by which one formally professes faith in the Buddhist religion. Irrespective of whether one is beginning a Buddhist life as a member of the lay or monastic community, recitation of the three refuge formula is part of the proceedings. It involves a threefold repetition of the formula: "I go to the Buddha for Refuge; I go to the Dharma for Refuge; (and) I go to the Saṃgha for Refuge." It means that each individual puts his faith in Buddha as a man who accomplished what is ascribed to him in the tradition: that he put an end to suffering by uprooting its cause, becoming fully awakened in the process. It means that each individual puts his faith in the Dharma as reflective of those doctrines deemed by Buddha to be essential for practice leading to the eradication of suffering and the end of rebirth. It means that each individual puts his faith in the Saṃgha, the community of noble persons (ārya pudgalas) who have attained at least the first stage on the path, that of stream-winner (srotapanna). The completion of this refuge formula, in conjunction with acceptance of the five vows of the laity, constitutes acceptance into the traditional Buddhist lay community. The completion of this refuge formula, in conjunction with acceptance of the five vows of the laity, five additional vows, and a number of other requirements, constitutes acceptance into the traditional monastic community. (See also TRIRATNA.)

⌘ TṚṢṆĀ ⌘

Second of the famous Four Noble Truths, cornerstone of Buddha's Dharma or "Teaching." In his first sermon, Buddha is reported to have said that tṛṣṇā or "craving" is the root cause (samudaya) of suffering (duḥkha). In this second truth, Buddha identifies three essential kinds of craving: (1) craving for sensual desires (kāma-tṛṣṇā), (2) craving for becoming (bhava-tṛṣṇā), and (3) craving for nonexistence (vibhava-trṣṇā). Of course the antidote for craving is revealed in the fourth noble truth, that of the eightfold path. Nonetheless, it is clear that only by completely *uprooting the cause of suffering* can nirvāṇa be attained. Simply treating the symptoms of craving will not eliminate their reappearance any more than mowing a lawn full of dandelions will produce anything more than a temporary result. (See also ĀRYA SATYAS.)

⌘ TRUNGPA, CHÖGYAM ⌘
(1940–1987)

Contemporary Buddhist leader and author, founder of a number of highly successful Buddhist communities worldwide, and prior to his untimely death, considered to be one of the most important figures in the development of American Buddhism. In infancy he was determined to be an incarnation (sprul-sku, or more commonly, "tulku") of the tenth individual in the Trungpa lineage. Accordingly, he was enthroned in 1941 as the eleventh incarnation in this lineage, inheriting rule of the Surmang monasteries in eastern Tibet. While these monasteries were ruled through a regent, in keeping with the Tibetan tradition, Trungpa was given a proper monastic education and training. He fled Tibet in 1959 to avoid the Communist Chinese, taking up residence in India. He attended Oxford University (1963–1967), published his autobiography (in 1966), and established Samyê-Ling Meditation Center in Scotland. Following a stroke which left him partially paralyzed, Trungpa renounced his monastic vows, marrying Diana Judith Pybus the following year. In 1970 he traveled to North America, establishing Tail of the Tiger meditation center (now renamed Karmê-Chöling) in Barnet, Vermont. Trungpa eventually moved to Boulder, Colorado, where he founded Vajradhatu Foundation in 1973 to serve as the religious unit of his organization and Nalanda Foundation in 1974 to serve as a nonprofit educational unit. In 1976, Trungpa passed on leadership to one of his American students, Vajra Regent Ösel Tendzin (formerly known as Thomas Rich). Trungpa was thus enabled to devote time to writing, lecturing, and his own spiritual development. He later moved to Halifax, Nova Scotia, where he died on April 4, 1987. He was a prolific author, perhaps best known for his books *Meditation in Action*, *Cutting through Spiritual Materialism*, *Shambhala: The Sacred Path of the Warrior*, and a number of others. Although his Vajra Regent also died (on August 25, 1991), Trungpa's work in North America and worldwide has been continued by his son Mipham Rimpoche, the oldest of five children, and now lineage holder.

⌘ TSONG-KHA-PA ⌘
(1357–1419)

Important Tibetan Buddhist who founded the influential dGelugs-pa school of Tibetan Buddhism. Born in northeast Tibet, he entered the Buddhist order as a novice during his childhood. He studied in central Tibet, examined all the basic areas of Buddhist scholarship, and was especially fond of both logic and Vinaya. Tsong-kha-pa took full ordination at age twenty-five, and began what was at first a modest teaching career. Within a quarter-century he was a major figure in Lhasa, had moved away from the bKa-gdams-pa school and begun the dGe-lugs-pa school or "School of the Virtuous." It was so named because Tsong-kha-pa underscored *both* an emphasis on Vinaya *and* doctrinal study. Tsong-kha-pa was regarded as a great scholar, implementing a monastic curriculum that led to a sort of spiritual Ph.D. known as the *Geshe* degree. His writings fill more than a dozen volumes, includes the voluminous Lam-rim chen-mo, an exceedingly important text on the stages of the Buddhist path. The sect he founded continues today, known as the "Yellow Hat School," because they rejected the traditional red hat of the prior Tibetan Buddhist schools. The lineage of the Dalai Lama also was established within the school founded by Tsong-kha-pa, making the school a political as well as religious force. (See also DGE-LUGS-PA.)

⌘ TSUNG-MI ⌘

(780–841)

Fifth (and last) Hua-yen patriarch in Chinese Buddhism. Although he first followed the Ch'an school, and was considered a master, he joined the Hua-yen school after reading a commentary on the Hua-yen-sūtra by Ch'eng-kuan. In deference to his reputation, he was afforded the title "Master of the Purple Robe" by the emperor and given the posthumous title "Dhyāna Master of Concentration and Insight." Shortly following his death, the Buddhist persecution of 845 ensued, effectively eliminating Hua-yen from the Chinese landscape.

⌘ TUNG-SHAN LIANG-CHIEH ⌘

(807–869)

Along with his student Ts'ao-shan Pên-chi (840–901), one of the founders of the Ts'ao-tung school of Chinese Ch'an Buddhism. Having taken full ordination at age twenty, he studied with a number of influential Ch'an masters, eventually coming to

Yün-yen T'an-sheng (780–841), whose Dharma successor he became. He is credited with creating the important scale known as the "five degrees of enlightenment." Sometime after fifty years of age, he became abbot of the monastery on Mt. Tung-shan, from which his name is taken. His teaching is captured in the Shui-chou Tung-shan Liang-chieh-ch'an-shi yu-lu or Record of the Teaching of Tung-shan Liang-chieh, the Ch'an Master from Shui-chou. The school that he founded was later taken to Japan by Dōgen Zenji as Sōtō Zen. (See also FIVE DEGREES OF ENLIGHTENMENT.)

⌘ TUN-HUANG ⌘

Location in northwest China, housing a series of caves best known for their Buddhist art and as a repository for Buddhist texts. Despite dating from the fifth century, nearly 500 caves are still preserved today. The Mo-kao-k'u, as they are known, was discovered by a local farmer around 1900. The site was visited in 1907 by Sir Mark Aurel Stein and again the following year by Paul Pelliot. Pelliot removed thousands of the scrolls containing Buddhist sūtras. The value of the art work and literary masterpieces preserved at Tun-huan, in terms of their information on both Central Asian and Chinese Buddhism, is simply immeasurable.

⌘ TU-SHUN ⌘
(557–640)

Founder and first patriarch of the Hua-yen school of Buddhism in China. He was also called Fa-shun. Having originally joined the army, Tu-shun renounced the world and began to practice meditation diligently. He became known as a miracle-worker. He became a specialist in the Hua-yen-sūtra, and his disciple Chih-yen (602–668) became the teacher of Fa-tsang (643–712), the organizer of the school. (See also HUA-YEN.)

— U —

⌘ ULLAMBANA ⌘

Festival of the hungry ghosts. Based on the Ullambana-sūtra, the festival presumably takes it origin from a legend surrounding

Buddha's disciple Mahāmauduglayāyana. The faithful disciple utilized his supernormal powers (abhijñā) to discover that his mother had been reborn as a hungry ghost (preta), and wanting to save her from this terrible destiny, made all sorts of offerings as a gesture of filial piety. On the day of the Ullambana festival, sūtras are recited, and offerings of money, food, clothing, flowers, and other goods are made. The festival has been especially popular in Chinese Buddhism, dating from the T'ang Dynasty, and is still celebrated today.

⌘ UPĀLI ⌘

Former barber and early disciple of the Buddha, regarded as being the foremost specialist on matters concerning the disciplinary tradition (Vinaya Piṭaka). When Buddha returned to Kapilavastu to see his family a few years after attaining enlightenment, he initiated a number of young men into the saṃgha. Among these initiates were his cousins Devadatta and Ānanda, his son Rāhula, and also a barber named Upāli who served the Śākyan clan. Because he was ordained early in Buddha's ministry, with seniority counted from the moment of ordination, Upāli was senior to many of Buddha's most well-known disciples. He also distinguished himself by learning all of the disciplinary requirements for the monastic community. As such, at the first council, held in Rājagṛha during the first rainy season following Buddha's death, Upāli recited the entire Vinaya Piṭaka or "Basket of Discipline." In so doing, he became the first master of Vinaya, beginning a lineage that, according to the Pāli tradition, was unbroken at least until Aśoka's reign. (See also COUNCILS-RĀJAGṚHA.)

⌘ UPĀSAKA ⌘

Technical term for male Buddhist lay disciple. Becoming a lay disciple in the early Buddhist tradition requires a recitation of the triśaraṇa or "three refuges" and the formal acceptance of the pañca-śīla or "five moral precepts." In so doing, an upāsaka sets out on the Buddhist path attempting to perform good karma, thus accruing the corresponding merit (puṇya), and moving on to a more favorable rebirth, perhaps one in which he might be able to renounce worldly life and join the monastic community. It is also the responsibility of the laity to provide for the welfare of the monastic community through offerings of clothing, food, and the like. Although there are some records in early Buddhism of members of the laity actually attaining nirvāṇa, these cases are extremely rare, thus establishing the monastic life as a clearly more desirable path. In Mahāyāna, where the bodhisattva ideal is predominant, with enlightenment clearly more accessible to all disciples, more emphasis is placed on the laity, thus upgrading the lay disciple's overall status in the community. (See also UPĀSIKĀ.)

⌘ UPĀSIKĀ ⌘

Technical term for a female Buddhist lay disciple. Although the upāsikā recites the same triśaraṇa as the male lay disciple, and adheres to an identical pañca-śīla, in the earliest tradition, her status is theoretically equal to but pragmatically inferior to the male lay disciple. Like her male counterpart, she attempts to perform good karma, cultivates merit through acts of giving, and hopes to be reborn *as a male,* in order that she have a geuinely more accessible opportunity for the attainment of nirvāṇa. (See also UPĀSAKA.)

⌘ UPĀYA ⌘

Sanskrit technical term literally meaning "skillful means" or "skill-in-means." Although the term is not unheard of in early Buddhism, it is almost always applied to the Mahāyāna tradition, where it is counted as one of the pāramitās or "perfections." Identified as the seventh perfection, it follows attainment of the perfection of wisdom (prajñā). Since one of the critical aspects of Mahāyāna teaching is that bodhisattvas must have compassion (karuṇā) for all sentient beings, it is logical for Mahāyāna adepts, at a certain stage of development, to *know precisely how to apply the wisdom they have experienced.* Upāya provides that aspect of the teaching. Upāya enables the individual who is teaching to find precisely the method of instruction that is appropriate for the person being instructed. Whether a Dharma discourse or shout, meditation instruction or a slap, upāya is the skillful means by which a genuine teacher demonstrates the truth of enlightenment.

⌘ U-RGYAN (URGYAN) ⌘

According to Tibetan tradition, the birthplace of Padmasambhava. The Tibetan name corresponds to the Sanskrit Uḍḍiyāna, a location in the modern Swat valley of Pakistan. The location was long a center of Tantric Buddhism, mentioned by such Chinese pilgrims as Hsüan-tsang.

— V —

⌘ VAIBHĀṢIKA ⌘

Name of the orthodox Sarvāstivādin school taking its doctrinal stand according to the tenets preserved in the text known (in short) as the Mahāvibhāṣā. It is widely acknowledged that the Sarvāstivādin school compiled a commentary on the Jñānaprasthana at Kaniṣka's council, held at Gandhara. This text, basically upholding the views of the great Sarvāstivādin scholar Vasumitra, was known as the Abhidharma-mahāvibhāṣā-śāstra (generally referred to, in short, as noted above). In time, rival viewpoints appeared, in consequence of which those individuals maintaining the orthodox position established by the Mahāvibhaṣa identified themselves as "Vaibhaṣikas." (See also MAHĀVIBHĀṢĀ.)

⌘ VAIPULYA-SŪTRAS ⌘

Class name of a category or group of texts generally referred to as "Extended Sūtras." The Sanskrit term vaipulya literally means "lengthy" or "extended" and refers to a means by which Buddha taught the Dharma through "extending" a story or description. This type of approach is particularly applicable to various Mahāyāna sūtras such as the Prajñāpāramitā texts, the Avataṃsaka-sūtra, and many others.

⌘ VAIROCANA ⌘

Literally "Shining Out," one of the five Celestial Buddhas of Mahāyāna Buddhism. Although he did not become popular until around the seventh century C.E., in Tantric Buddhism he is located at the center of the cosmic maṇḍala, surrounded by the other four Celestial Buddhas. His symbol is often represented as the Dharmacakra or "Wheel of the Teaching," and is sometimes shown making the "supreme wisdom" mudrā in which the right index finger is held by the fingers of the left hand. His is regularly associated with the Celestial Bodhisattva Samantabhadra. Some traditions identify him with the earthly Buddha Krakucchanda, but he is also noted, in the Chinese scholastic tradition, to be the Dharma-kāya of Śākyamuni Buddha. Vairocana is regarded in some traditions to be the Ādi-Buddha or primordial Buddha. In the iconography, he is depicted as white in color. (See also AKṢOBHYA; AMITĀBHA; AMOGHASIDDHI; RATNASAMBHAVA.)

⌘ VAIŚĀLĪ ⌘

Famous city in early Indian Buddhist history, located about twenty-five miles northwest of the modern city of Patna. Originally noted as being located in the Vṛji republic and serving as capital of the Licchavi confederacy, it was frequently visited by Buddha. It was also the site of an early vihāra or monastic settlement given to the saṃgha by the courtesan Āmrapālī. By far, its most important role in Buddhist history centers around the second historical council, said to have been held in Vaiśālī one hundred years after Buddha's death. It was this council that marked the rapidly approaching onset of sectarianism in the Indian Buddhist tradition. (See also COUNCILS-VAIŚĀLĪ.)

⌘ VAJRACCHEDIKĀ-PRAJÑĀPĀRAMITĀ-SŪTRA ⌘

See DIAMOND-SŪTRA

⌘ VAJRAYĀNA ⌘

"Diamond Vehicle," the third major school of Indian Buddhism, arising predominantly in northwest India during the middle centuries of the first millennium C.E. It is also sometimes called the Tantrayāna or Mantrayāna as a further delineation of the main tenets of the school. It combined elements of Mahāyāna philosophy with the esoteric physiological and psychological practices of the emergent Tantric oral literature to form a powerful, unorthodox, and highly successful methodology for attaining enlightenment. Written Vajrayāna literature developed somewhat late in the school, thus necessitating a primary emphasis on the role of the guru or spiritual master. These teachers, often unconventional in their approach, utilized mantras, maṇḍalas, mudrās, and the like to bring about dramatic results for their disciples. While the monastic tradition was not abandoned, a highly complex series of initiations, empowerments, and other rituals was integrated into monastic life. The great saints of Vajrayāna were called Mahāsiddhas, notorious for possessing magical powers and having developed an extensive oral and written tradition. The Vajrayāna tradition was rather quickly exported, first to Central Asia, and later to Tibet and throughout East Asia. It is most readily seen today in the various schools of Tibetan Buddhism and the Shingon tradition of Japanese Buddhism. (See also CHÊN-YEN; HĪNAYĀNA; MAHĀYĀNA; SHINGON.)

⌘ VASUBANDHU ⌘

Indian Buddhist scholar, of somewhat uncertain history, who is reputed to be the author of the Abhidharmakośa, but later a primary figure in the development of the Yocācāra school of Buddhism. General consensus identifies Vasubandhu as the younger brother of Asaṅga, probably born in Puruṣapura (i.e., modern Peshawar) in the fourth century C.E. (and quite possibly 320–400). He is said to have lived around Kaśmīr and died in Ayodhyā. Originally a member of the Sarvāstivādin school of Buddhism, over time he became critical of its views as established in the Mahāvibhāṣā, and composed the Abhidharmakośa, literally meaning "sheath" or "storehouse" of Abhidharma, to critique that position. This text establishes Vasubandhu as a proponent of the philosophy of the Sautrāntika Buddhist school. Apparently later, however, Vasubandhu is converted to the Yogācāra school of Mahāyāna Buddhism by his brother Asaṅga. As a Yogācārin, Vasubandhu is recognized as the author of at least two major texts, the Viṃśatikā or "Twenty Verses" and the Triṃśikā or "Thirty Verses." Each of these texts develops the theory of consciousness-only, critical for Yogācāra philosophy. It is admittedly difficult to reconcile how an individual could embrace so many differing viewpoints, and so passionately, during the course of one lifetime. A possible explanation was voiced by the German scholar Erich Frauwallner who suggested that there were actually *two Vasubandhus*. He claims that Vasubandhu the younger lived from 320–380, was Asaṅga's brother, and was *a Mahāyāna philosopher* exclusively. According to Frauwallner, Vasuabandhu the elder lived from 400–480, was *a thorough-going Hīnayānist*, and the author of the Abhidharmakośa. This viewpoint, although interesting, has been rather thoroughly discredited. (See also ABHIDHARMAKOŚA; ASAṄGA, YOGĀCĀRA.)

⌘ VASUMITRA ⌘

Indian Buddhist scholar reported to have been president of the Buddhist council held by King Kaniṣka in Gandhāra around 100 C.E. The council, in its proceedings, prepared a commentary on the Jñānaprasthāna known as the Mahāvibhāṣā. This text presumably relies heavily on the positions of Vasumitra and verifies his status as one of the primary Sarvāstivādin philosophers. He is also the author of the Samayabhedoparacanacakra, an important text providing much data on Indian Buddhist history.

⌘ VĀTSĪPUTRĪYA ⌘

Primary Indian Buddhist sect belonging to a group collectively referred to as "Personalists" (Pudgalavādins) because of its position regarding the nature and content of rebirth. Taking its name from the founder of the sect, Vātsīputra, it appears to have emerged around 200 years after Buddha's death or sometime around 280 B.C.E. The Sri Lankan tradition identifies this group with the so-called Vṛjiputraka monks living in Vaiśālī at the time of the second Indian Buddhist council, but this account cannot be verified. In any case, the name Vātsīputrīya identifies the main trunk of a group that later subdivides internally into a group of (probably) four sects. This group of sects is unique in claiming that something identifed as a "pudgala" transmigrates from life to life, carrying accumulated karma with it, and thus maintaining continuity from one life to the next. Although the group argues that the pudgala is neither the same nor different from the five aggregates (skandhas), the school was quickly criticized as establishing a functional equivalent to the ātman, a sort of *surrogate ātman*, and thus dismissed for preaching heretical doctrines contrary to Buddha's primary teaching on the subject. Despite much philosophical travail, the subdivisions of the school appear to have enjoyed a long history in India, having been cited regularly by Chinese pilgrims such as Hsüan-tsang and I-ching nearly a millennium after the appearance of the group. (See also PUDGALAVĀDA.)

⌘ VAṬṬAGĀMAṆĪ ⌘

King in Sri Lanka, dethroned in 43 B.C.E., but later restored to the throne from 29–17 B.C.E. In the fourteen years that Vaṭṭagāmaṇī was absent from the throne, famine and political turmoil were rampant. Upon reclaiming the throne, the king built Abhayagiri monastery in the capital of Anuradhapura. Unlike the Mahāvihāra, given to the saṃgha by King Devānaṃpiya Tissa, Abhayagiri was given to an individual monk. Such an act, the first gift of a monastery to an *individual*, caused a conflict with the monks of the Mahāvihāra, and a split developed between the monks of the two locations, resulting in an internal sectarian division in Theravāda Buddhism on the island. Despite such essentially political turmoil, during the reign of King Vaṭṭagāmaṇī the Pāli Canon was committed to writing for the first time, a momentous event in the history of Buddhist literature.

⌘ VIBHAJYAVĀDA ⌘

Name of a major trunk within the Indian Buddhist sectarian lineage known as the Sthaviras, from which the Mahīśāsakas, Theravādins, and Kāśyapīyas later subdivided. The sect name literally translates to "Distinctionists," and it was this group that King Aśoka's council at Pāṭaliputra found to be "orthodox." We really know quite little about the group's doctrinal positions, but can assume that the Pāli Abhidhamma text known as the Kathāvatthu, presumably compiled as a result of the council, captured their essential positions. It is at least safe to say that they opposed the doctrinal stance taken by the Sarvāstivādin school, which was, accordingly, expelled from Aśoka's kingdom as heretical.

⌘ VIHĀRA ⌘

General term for a Buddhist monastery. In the earliest Buddhist tradition, when monks and nuns essentially wandered through the countryside settling down only during the rainy season, the word vihāra was used to designate an individual *hut* within the rainy season retreat known as an āvāsa or ārāma. In time, as the eremitical ideal largely disappeared in Buddhism, and Buddhists began to develop permanent, settled dwellings, the term vihāra came to be designated as *an entire monastery*. As such, it is usual throughout the Buddhist world to refer to monasteries by the now generic term vihāra. As times changed, and the needs of the saṃgha began to reflect a growing institutionalization, some vihāras became enormously large, complex, and *wealthy* units with elaborate administrative hierarchies, straining the organizational capacity of the codes preserved in the Vinaya Piṭaka to their limits of applicability. Nonetheless, the vihāras also provide a common meeting place for the monastic community and laity, a place for Dharma instruction, personal training, and inspiration. (See also ĀRĀMA; ĀVĀSA.)

⌘ VIJÑĀNA ⌘

Sanskrit technical term usually translated as "consciousness." It is derived from the Sanskrit prefix *vi* + √ jñā. Traditionally, six types of consciousness are identified, each reflecting the contact of a specific sense organ with an object in the external world. Consequently, we can identify eye, ear, nose, tongue, body, and mind consciousness. Consciousness is also listed as the fifth aggregate in the skandhas and as the third link in the chain of dependent origination (pratītya-samutpāda). It is a category that was vigorously investigated during the period of composition of the Abhidharma Piṭaka.

⌘ VIJÑĀNAVĀDA ⌘

See YOGĀCĀRA

⌘ VIMALAKĪRTI-NIRDEŚA-SŪTRA ⌘

Mahāyāna sūtra titled "Sūtra on the Discourse of Vimalakīrti." One of the most important, and frequently quoted Mahāyāna sūtras, this text relates the story of a famous Buddhist lay disciple named Vimalakīrti who, despite being engaged in wordly activities through his livelihood as a banker, manages to lead an exemplary life as a bodhisattva. The story of the sūtra focuses on a Dharma discourse being delivered by Buddha in the town of Vaiśālī. Buddha was surrounded by 8,000 monks and 32,000 bodhisattvas, but Vimalakīrti was absent due to an illness. In seeking to learn of Vimalakīrti's condition, Buddha wants to send any of the disciples so inclined. Each declines due to Vimalakīrti's superior position until the bodhisattva Mañjuśrī offers to go, at which point all follow. When queried about his illness, Vimalakīrti offers a response brimming with Mahāyāna philosophy. He attributes his illness to his compassion for the sickness of all sentient beings, noting that he will become cured *only when all other sentient beings are cured*. What follows is a long discussion on various aspects of Mahāyāna doctrine. Eventually, Vimalakīrti poses the question that provides the highlight of the sūtra: he asks how a bodhisattva can enter the Dharma-door of nonduality? Thirty-one replies follow, each somewhat more insightful and sophisticated than the preceding, but each lacking in *complete* understanding. When it becomes Mañjuśrī's turn, he simply says (from page 77 of Robert Thurman's translation, *The Holy Teaching of Vimalakīrti*): "Good sirs, you have all spoken well. Nevertheless, all your explanations are themselves dualistic. To know no one teaching, to express nothing, to say nothing, to explain nothing, to announce nothing, to indicate nothing, and to designate nothing—that is the entrance into nonduality." Mañjuśrī then requests Vimalakīrti's answer to his own question. Vimalakīrti's response: *complete and total silence*. In so doing, he has provided the only perfect answer! Because of the sūtra's high relevance for *all* of Mahāyāna, it became important in virtually every Buddhist country where Mahāyāna flourished.

⌘ VINAYA PIṬAKA ⌘

The first portion of the Buddhist canon, generally rendered as the "Basket of Discipline." It consists of three basic parts. First there is a compendium of rules (called the Sūtravibhaṅga) for the *individual behavior* of the monks and nuns. The formal canonical text is an extension of the brief monastic liturgy known as the Prātimokṣa-sūtra, an eight category inventory of offenses arranged in decreasing order of severity. It extends the text by offering a story or stories surrounding the promulgation of each specific rule, presents the rule itself, continues with a word-for-word commentary on the rule, and concludes with further stories identifying mitigating circumstances in which exceptions to the rule or deviations in punishment might be made. There are separate versions of this first portion for the monks and for the nuns. The second portion of the canonical text, known as the Skandhaka, deals with the *collective rules* for the smooth and proper running of the saṃgha as a religious institution. This section is divided into approximately twenty chapters, considering such topics as ordination, schisms, rainy season retreat, and the like. The third general section of the text includes appendices that consider matters best termed "miscellaneous." Virtually every major Hīnayāna school preserved its own version of the Vinaya Piṭaka, manifesting a high *general agreement* regarding the basic content of the rules, but *differing significantly* in several areas, thus affording a glimpse as to how individual Buddhist schools changed in response to differing times and locations. We have the complete Vinaya Piṭaka for only one school in its *original language*: the Pāli Canon of the Theravāda school. A number of other schools present Sanskrit fragments and mostly complete translations into Chinese and/or Tibetan. A significant amount of "paracanonical" literature, or texts that preceded the actual, finalized canonical versions, has also been preserved in a variety of languages, as well as copious volumes of commentarial material. (See also ETHICS; PRĀTIMOKṢA-SŪTRA; TRIPIṬAKA.)

⌘ VINAYA SCHOOL ⌘

See LÜ SCHOOL; RITSU SCHOOL

⌘ VIPAŚYANĀ ⌘

Meditational term denoting "insight" of the mind, generally following a preliminary period of calming the mind (known as śamatha). The goal of Buddhist meditation necessarily is the attainment of enlightenment. Each Buddhist school that emphasizes meditation generally describes a practice that begins with calming, intending to lower physiological body function and eliminate mental clutter, in order that insight and the higher practices be attainable. Winston King, in his influential book *Theravāda Meditation*, says (on page 82), "Vipassanā (insight) is the heart of the Theravāda meditational discipline. As the technique for attaining Nibbāna par excellence, it is the living, existential essence of the Theravāda worldview and the mode absolutely essential to achieving final salvation." To be sure, insight is achieved in various way by the different schools. Nonetheless, irrespective of whether one employs Tantric visualizations or Zen kōans, insight is a necessary component of the enlightenment experience. (See also ŚAMATHA.)

⌘ VISUDDHIMAGGA ⌘

Famous Pāli text written by Buddhaghosa, the title of which means "Path of Purity." The text is a systematic compendium of Theravāda Buddhist doctrine and practice. It is divided into three parts: (1) the "purification of virtue" (śīla), (2) the "purification of concentration" (samādhi), and (3) the "purification of wisdom" (prajñā). The first part, covering two chapters, is a thorough explanation of the moral guidelines of the school. The second part, covering eleven chapters, is regarded as the foremost Theravādin meditational handbook. The third part, covering ten chapters, reveals the philosophic insight that emerges from proper cultivation of the first two parts. The Visuddhimagga remains the most comprehensive, clearly structured handbook of Theravāda Buddhism available. (See also BUDDHAGHOSA.)

— W —

⌘ WARREN, HENRY CLARKE ⌘
(1854–1899)

American scholar noted for his work with Sanskrit and Pāli Buddhist texts. Born in Boston, Warren was severely injured in a childhood accident, limiting his mobility for the rest of his life. He received a degree from Harvard University in 1879, after which he studied Sanskrit with Charles Lanman at Johns Hopkins. He eventually followed Lanman back to Harvard, where the two were instrumental in beginning *The Harvard Oriental Series.* Warren's volume *Buddhism in Translations,* an anthology still highly praised today, became the third volume in that series. He also edited the Pāli text of Buddhaghosa's Visuddhimagga, which, when revised by Dharmananda Kosambi, was published as volume forty-one in the series. Possessed of a remarkable sense of humor despite his debilitating disability, he worked almost up to the very end of his life by kneeling on a chair while leaning over his desk and sleeping on the floor of his study.

⌘ WAYMAN, ALEX ⌘

Modern American scholar of Buddhism, best known for his work as a professor at Columbia University and his prolific publication record on a variety of Buddhist topics. The vast majority of Wayman's scholarly publications are devoted to topics in Tibetan Buddhism, traversing the field from sophisticated philosophy and philology to studies of meditational texts. However, to see Wayman as merely a Tibetologist would fail to do him justice. He possesses a firm grounding in the Indian Buddhist tradition, and has written creatively on it as well. Moreover, his books and articles are often provocative and even occasionally filled with wit. He has also produced a number of highly qualified students who earned their Ph.D. degree under his tutelage. He continues to be active in professional organizations specific to his discipline. No doubt, along with Edward Conze, Masatoshi Nagatomi, Richard Robinson, and perhaps one or two others, he has developed and shaped the study of Buddhism as an academic discipline in the United States.

⌘ WHEEL OF BECOMING ⌘

See BHAVACAKRA

⌘ WHITE LOTUS SOCIETY ⌘

Society formed by Mao Tzu-yüan in the twelfth century, and devoted to the worship of Amitābha. Although especially interested in T'ien-t'ai meditation, Mao Tzu-yüan was inspired by Hui-yüan (334–416) and organized a loose association of laymen and monks who were devoted to restraint of the passions and rebirth in the Pure Land. The resulting White Lotus Society engaged in daily recitation of penance, worked at performing good karma, and recited Buddha's name as a regular part of their religious practice. They restricted their diet, avoiding all wine, milk, onions, and meat. The society was accused of a variety of offenses, including being involved with demons, resulting in their withdrawal into secrecy. In 1313 they were able to come into the open once again, but were banned nine years later.

⌘ WON BUDDHISM ⌘

Form of modern Buddhism in Korea, started in 1924 by Soetae San (1891–1943). Won Buddhism is a "reformed" school of Buddhism whose religious practice involves worship of a black circle said to represent the Dharma-kāya. For this reason, it is called the "round" or "circular" school. Won Buddhism is not exclusively monastic, as monks are permitted to marry. Since 1953 it has been on the rise in Korea, with over 500,000 disciples and 200 temples by 1975.

⌘ WORLD FELLOWSHIP OF BUDDHISTS ⌘

Buddhist organization founded by the Sri Lankan scholar G. P. Malalasekera in 1950. Its mission is to propagate Buddhism worldwide and to try to unite Buddhists of all countries. In a spirit of ecumenism, the World Fellowship of Buddhists has sponsored a series of conferences in various Buddhist countries, the first of which was held in Sri Lanka in 1950. The organization flies a six-colored flag emblazened with the dharmacakra or "Wheel of the Teaching."

⌘ WORLD PARLIAMENT OF RELIGIONS ⌘

Major event held at the Chicago Columbian Exposition in 1893. This conference was one of the very first occasions in which Asian religions in general were presented to the American public in an organized fashion. Anagārika Dharmapāla and Sōyen Shaku, well-known Asian Buddhists were in attendance, as well as representatives from a number of other traditions. Also present was Paul Carus, the editor of Open Court Press, who was later to become an important voice for the infant American Buddhist movement. In the aftermath of the Parliament, a growing number of Buddhists, particularly from the various Japanese schools, but also including representatives from other traditions, were to appear on American soil. (See also CHICAGO COLUMBIAN EXPOSITION.)

⌘ WU ⌘

Chinese equivalent term for the Japanese satori or "enlightenment." Like its counterpart terms in other traditions, such as bodhi in Sanskrit or kenshō in Japanese, it represents a breakthrough to enlightenment, an experience potentially available to the practitioner at any time. It is dramatic, visionary, impossible to capture in descriptive, conceptual terms, but always available under the proper circumstance. It is not to be considered the culmination of practice, but an experience that can be continually deepened. (See also BODHI; ENLIGHTENMENT; KENSHŌ; SATORI.)

⌘ WU-MÊN HUI-K'AI ⌘
(1183–1260)

Chinese Ch'an master from the Yang-ch'i line of the Lin-chi school, and Dharma heir to Yueh-lin Shih-kuan (1143–1217). Perhaps the most significant Ch'an master of his era, he is most famous for composing a text known as the Wu-mên-kuan or The Gateless Barrier, a compilation of 48 kung-ans (Japanese: kōan) with commentaries. One of his disciples from Japan, Kakushin (1207–1298), took a copy of the Wu-mên-kuan with him on his return to Japan in 1254. In 1246 Wu-mên became abbot of a large Ch'an monastery, where he lived until shortly before his death, when he took up residence in a small mountain monastery. The emperor of the Southern Sung Dynasty gave him the title "Zen Master of the Buddha Eye." (See also WU-MÊN-KUAN.)

⌘ WU-MÊN-KUAN ⌘

Famous text by Wu-mên Hui-k'ai containing a collection of 48 kung-ans or "public cases" and commentaries, utilized in facilitating the enlightenment experience in Ch'an disciples. The collection, whose title literally means "The Gateless Barrier," was originally published in 1229. It was brought to Japan in 1254 by Wu-mên's Japanese student Kakushin. The Japanese text, known as the Mumonkan, has been extremely important in Rinzai Zen in Japan. Along with the Hekigan-roku (Chinese: Pi-yên-lu), it remains one of the two most famous and useful kōan collections. The text has also attracted a great deal of attention in the West, having been translated into English a number of times by various individuals. (See also KŌAN; WU-MÊN HUI-K'AI.)

⌘ WU-WEI ⌘

Traditional Chinese Taoist term often translated as "nonaction," utilized as an early translation equivalent for nirvāṇa.

Taken from its usage in Lao-tzu's Tao-te Ching, wu-wei actually means more than simple nonaction. It represents action that is not tainted by worldly desires or motivation. Nonetheless, the early Buddho-Taoists, in seeking to make Buddhism and Buddhist ideals understandable to a Chinese audience, utilized a term in Taoist vocabulary that *seemed to approximate* the Buddhist notion of nirvāṇa. That it was not an especially good match was soon to be remedied as a distinctly Chinese Buddhist vocabulary was on the near horizon. (See also BUDDHO-TAOISTS.)

— Y —

⌘ YAMA ⌘

According to Buddhist mythology, the ruler of the various hells. The Buddhist hells are often described in painstaking detail, presumably as an encouragement for individuals to lead a proper life. Nonethless, for those who are unfortunately reborn in one of the hells, Yama and his retinue have an incredible array of tortures with which to continually torment evildoers. (See also HELL.)

⌘ YĀNA ⌘

Sanskrit technical term meaning "vehicle." It is compounded with a variety of "path" words descriptive of particular approaches to spiritual progress and development. In so doing, large *groups* of adepts, each maintaining a particular doctrinal and pragmatic position, are identified generically. Thus, the Hīnayāna is rendered as the "Lesser Vehicle," while the Mahāyāna is called the "Greater Vehicle." The Vajrayāna represents the "Diamond Vehicle." Vajrayāna is also sometimes referred to as the Mantrayāna (i.e., "Mantra Vehicle") or the Tantrayāna (i.e., "Tantric Vehicle"). Occasionally, as in the Lotus-sūtra, the term Ekayāna or "One Vehicle" is employed to suggest that all vehicles are simply manifestations of one, true vehicle. Sometimes the word is appended to the title of a particular kind of practitioner in order to generalize that approach to the religious path. Consequently, we identify Śrāvaka-yāna, the vehicle of the "hearers," or Buddha's early disciples. Further, there is the Pratyekabuddha-yāna, the vehicle of the "private Buddhas," or those individuals who attain enlightenment on their own, never to embark on a teaching career. Finally, there is the Bodhisattva-yāna, those persons following the "Bodhisattva vehicle," pursuing Buddhahood according to the Mahāyāna tradition.

⌘ YAŚODHARĀ ⌘

Wife of Siddhārtha Gautama and mother of his only child, Rāhula. As was customary in families such as his, Siddhārtha Gautama was married on an appropriate and auspicious occasion to a fair maiden in the kingdom. In due course, their union produced a son, but unfortunately, by the time of Rāhula's birth, Siddhārtha was ready to renounce the world in pursuit of a solution to the problem of old age, sickness, and death. Consequently, Yaśodharā was left behind as her husband pursued the mendicant's path. After attaining enlightenment, he eventually returned to his clan, but at that time accepted Rāhula into the saṃgha as a monk, infuriating Yaśodharā because of the child's tender age. Thus, Yaśodharā lost both her husband and only child to the religious vocation.

⌘ YASUTANI, HAKUUN RYŌKO ⌘
(1885–1973)

Japanese Zen master who was important in the transmission of Zen to America. In his early years he was a schoolteacher, married at age thirty, and raised five children. Yasutani Rōshi became a student of Harada Rōshi when he was around forty years old, gaining Dharma transmission from him in 1943. He utilized both shikantaza (or "just sitting") and kōan practice in his teaching, thus bridging the gap between traditional Sōtō and Rinzai Zen. He visited the United States for the first time in 1962, holding intensive training sesshins in several major American cities. He conducted similar tours in England, France, and Germany. He continued to visit the United States regularly until his death.

⌘ YIDAM ⌘

In Vajrayāna Buddhism a personal deity, matching the disciple in nature. Considered to be manifestations of the saṃbhoga-kāya, yidams are visualized in meditation practice, may be of either gender, and possessed of a variety of qualities.

⌘ YOGĀCĀRA ⌘

Indian Mahāyāna Buddhist school founded by two brothers, Asaṅga and Vasubandhu, emphasizing the doctrine of cittamātra or "mind only" as the basic mode of knowing and experiencing phenomenal reality. Beginning in the fourth century C.E., the Yogācāra school is so named because it argues for the "practice of yoga" as the primary means of religious attainment. Its name notwithstanding, the main emphases of the school are predominantly philosophical and psychological. Drawn not only from the writings of Asaṅga (which include primarily the Mahāyānasaṃgraha and the Abhidharmasamuccaya) and Vasubandhu (focusing on the Viṃśatikā and Triṃśikā), the school utilizes a wealth of Mahāyāna texts such as the Saṃdhinirmocana-sūtra, Laṅkāvatāra-sūtra, Madhyānta-vibhāga, and others stressing the bold new doctrine of the world of perception as a manifestation of mind. In addition to the primary doctrine of cittamātra, the school offers a new theory of eight consciousnesses, adding manas or "mind" and ālaya-vijñāna or "storehouse consciousness" to the traditional six consciousnesses of earlier Buddhism. For this reason, the school is sometimes called Vijñānavāda (literally "holders of the doctrine of consciousness"). Although it affirms the traditional Mahāyāna notion of emptiness (śūnyatā), it replaces the Mādhyamika school's theory of two levels of truth with "three natures" including: (1) an imagined or mentally constructed level known as parikalpita, (2) a relative reality known as paratantra, and (3) ultimate reality known as pariniṣpanna. The notion of "three bodies of the Buddha," also develops within the Yogācāra literature. The practical teaching of the school, including a description of its religious path, is embodied in Asaṅga's text called the Yogācārabhūmi-śāstra. The school reached its peak in the middle centuries of the first millennium C.E., as witnessed by its importance at the Nālanda University. The school became exceedingly important in the development of a number of Chinese and Japanese Buddhist schools as well. (See also ĀLAYA-VIJÑĀNA; ASAṄGA; FA-HSIANG; HOSSŌ; VASUBANDHU.)

⌘ YÜN-KANG CAVES ⌘

Large complex of grottoes carved into a cliff near the Northern Wei capital of Ta-t'ung dating from around 460 C.E. Following the Buddhist persecution of 446 by Emperor Wu, T'an-yao became chief of monks around 460. After seeing how easily wooden and metal Buddha images were destroyed in the persecution, T'an-yao helped to convince the new rulers following Emperor Wu that more lasting images were necessary. Apparently the caves now identified as numbers 16–20 on modern charts were carved first, housing five large Buddha figures, the tallest being 70 feet. Caves 5–10 followed next, with many others being constructed over the next century. More than fifty caves have been identified on the site, housing approximately 50,000 images and artifacts. Caves 5 and 6 appear to be most important, portraying the story of Buddha's life up to his enlightenment experience. Modern scholars have noted a strong influence of art forms from Gandhāra and Central Asia in the Yün-kang caves. It is certainly among the most ambitious projects of its kind in Buddhist history.

⌘ YÜN-MEN WEN-YEN ⌘
(864–949)

Eminent Ch'an master, known for short, abrupt answers which Zen scholar Heinrich Dumoulin calls "one word barriers." He joined the Buddhist community at an early age, following the Vinaya rules of monastic life rigorously, but eventually assuming an itinerant lifestyle in pursuit of religious illumination. Following an enlightenment experience under Ch'en Tsun-su, he practiced with Hsüeh-feng I-ts'un, becoming his Dharma heir. Following another brief period as a wandering monk, he became abbot of Ling-shu-yüan, until such time as a monastery was built for him on Mt. Yün-men. There he attracted a large number of disciples. His style was somewhat eccentric, often relying on shouts, blows with a stick, and the "one word barriers" mentioned above. Nonetheless, stories about Yün-men abound in the Ch'an literature, especially in the Wu-mên-kuan and the Pi-yên-lu. The school he founded is included as one of the "five houses of Ch'an," and a number of his disciples (especially Tung-shan Shou-ch'u, d. 900) became quite famous in their own right.

— Z —

⌘ ZABUTON ⌘

A "sitting mat" for practicing zazen. A zabuton is a small square mat, covered with dark material and stuffed (usually) with kapok. It is of sufficient size for one person to sit on in meditative posture while doing zazen. (See also ZAZEN.)

⌘ ZAFU ⌘

A "sitting cushion" for practicing zazen. A zafu is a small round cushion, perhaps eighteen inches in diameter, stuffed (usually) with kapok and quite firm. It is of sufficient size for one person to sit on in meditative posture while doing zazen. The zafu is sometimes placed on top of the zabuton. (See also ZABUTON.)

⌘ ZAZEN ⌘

Literally "sitting in meditation," a technical term for the primary religious practice in Zen. Utilized in all the schools of Zen, zazen is intended to provide the occasion for both discipline and insight. While enlightenment can occur at any time, and on any occasion in Zen, sitting meditation seems to offer the most fruitful approach to the awakening of realization. As such, it may result in kenshō or satori. Because zazen is often undertaken for several hours per day in Zen monasteries, and for very *many* hours during the intensified training periods known as sesshin, it is often combined with periods of walking meditation called kinhin. This latter practice enables the practitioner to stretch one's legs and thus retain a continued ability to make spiritual progress.

⌘ ZEN ⌘

Japanese technical term (short for Zen-na) said to be a transliteration of the Chinese term Ch'an or Ch'an-na, which in turn, is a transliteration of the Sanskrit technical term for meditation or dhyāna. It refers to a meditative practice in which one seeks to bring the mind under control as a step in the process of attaining enlightenment. Although a variety of Zen "schools" developed in Japan, they all emphasize Zen as a teaching that does not depend on sacred texts, that provides the potential for direct realization, that the realization attained is none other than the Buddha nature possessed by each sentient being, and that transmission occurs outside the teaching. This last statement is traced to the apparently initial transmission of the teaching from Buddha Śākyamuni to Kāśyapa in a silent sermon on Vulture's Peak. In so doing, a *lineage* was established which is considered unbroken, despite Buddhism's transmission into a large variety of cultures in its 2,500 year history. (See also CH'AN.)

⌘ ZENDŌ ⌘

Japanese technical term used to indicate the meditation hall. It is a large, sparsely furnished hall in Zen monasteries or centers in which zazen is practiced. It is purposely designed to be extremely quiet and intended to produce no external distractions, in order that each meditator pursue rigorous zazen with diligence.

About the Author

CHARLES S. PREBISH (B.A., Western Reserve University; M.A., Case Western Reserve University; Ph.D., University of Wisconsin) is Professor of Religious Studies at the Pennsylvania State University. His prior books include *Introduction to Religions of the East: Reader* (co-edited with Jane I. Smith), *Buddhist Monastic Discipline, Buddhism: A Modern Perspective, American Buddhism, Buddhist Ethics: A Cross-Cultural Approach, Religion and Sport: The Meeting of Sacred and Profane, A Survey of Vinaya Literature, Buddhism and Human Rights* (co-edited with Damien Keown and Wayne Husted), *The Faces of Buddhism in America* (co-edited with Kenneth K. Tanaka), and *Luminous Passage: The Practice and Study of Buddhism in America*. He has published nearly fifty professional articles and chapters in such journals as *The Journal of Asian Studies, Journal of the American Oriental Society, History of Religions*, and *Buddhist Studies Review*. In 1976 he was elected to a five-year term as Associate Secretary of the International Association of Buddhist Studies, and was elected to two further terms on the Board of Directors. In 1981 he was elected to a five-year term as Co-Chairman of the Buddhism Group of the American Academy of Religion. He has been active in a number of other professional organizations, including the Association for Asian Studies, American Oriental Society, Pali Text Society, Society for Asian and Comparative Philosophy, and Society for Buddhist-Christian Studies. In 1993 he was invited to hold the Numata Chair in Buddhist Studies at the University of Calgary during the fall semester. In 1994 he became founding co-editor of *The Journal of Buddhist Ethics*, the first online scholarly, peer-reviewed journal in the field of Religious Studies. In 1997–98 he held a Rockefeller Foundation National Humanities Fellowship at the Centre for the Study of Religion at the University of Toronto. He is currently co-editor of the "Critical Studies in Buddhism" series published by Curzon Press.